INFLUENCE

INFLUENCE

How Women's Soaring Economic Power
Will Transform Our World for the Better

Maddy Dychtwald

with Christine Larson

voice

Hyperion   New York

Library of Congress Cataloging-in-Publication Data

Dychtwald, Maddy
  Influence : how women's soaring economic power will transform our world for the better / Maddy Dychtwald with Christine Larson.
    p. cm.
  ISBN 978-1-4013-4102-2
  1. Labor market—Sex differences.   2. Women—Employment.   I. Larson, Christine, 1968 II. Title.
  HD5706.D93   2009
  331.4—dc22

                          2009047446

SUSTAINABLE FORESTRY INITIATIVE   Certified Fiber Sourcing   www.sfiprogram.org

To my beloved daughter, Casey;
my mother, Sally; and my mother-in-law, Pearl:
three amazing women who inspire and nourish me,
each in her own unique way.

—Maddy Dychtwald

To my mother, Peggi Berge,
and my mother-in-law, Diana Rojo,
with all my love and thanks.

—Christine Larson

Contents

INFLUENCE

Power Shift
on the Horizon

In the village of Kampala in Uganda, Joan Ahimbisibwe, an HIV-positive mother of three, recently bought a piglet. For most of her life, Ahimbisibwe has lived on less than $1 a day, which is not enough to feed her family, let alone buy the school uniforms necessary to send her children to school—and certainly not enough for a lucrative investment like a piglet. Then Ahimbisibwe started making beads out of recycled magazine paper with a group of other women in her village. When two women in Colorado, Ginny Jordan and Torkin Wakefield, started a nonprofit called BeadforLife, which sells the beads at private parties and on the Internet, Ahimbisibwe started making $5 or $6 a day, about what a Ugandan policeman earns.

With her newfound financial stability, Ahimbisibwe saved enough money to buy her pig, which she raised then resold at a nice markup. With her profits, she moved her family into a storefront complete with mattresses, a big step up from the mud hut in which they'd been living and where they'd slept on the ground. Through the storefront, Ahimbisibwe sells vegetables and sugar, upping her earnings yet again. Ahimbisibwe's daughter is now in private boarding school, which means that her chance of escaping the vicious cycle of African poverty has just changed forever.

Ahimbisibwe's adult life so far is the story of one woman's rising, and it's the story of women helping women. Most of all, it's an illustrative account of twenty-first-century female economic emancipation, an emancipation more fast-paced and far-reaching than any the world has seen before.

Around the world, from developing nations like Uganda to economic giants like the European Union and the United States, women are finally starting to control their economic destinies and those of their families. Take Sara Wood, thirty-eight, who grew up in the Deep South in the United States as the daughter of struggling Louisiana farmers. One of five siblings, including a brother who died young, Sara didn't see many paths she wanted to follow. Many of the girls in her town were knocked up and headed for the altar by the time they graduated from high school: She didn't know any women with high-earning careers, let alone with lives that didn't revolve around their children and depend, utterly, on their husbands. Today, after managing product development for several technology start-ups, Wood earns more than she ever dreamed possible, owns multiple properties on two continents, and supports her two children, whose father makes less than one-third of what she does. Wood wasn't saved from her narrow, small-town existence by anyone but herself. No prince swept in and brought her back to his castle. Wood built her position in the world through her ability to function, and function highly, in the marketplace. Hers is also a twenty-first-century story of economic emancipation.

Limerick, Ireland, when Anne Fleming was growing up in the seventies, was a place of pink slips and beer in the afternoons. No one expected to get rich, especially not little girls. The women Anne knew were moms; the professional women were teachers and nurses. Today, Anne lives in Dublin, where she's a high-level financial advisor to one of Ireland's biggest investment companies, negotiating multibillion-dollar deals. She drives a BMW convertible and already has enough in savings to retire and live comfortably for the rest of her life. Although she thinks she'd like to get married one day, she hasn't yet and feels no pressure to do so. If anything, she worries about finding a man who can keep up with her.

If Anne had been born even ten years earlier, it's doubtful she would have taken such a path. It probably wouldn't have crossed her mind that such a future could be hers. Would she have gotten the MBA that gave her the skills to get her job? Would it even have occurred to her to explore a career in finance? And if it had, what are the chances the marketplace would have allowed a place for her?

It's not that success equals monetary riches; I'd be shallow indeed if that were my point. What I'm talking about is economic emancipation— women around the globe becoming financially powerful enough to stand on their own two feet and tip the world's power balance, starting with home life, extending to work life, and finally affecting general society.

This twenty-first-century phenomenon is on par with other remarkable human leaps forward—including other great moments of progress for women, such as women achieving the right to own property, to vote, to leave an unhappy marriage, to get a higher education, and to control their own reproductive systems. In many ways, what is happening now is a bigger breakthrough than any one of those others; as if those essential rights have intertwined and grown upward like so many morning glories, so that this new, taller flower can burst open—an essential bloom that couldn't exist without all that came before, and one toward which all those steps were, ultimately, aiming: freedom from dependence, the chance for real power, and the opportunity to influence the workings of the world.

This narrative is not a feminist treatise. These are just facts. This is simply history, the logical outcome of the last hundred years and all the hundreds of years that came before that. It's hardly an exaggeration to say that for all of recorded history, women have basically been second-class citizens in a male-dominated world. And it's not ideology to assert that the status of women is changing. What we're seeing now—exponential gains toward self-sufficiency, soaring education rates, mass economic empowerment around the world—are facts. They are history rushing forward. Nothing more, nothing less.

Until the last few years, the massive entry of women into the paid workforce seemed important mostly because it was a victory for social justice. Only recently has another, even more significant implication of women's success become clear: The health of the global economy now demands that women realize their full potential as economic participants. This transformed world, where women hold economic power equal to men's, is inevitable not only because it's fair and just (which it is), but because human economic success now depends on it. In the coming decades, countries that harness women's economic power will win; those that fail to do so will lose.

In the past few years, prominent economists and policy makers have abruptly woken to the fact that women's equality in the workplace is not a "women's issue" but a serious factor in global economic competitiveness.

In Geneva, for example, the World Economic Forum—a global group of influential economists and policy makers—launched a comprehensive annual *Global Gender Gap Report* in 2006. The report, developed by the WEF's Global Competitiveness Network, looks at gender economic equality as a serious factor in determining a nation's economic success. Every annual *Global Gender Gap Report* since the first full issue in 2006 has found a direct connection between a country's ability to tap the skills and talents of women and its economic success. According to the 2007 report, "A nation's competitiveness depends significantly on whether and how it educates and utilizes its female talent."

"In every country in the world, half of the potentially available human resources are women," points out Saadia Zahidi, associate director and head of constituents for the World Economic Forum. "If that half is not educated or not healthy, they're unlikely to be channeled into the economy in the most effective way."

All of this makes an obvious kind of common sense: What happens when a country actively suppresses half its population's economic contributions? It gets half the ideas, half the labor, half the productivity. No country can afford this kind of waste. As journalists Nicholas Kristof and Sheryl WuDunn make clear in their important 2009 book, *Half the Sky: Turning Oppression into Opportunity for Women Worldwide,* the appalling and routine violation of women's human rights around the world undermines the economic power of entire nations. A mirror image to that argument is also becoming clear: When countries treat women equally to men and make it possible for both genders to have families and careers, national economies prosper.

Of course, transforming a culture that discriminates against women to one that unleashes women's full economic potential is far from easy. It's a process that can and will alter entire economies. But it also opens a Pandora's box of societal anxieties. A world transfigured by women's earning power challenges the very notion of what it means to be a woman. And if we must reconsider what it means to be a woman, then we must also reconsider what it means to be a man and, by extension, revisit all of our fundamental assumptions about family, society, the workplace, leadership institutions, and overall, how we believe the world works and should work.

Sweeping as it may sound, this kind of reconsideration is already happening in almost every country in the world, and yielding concrete results. Those results manifest differently from country to country, from culture to culture. But in regions spread across the globe, one thing is clear: Change is happening. As I write, as you read, the future is becoming the present. Health and education gaps between men and women are closing in even the poorest nations on earth, redirecting women away from poverty and toward economic and political opportunities.

A world of financially empowered women is a world changed for the better, and this reality is approaching with the speed of an almighty storm. Even now, you can see the lightning flash in the distance. More women than men are graduating from high school, college, and graduate programs in the United States. Women hold more than half the parliamentary seats in Rwanda. In China, a country flush with newly minted millionaires, a woman, Zhang Yin (a paper-recycling entrepreneur), is the richest of the rich (a multibillionaire). This is a moment that historians will look back on, pointing their fingers and tracing the era on timelines for students of the future: See it there! See the rise of the woman at the dawn of the twenty-first century! This is when women achieved economic emancipation after thousands of years as dependents.

The lightning's moving closer; the storm is about to break. Like it or not, we'll all feel the downpour soon.

In 2009, in the United States, women held 49 percent of all non-farm jobs. The number of women earning $100,000 or more tripled between 1991 and 2001. Between 2000 and 2008, women's average weekly wages grew steadily, while men's didn't grow at all. "Women are catching up to men," says Heidi Hartmann, president of the Institute for Women's Policy Research. Adds Robert Reich, former U.S. secretary of labor and now a professor of public policy at the University of California, Berkeley: "I wouldn't be surprised if, in ten years, the typical woman in the workforce was earning more than the typical man."

Women are not only earning more than they used to, they're taking on different types of jobs—in fields that pay more and command more esteem and, sometimes, more power. Today, women hold 51 percent of all management, professional, and related positions in the United States.

American women are starting their own businesses at nearly double the national average. Already, about 40 percent of U.S. private firms are women-owned, compared to only 26 percent in 1997.

These developments in business are not exclusive to the United States. In Cuba, women hold more technical and professional jobs than men do. And all over the world, as Joan Ahimbisibwe's story reveals, women are starting their own businesses. These changes speak to myriad shifting impulses, ideas, roles, and realities in less than a lifetime.

At the same time these business patterns are changing, the global economy happens to be undergoing other fundamental shifts, the most profound of which is the switch from an industrial to a knowledge economy. "The economy of the future is one that depends less on physical strength and more on the ability to solve problems—to critically collaborate and empathize, and pick up on subtle emotional cues. The more people, both men and women, are able to do that, the stronger our overall economy will be," says Robert Reich. The information economy doesn't give men an advantage over women, as did more agricultural or manufacturing-oriented economies—where physical strength matters. A knowledge-based economy doesn't reward strength, it rewards smarts. And women, who now equal or exceed the education levels of men in numerous countries, are poised to reap a massive benefit from the shifting economy.

In fact, they're already reaping it.

In the United States, women already control 51.3 percent of the nation's private wealth. One reason for this is women's growing earning power; another is that women, in general, outlive men and inherit their wealth. Just imagine how the balance of wealth will shift between genders when those women born during the baby boomer era start to inherit their parents' and their husbands' assets. Meanwhile, women in the United States already control some 80 percent of all household spending decisions, according to research firm A. T. Kearney. All told, American women have a purchasing power of more than $5 trillion. That's more than the entire economy of Japan ($4.9 trillion in 2008).

These economic forces are impossible to ignore. We're on the brink of a massive power shift, a grinding of the gears of history into a new human condition, one where women are no longer most of the world's poor, no longer the least educated and least powerful, a world where women can, if they choose, seize the reins of economic control.

What will a world with women in power look like? Will Anne Fleming in Dublin become a terror with her newfound riches, as bad as any stereotypically bad male boss who ever terrorized his underlings? As Sara Wood continues her way up the ladder, what kind of a leader will she become? Will Joan Ahimbisibwe's daughter use her education to take another step out of poverty? And what of the women in Colorado who came up with the program that gave Ahimbisibwe the chance to educate her daughter? Will they continue to use their Western wealth to raise women in developing countries out of poverty?

It's typical in Western culture to see things as either/or, as black or white: You're either at the top or on the bottom. But it doesn't have to be that way. Women are on their way to being in power. Gender roles and all that they imply will be transformed—are already transforming—probably beyond anything our turn-of-the-century eyes will recognize. But must one gender rule the other? Is it possible instead that the economic emancipation of women will lead to a more balanced world, where neither sex dominates but both work together in a kind of harmony? Pollyannaish, perhaps. Possible? Definitely.

But First, a Little History

Connecting the dots of women's emancipation in the last hundred or so years brings home how quickly women's status has changed yet also reminds us that freedom is not something achieved overnight. One obstacle was overturned, then another, until now the road ahead is no longer rife with roadblocks but is a clear, broad path stretching toward the future, with far fewer hurdles ahead.

As recently as 150 years ago, when a woman married in the United States, all of her property became her husband's, by law. Whether or not the husband willed a wife's inheritance back to her at the time of his death depended on his whim. Even personal items, like clothes, trinkets, and pictures, belonged to the husband. In the 1850s, and only in some states (mostly northern, Midwestern, and mid-Atlantic), married women at last were allowed to own property separate from their husbands; even then, though, a woman couldn't sell her property without her husband's consent—which meant she couldn't use the value of the property to build her own economic independence. If the man and the woman divorced, the law, in all but the rarest of cases, would see the property revert back to the man, who would also keep custody of any children. So while divorce was never illegal in most of the United States, it was nearly impossible for a woman to separate herself and become financially independent—let alone hold on to her children. The briefest overview of women's property rights at that time reveals how near to impossible it would have been for a woman to support herself if she left her husband. Legally, women were essentially property of their husbands. (Even today, there are countries, such as Uganda, where Joan Ahimbisibwe lives, where most women are still their husband's property in practice, if not in law.)

In the United States and Europe, circumstances changed again for women at the turn of the last century, when agricultural economies evolved into industrial ones and people became more dependent for survival on jobs than on property. Women could, and frequently did, take factory jobs in cities like London, Berlin, and New York. But a factory job during the Industrial Revolution was hardly the ticket to financial independence. Whether she worked or not, a snapshot of a young woman's life at the turn of the last century shows she had none of the opportunities we take for granted today:

- She couldn't vote.
- She couldn't choose when to get pregnant.
- She couldn't pursue higher education.
- She couldn't expect to find a job outside domestic work or factory labor.

It's easy to forget how new women's freedoms really are and what a radical departure they are from most of human history. ("My mother was born before women could vote," Hillary Clinton reminded the Democratic National Convention in 2008. "But in this election, my daughter got to vote for her mother for President.") The right to vote, to choose when to have children, to educate ourselves and support ourselves—these fundamentals seem so basic we barely notice them today. But almost none of those freedoms were possible for a woman at the turn of the twentieth century, not in the United States or anywhere else. The idea of granting women the right to vote was so radical that Susan B. Anthony named her magazine about women and the vote *The Revolution*. (Motto: "The true republic—men, their rights and nothing more; women, their rights and nothing less.") Women first got the vote in New Zealand in 1893; in the United States, the Nineteenth Amendment, granting women's suffrage, didn't pass until 1920; and, worldwide, the fight for a woman's right to vote continues: Kuwaiti women won the vote in 2005, and women in the United Arab Emirates will likely have suffrage by 2010. It's been a long struggle indeed—but one that I believe is nearly at an end.

If the idea of voting was controversial, the concept of women choosing whether and when to have children was literally criminal. In 1873, the United States outlawed the sale or delivery of contraception (back then, just condoms or diaphragms) through the mail. Even publishing information about how to avoid pregnancy was illegal. Margaret Sanger, a nurse on the Lower East Side of Manhattan, published a magazine describing ways to avoid pregnancy for women too poor or sick to raise children. She had to flee the country or face prosecution.

All this ruckus was over relatively primitive, ineffective methods of birth control. The real brouhaha began at a dinner party in 1951, when Sanger, then in her seventies, met a scientist named Gregory Pincus. Pincus had a theory that injections of progesterone could stop ovulation. Sanger introduced him to Katharine McCormick, heir to the International Harvester fortune, who had joined the fight for birth control because of her own experiences: Her husband had schizophrenia and she didn't want to pass the disease along. Ultimately, she provided $16 million in today's dollars to develop the birth control pill. Her economic power made possible the Pill's introduction in 1960, changing women's lives forever.

And when the Supreme Court legalized abortion in 1973 (after more than a decade of protests, marches, and intense legal debate), safer abortions became a reality, allowing women further reproductive choice.

In the 1960s and 1970s, feminists lobbied for equal rights in all spheres, and their push for equality took hold in academia, which until the

1970s had been heavily segregated. Columbia University did not start admitting women undergraduates until 1983. (To be fair, Barnard College still does not admit men.) Common thought held that wives, sisters, and daughters shouldn't be intellectuals and that a professional education in law, medicine, or business would be wasted on women, who were going to stay home raising children and weren't going to enter the marketplace.

Today, women hold 57.5 percent of all U.S. college bachelor's degrees, 61 percent of all master's degrees, and 49 percent of all doctorate degrees.

"Education has been a prime driver for women's income growth in the U.S. and around the world," says Heidi Hartmann. The powerful impact of women's education on earning power is now sweeping the globe, and its effects will be dramatic. "In Latin America, education gaps are starting to close, in patterns similar to those seen in Western countries, and women are starting to be present in higher education in bigger numbers than men," says World Economic Forum's Zahidi. In the Arab world, literacy rates for women climbed from 16.6 percent in 1970 to more than 50 percent in 2000. In the years ahead, countries that let these educated women put their knowledge into the marketplace will reap dramatic dividends.

From Survival to Influence: The Stages of Economic Power

Together, these revolutions, in suffrage, birth control, and education, unshackled women and provided them with the tools any person needs to improve his or her lot—independence, knowledge, and the ability to work. The challenge before us is to continue women's progress, to identify what still holds women back, and to prepare ourselves for full economic equality. To do that, we need to understand the steps in the journey ahead. In many ways, the fight ahead is an internal one—understanding what women's newfound economic power means to each of us personally and to our society, and figuring out how we want to use it.

In 1970, distinguished psychologist Abraham Maslow published a groundbreaking paper called "A Theory of Human Motivation," wherein he outlined his now-famous theory on the hierarchy of needs: Only after certain fundamental needs have been met, he argued, do we seek to fulfill the next set of needs. We need to eat and have basic shelter before we can worry about finding love and affection; we need love and affection before we can seek social status or strive to change the world for the better.

I believe Maslow's hierarchy is directly applicable to understanding the full range of women's economic rise. Most women are in the two early stages of what I call the Three Stages of Economic Power, an idea built on Maslow's hierarchy. A combination of extraordinary forces are now in place to help raise women to the third and highest level of economic power—influence—if women will choose to make the leap.

THREE STAGES OF ECONOMIC POWER

The first of Maslow's needs are physiological—the drive for food, water, sleep, and shelter. The basics. In the Three Stages of Economic Power, we call the first stage *Survival.* Survival is a woman earning enough money to put a roof over her family's heads and feed and clothe her children, but not much more. Survival is Joan Ahimbisibwe before she began making beads for BeadforLife.

The second stage of economic power I call *Independence.* I don't mean that women in this sphere are independently wealthy and don't need to work. Far from it. I mean they're free from daily worries about food and shelter and can rely on themselves to provide the basics—and, gradually, much more. (In my adaptation of Maslow's theory, this second step, of independence, is equivalent to the stages that Maslow called security, love, and self-esteem.)

When women reach this stage, they're eating well and living in reliable housing—and as their confidence grows, they're investing in their own futures. At one end of the spectrum of independence is Joan Ahimbisibwe, making sure her family will have enough to eat today, taking entrepreneurial steps to improve her family's future. At the other is Anne Fleming, with a lifetime of savings socked away. Many women fall somewhere in between. In fact, women around the world have done a phenomenal job moving into this middle place.

And significant numbers of those women will soon learn that there is even more to life than security and independence.

At the top of Maslow's hierarchy is the stage he called "self-actualization." Self-actualization occurs when one can project one's self—one's best self—onto the world and, in so doing, change the world. For our purposes in understanding the Three Stages of Economic Power, we call this third stage *Influence*. Katharine McCormick was certainly in the influence stage when she funded the development of the Pill. She was imprinting her vision on the world through her economic power.

Powerful men are in the habit of thinking about their lives as historically meaningful. They are accustomed to asking, "What effect do I have?" "What will my legacy be?" They consider it normal to think that they *ought* to leave a mark, that they have the right to do so. But acknowledging and using their influence is new territory for many women. For most of history, women have had only one powerful way to make their mark on the world—the character they establish in their homes and in their children. The time has come for women to make their mark in the public sphere as well. What will we do? It's one of the central questions facing the world in the twenty-first century, and how women answer it will affect both men and women in every corner of the globe: How will women use their newfound economic independence to self-actualize? What will that mean for the world? For men? For our families? That's why I wrote this book: to take a peek at the future that's arriving faster than we can write.

Urgent Choices

In the chapters ahead, you'll learn about women around the globe who are using their influence to change the fundamentals of the family, the workplace, the marketplace, and politics. How are these women rewriting the rules of the game, questioning old assumptions and inventing new paradigms? How are powerful economic forces—including globalization, demographic change, environmental challenges, and new technology—converging to add new urgency to women's choices?

In unprecedented numbers, women have already moved into that middle stage of economic power—the stage of independence—but now our families and our countries need us to take the next step. As the global economy emerges from the economic tumult of the early twenty-first century, countries and companies are entering a unique time of rebuilding. There are unprecedented opportunities to throw out old models and try new ones. In the decade beyond 2010, women—and men—will be shaping a "new normal."

We are at a turning point in history. For the first time, the smartest nations, corporations, and communities know that they must seek better ways to nurture and harness the full talents of their entire population, both women and men. And there is ample hard evidence to show that tapping women's talents, in every sphere, will make the world more equitable and more prosperous.

When a country educates its girls and women, its gross domestic product grows. When a corporation adds more women to its senior leadership, the company performs better financially than if there are only men at the top. When a nation makes it easier for two-income families to work and have a balanced life, its children and its economy thrive.

Countries and companies face a unique opportunity, here and now: to create a world where both women and men can bring their wide array of talents to bear on the problems of the world. But this moment won't last forever. Those countries and companies that heed the call—accepting and facilitating women's rising power—will emerge as winners in the economy of the future. Those that don't will be left behind. For women, too, this is an unparalleled moment: For the good of families, personal economies, countries, and women around the world, it's time for women to take the step to influence. It's time not to seize power from men, but to shift it, so half the world's citizens hold half the world's economic influence.

Once the power shift happens, the world will never be the same.

TWO

Global Change and Whole Wheat Pizza

PROFILES OF INFLUENCE

Tecate, Mexico, is a little Baja town known for two big things: the pale, bitter brew of Tecate beer, and Rancho La Puerta, an organic farm and health spa that's been coaching guests on healthy living for more than sixty years. Founder Deborah Szekely takes an interest in demographic changes—my own area of expertise—and from time to time she invites my husband, Ken, and me down to the three-thousand-acre ranch to share our findings with her guests.

So on a crisp January day not long ago, Ken and I hiked the half mile from our guest casita, passing boulders and sagebrush, to join Deborah and several others for lunch in the Spanish mission-style dining hall. I found my petite white-haired hostess chatting with an illustrious guest, civil rights activist Marian Wright Edelman. They were an impressive duo: Deborah, a smashingly successful businesswoman; Edelman, the first African-American woman admitted to the Mississippi bar and the founder and president of the Children's Defense Fund, the preeminent advocacy organization for the rights of poor, abused, and neglected children in the United States. Edelman was at the ranch finishing up a new book about hardships facing American children.

As we dined on delicious whole wheat pizza and salads from the organic garden, Deborah and Marian brainstormed about another crusade. Deborah wanted to launch an effort to bring healthier foods into American schools, encouraging garden-to-table experiences for sixth graders. Marian knew exactly what connections Deborah would need to raise money for a pilot project.

"You know who you should talk to?" Marian said. She mentioned a prominent foundation with a new interest in the kind of program Deborah wanted to promote.

"Great," said Deborah. "Do you know anyone there?"

"Absolutely," Marian replied.

Without missing a beat, Deborah asked, "Can you introduce me?"

Marian grinned. "Of course."

Before I'd finished my first slice of pizza, Marian was making a list of names and numbers.

As I reached for seconds, it occurred to me that I was witnessing a critical moment in history: two powerful, economically independent women helping each other change the world. This moment was nothing less than the culmination of women's progression from survival to independence to influence, a progression that, at least in Deborah's case, occurred in the course of a single lifetime.

Deborah didn't start out lunching with luminaries. When she launched Rancho La Puerta in 1940, she did it for survival, that first stage of economic power. "We had nothing," she told me. "Our priority was food." It was World War II, and her husband, a Hungarian intellectual, could neither return home nor remain legally in the United States. So the couple scratched out a living by inviting American friends to visit the ranch in Mexico for a health vacation; the friends would stay in tents and work on the farm, all for the kingly sum of $17.50 a week. Deborah's husband lectured to guests on healthy living while Deborah did the manual labor. "In the beginning, there was just me, doing the laundry and the cooking and all the letter writing to invite guests," she says. "I had no identity and I was too tired to establish one because after I worked all day, I wrote letters all night."

Over time, the ranch grew from a desperate gambit for financial survival to the thriving spa it is today.

Nearly twenty years later, in 1958, when Deborah started her second spa, the fabled Golden Door, she did it for *Independence*, the second stage of economic power. Specifically, she wanted to have children, but to do so she needed the steady income that her much older husband, who had little interest in starting a family, was both unwilling and unable to provide. The success of Rancho La Puerta—which by now boasted running water, small guest houses instead of tents, and celebrity guests from around the world—gave Deborah the confidence to launch her new spa, the Golden Door, in Southern California.

Under Deborah's leadership, the Golden Door soon became a synonym for health and fitness delivered with a strong measure of Zen luxury. Based on its success, Deborah shifted into that top stage of economic power, *Influence*—the ability to use financial and personal resources to make a difference in the broader world. Deborah founded a school in Tecate, then a library. She launched an arts fund in San Diego. Then in the 1980s, she went to Washington and became president of the Inter-American Foundation, channeling American aid to poor people in Latin America and the Caribbean.

On this cold, clear January day, here she was again, still bent on influencing the world—and working with another influential woman to make it happen. "I have nothing to lose and no time to waste. Maybe it's time women showed men how we get things done," Deborah told me later.

When I look at Deborah and Marian and how seamlessly they worked together, using their influence, resources, and vast networking power to impact their world, I see something old and something new. Women helping women? That's the oldest tale in the book. In some ways, what they were doing that day in the dining hall was no different from moms swapping babysitter names on the playground. But that kind of age-old women's networking and advice gets a powerful boost when there's serious women-controlled money behind it—and that *is* new. This mighty influence is just starting to change the world and in ways we can only begin to fathom.

From Survival to Influence: A Move to the Middle

Of course, not everyone is Deborah Szekely or Marian Wright Edelman. Far more women are like Rosa Acosta, a housekeeper in Phoenix who earns about $8 an hour. (Note: Rosa's one of just four people in this book who asked me to change her name: I'll tell you when I've changed the others.) A single mom of three, she had lived in three apartments within the past year when I first spoke with her. When she needed minor surgery, she paid for it out of pocket. During her three-week, unpaid recovery, she lost some of her cleaning clients and couldn't afford her rent or the much needed repairs to her car. She and her three children lived with friends for a while, but she found the neighborhood too dangerous for her kids. A few months after I first met her, Rosa launched her own version of a micro-loan program, asking her employers to advance her a month's pay so she could buy an old motor home from another client. It worked. She paid back the advances, and she and her children now live in a safer area. She's a loving mother, a hard worker, and her life is exhausting.

Globally, more women than not are like Rosa, struggling to find food and shelter. Poverty is not equally shared by both genders: Most poor people are female. Of 1.1 billion people living in abject poverty around the world, a whopping 70 percent are women. In India, more than a third of working women earn less than $1 a day—and that's just the women who *have* jobs. Much of women's disproportionate poverty in developing countries is related to government, tribal, or religious suppression of women's most basic rights (to move about freely, to be educated, to own property, to earn money). By contrast, here in the United States, having children and supporting them when fathers are absent is a major indicator of poverty: A woman like Rosa, who's the female head of a household with no man present, has a one-in-four chance of living in poverty. That's twice the number of male heads of households who live in poverty.

It's a human tragedy that so many people live in poverty. To deny the enormity of this problem around the world would be to sweep massive injustice under the rug. But there is good news regarding women and poverty: In recent years, women have been making steady progress out of the survival level of power into the beginnings of economic independence. Two decades ago, Rosa's chances of living in poverty, as a single female head of household, were significantly greater than they are now—more than one in three, instead of today's one in four. Things are getting better.

"Single mothers are still the poorest family group in society, but the good news is that they're less poor than they used to be," says Heidi

Hartmann of the Institute for Women's Policy Research. In the past twenty years, the percentage of female heads of household living in poverty has dropped nearly 10 percent.

This move out of poverty comes directly from women's education and improved earning power. "By getting an education, women have become more able to support their children," Hartmann says. Women's incomes have climbed steadily since 1980.

"The trends are unmistakable," says Robert Reich. "The typical male worker today is earning no more than the typical male worker thirty years ago, adjusted for inflation. But the typical woman is earning much more today than the typical woman earned thirty years ago."

All this adds up to real change for women like Rosa. And it's happening around the world.

Gradually, quietly, slowly, women have been becoming a larger share of the workforce, entering increasingly well-paid jobs, and inching up the income ladder. Continent by continent, you can trace women's global progress on the income charts as easily as you can watch the tide lap up a beach. In Sub-Saharan Africa, the number of people living on less than $1.25 a day (a group, globally, made up of far more women than men) fell by 6 percentage points between 1990 and 2005. In Southeast Asia, that number fell by 20 percentage points. In all developing regions as a whole, the quantity of people living on less than a dollar a day has dropped 42 percent to 25 percent. That's real progress.

Clearly, women's expanding earning power isn't just improving life for individual families. It's influencing the entire global economy.

"For the past two decades, the increase in female employment in the rich world has been the main driving force of growth," *The Economist* magazine reported in 2006. "Those women have contributed more to global GDP growth than have either new technology, or the new giants, China or India."

A bigger impact on the global economy than *China* or *India*. That's simply astounding: The development of those two booming countries, particularly the growth of their middle class, contributed nearly $5 trillion to the global economy between 1998 and 2006. If, as *The Economist* asserts, women's growing employment *just in wealthy countries* has added more than that, imagine what will happen when women's full economic power, worldwide, is unleashed.

Talk about the power of the purse!

Influence Defined

While there are still far too many women living in poverty, it's encouraging to see how many women like Rosa are moving to the middle stage of economic power, *Independence.* Let's not underestimate this. In one hundred years women have moved from *being* property to *owning* property.

But figuring out how many women are making the next step, from independence to influence, is a tougher task. First of all, these stages of economic power aren't necessarily a one-way trip. Making it to independence doesn't guarantee you'll stay there, let alone head upstairs to influence. Also, financial influence is a slippery concept. In the three stages of economic power, you can't draw simple income lines and say, "At $25,000 a year or less, a woman is surviving; at $26,000 she's independent." Nor can you say, "At $75,000 she's independent, and at $150,000, she has influence."

Instead, the stages of financial power are related to how women *use* their money. At the survival level, every dollar (or yuan or dinar or euro) goes toward food and shelter. At the independence level, the money goes toward a wider variety of things (which makes it tougher to track): education; nicer houses in safer neighborhoods with better schools; more reliable cars; healthier foods.

At the influence stage, women start using their money (and/or the security, independence, and financial power it brings) to impact the world beyond the circle of their loved ones and friends. In short, economic influence is the use of financial power (and all that comes with it) to affect the broader world. Influence is Melinda Gates starting the Bill & Melinda Gates Foundation with Bill; it's Deborah Szekely founding schools and libraries and arts organizations, and heading up Latin American aid efforts. It's Shelly Lazarus, chairman and CEO of ad and marketing giant

Ogilvy & Mather, making sure every bed at the children's hospital at Columbia Presbyterian in New York has video consoles for games and movies.

But influence isn't expressed only through philanthropy. Influence is any use of your resources to affect the world. In the corporate sphere, Indra Nooyi, chairman and CEO of Pepsico, adopted a new mission for the company: "performance with purpose." Under her leadership, the company reduced its use of fossil fuels in favor of wind and solar power, and launched global initiatives at its factories to reduce waste and use water more efficiently. The company sold off fast-food businesses like Pizza Hut and bought businesses making healthier foods, including juice maker Tropicana and oatmeal giant Quaker Oats. Nooyi vowed that within a few years, the company would earn half its profits from healthy products. Meanwhile, under her guidance, Pepsico launched an effort to train its farmer-suppliers in India in sustainable, water-efficient agricultural methods, which boosted the farmers' productivity and saved water—a win for the company, the farmers, and the environment. "Nobody's going to remember you for delivering earnings to stockholders," Nooyi told a standing-room-only crowd at New York's Asia Society in the spring of 2009. "They will remember you for the lasting impact you made on society and for being sustainable." Making positive changes people will remember—now *that's* influence.

Influence also happens in small business: In Northern California, Sally Thornton left the corporate world to cofound Flexperience, a consulting firm that connects experienced, talented women with part-time, flexible jobs with clients such as Genentech, Levi Strauss & Co., and Pixar. Thornton's firm is opening up all kinds of new work-life possibilities for women. As Thornton, Nooyi, and thousands of other women have shown, you don't have to be a philanthropist to exercise economic influence. Influence can happen in politics or investing or any other institution where you want to make a mark.

You don't have to be wealthy, either, to exercise influence. While in college at the Al Akhawayn University in Ifrane, Morocco, Kawtar Chyraa, twenty-two, became treasurer of Hand-in-Hand, a campus group promoting education for rural girls and women. During her term as treasurer, the group raised enough money to build a new school in Ain Lkhil, a poor rural area near the college. They didn't just build the school; they also funded power and water projects for it.

"Ifrane is a very poor area, so we also needed to raise money for the electrical infrastructure and to have a well dug," she says.

Two fun runs raised much of the needed money. Meanwhile, Chyraa and her colleagues persuaded a French NGO to donate two school buses. At the same time, Hand-in-Hand helped poor women in the community start a business baking bread at home and selling it on campus. "It's a very smart business, because most of the students on campus are starving for homemade bread," she says with a laugh.

Chyraa's efforts prove you don't need to be wealthy to exercise economic influence. What you *do* need is to understand how money works—what makes it flow, how to get it where you want it and to do what you want it to do. And you need the psychological freedom from hunger, fatigue, and constant need. Virginia Woolf argued, "A woman needs a room of her own and an independent income if she is to write." In the realm of economic influence, I would say that a woman needs a psychological room of her own and economic independence if she is to inscribe herself on the world.

It's also possible to be wealthy but *never* reach the stage of economic influence. Deborah Szekely didn't *have* to start a school or head an aid foundation. She could have stayed at her spas enjoying unlimited access to Pilates and massage. Shelly Lazarus, the CEO of Ogilvy, didn't have to fund bedside video consoles at a children's hospital. These women didn't choose to stay home and keep their wealth to themselves: They found ways to improve their world. At a certain point in highly successful careers, many women (and men) of substance feel keenly that the "he who dies with the most toys wins" philosophy fails to nourish their souls—and they begin to seek a philosophy that does.

The Power Shift: From Independence to Influence

While influence and wealth are not synonymous, money can serve as a pretty good *indicator* of influence—and it's an indicator we can measure. So far, women's progress into the upper echelons of wealth has been slow, far slower than their progress from survival to independence. But this progress toward influence is happening—slowly, but inexorably. Between 1991 and 2001, the number of women earning more than $100,000 tripled. By 2006, about 5 percent of all women (compared with 15 percent of men) made more than $75,000. In 2000, just 2.8 percent of women earned more than $75,000. Maybe jumping from "almost zero" to "very small" isn't enough to change the world—yet.

But this is the sign of things to come. And that's the point.

Globally, it's much harder to get figures tracing these earliest of movements of women into the top income ranks, because many countries don't measure income by gender, or if they do, there's little historical data. But where there are numbers, those numbers tell a striking story. In the UK, women will soon be richer than men, owning 60 percent of all personal wealth by 2025. Even in the Middle East, where women's social freedom is severely restricted, women control huge sums of money. Around 40 percent of high-net-worth assets in Saudi Arabia, Bahrain, Kuwait, Qatar, the United Arab Emirates, and the Sultanate of Oman are at least partially controlled by women.

These promising numbers aren't the only way—are maybe not even the best way—to follow women's economic emancipation. You can also track this change by the clues it leaves behind. Ever so slowly, the structure and rules of the world's most influential institutions are starting to change, largely in response to women's growing economic influence. At global consulting giant Deloitte, the "traditional" career path—work like crazy for fifty weeks a year, for forty-five years—no longer exists: Instead, the firm assumes every career will include periods of more or less intense work, sabbaticals, leave, part-time schedules, flex time, and other arrangements. The company didn't change because it makes Deloitte's executives feel good about themselves. The company needs to be flexible to retain top-quality women, or it will lose the battle for talent.

Likewise, Dove didn't launch its game-changing ad series "Campaign for Real Beauty," featuring women's honest-to-goodness bodies, as an antidote to negative messages about women's appearance: It wanted to sell soaps (and it did: Within two months of the U.S. campaign launch, sales of products featured in the series shot up 600 percent; six months after the campaign launched, sales were up by 700 percent in Europe!). Rwanda's constitution doesn't mandate that 30 percent of legislative seats go to women simply because equality is nice: More and more, decision makers of either gender see with increasing clarity that diverse points of view help countries and companies become more effective.

Overall, the easiest way to trace women's ascendance is to track the signs. And if you're a savvy tracker, those signs will show you not just where women have been, but where they are headed.

What's at Stake?

Of course, it's great news that women are pulling themselves out of lives of mere survival into independence and even, slowly, influence. But— aside from the obvious human benefits—so what? If my point were simply to call out the rather obvious evidence that women are starting to do better financially, you could close this book right now.

It turns out, though, that as women gain more and more control over money, the world is starting to *look* different. The difference isn't just that more women are moving to middle-class neighborhoods and sending their kids to better schools: When women have more money, they *use* it differently than men do. They make different choices. They invest it differently. They spend it differently. And they *feel* differently about money.

By starting to understand how men and women relate differently to money, we begin to see why and how they make different choices when they have it. We also begin to see why the gradual, inexorable shift of the world's money from "his" to "his and hers" will change ever more of the world's institutions, norms, and policies to "ours." Of course, there are barriers to these sweeping institutional transformations; paradigms rarely change overnight. Of course, this shift won't happen at the same pace everywhere. Of course, there's plenty that could go wrong. But if, as women, we're aware of these changes, understand why they're important, and continue to work to hasten change, the inevitable power shift will happen *sooner,* not later—and will benefit not just women but everyone.

Throughout this book, I'll show precisely how women's rising economic power has already started to affect specific institutions, including the family, the workplace, and politics. But for those transformations to make sense, we first need a better understanding of what a dollar means to a man and what it means to a woman.

Gender, Money, and Power: The Study

I'm not the first person ever to wonder about men, women, and money. Over the past decade, there have been many studies that have looked at gender and money, some led by academics trying to understand the progress women have made around the globe, others conducted by companies trying to sell more products to women.

But I wanted to go beyond the external records to get a psychological take on the issue. Surprisingly little has been done on the psychology behind women's choices when handling money—though this seems the very crux of women's economic progress. If a woman earns a million dollars a year, but is so terrified of losing it that she's afraid to part with a penny, how far has she come, really? Or if a woman doesn't negotiate for a bigger salary because she fears looking bitchy or unattractive, how much progress have we made?

To answer these questions, Age Wave, the company I cofounded with my husband, Ken Dychtwald, teamed up with financial services company Allianz and with Harris Interactive to launch an in-depth study of gender, money, and power. We started with a large, randomized survey of three thousand men and women around the United States. We asked how financially secure they felt, what they worried about, what money meant to them. We asked about their secret money lives: Did they have a stash their spouse didn't know about? Did they fantasize about someone rescuing them financially? Did they feel confident or insecure about making investment choices?

While one should always be wary of overgeneralizing, it was astonishing to see distinct trends emerge from the data. Of course, one can never say, "All women feel this way and all men feel that way." But in at least three critical areas, there was a clear gender split in attitudes and behaviors toward money—attitudes that have a direct impact on the choices men and women make with their money, their careers, and their families.

These startling results are why I found myself on a sunny day in Los Angeles observing focus groups of women talking about their relationships with money. I wanted to dig deeper, to put faces and names and hearts to the numerical trends we found. As women of all ages, income levels, and ethnic backgrounds talked about their feelings around money, I was struck by the passion they felt about the issues, and by their willingness to share, very frankly, their conflicts, challenges, and secrets. We convened more focus groups, in Chicago and Atlanta, and interviewed groups of men, too. The more I heard both genders talk about their different psychological relationships to money, the more I could make sense of changes I was already seeing all around me, at the grocery store, the office, the polling place. Three clear trends quickly emerged from our research—trends that were largely, on the surface, already supported by previous studies, but that hadn't been probed as deeply before. We saw *what* was happening with women and their money, and with men and their money, but also began to understand *why*—and what it means for the future.

Finding One: Money Means Security to Women, Freedom to Men

By a significant margin, the men we surveyed said the best thing about having money was having the freedom to do what they want; for women, it was the security that came with it. A startling two-thirds of women said security was the top benefit of money.

It's no surprise to learn that women want economic security. Most studies and secondary research support this finding. But additional questions helped us deepen our knowledge about this gender difference. We wanted to know why women value security so very highly. What we found was that women's fears of poverty run deep, at every income level. Those fears didn't go away when women had money. In fact, women who earned $100,000 or more were slightly *more* likely to fear losing it all. Sandy Lawrence, one of our San Francisco discussion group participants, called this phenomenon "delusions of poverty" and mentioned they'd haunted her for a long time.

She's the smart, savvy former CEO of a biotech company, but she was very familiar with the fear of landing out on the street—although years of exercising her own earning power eventually helped her escape these delusions.

Because women value security so highly (their value of security far outweighs their next two priorities, caring for family and financial freedom), financial insecurity can take a high toll. Fully a third of the women we surveyed did not feel financially secure at all; just 10 percent said they felt extremely secure. And, overall, women were far less optimistic and confident than men about money. In fact, men were fully *twice* as likely to describe themselves as optimistic. Men were also more confident about money than women: About 56 percent of men scored high on confidence (rating themselves as "confident," "responsible," and "not passive regarding money"), compared with 49 percent of women who rated themselves highly on these attributes.

These differences in security, optimism, and confidence had a clear influence on the choices women made about their money. Example: One in five women in our study said she had a secret stash of money her partner didn't know about—that's twice the number of men with a secret stash. Some 70 percent of the women with a stash said it was as a hedge against economic disaster—specifically, against financial emergency (52 percent) or desertion by her partner (18 percent). Said one focus group participant: "My mom was always hiding money in the back of the closet, and even though my husband is very generous, I find myself doing the same exact thing." As women's wealth and economic power grow, will these trends change? Will fear, delusions of poverty, and economic self-doubt continue to affect the way women influence the world? Or as women have more money, will their confidence grow? The answers to these questions will have a big impact on the way women use their economic independence and influence in the future.

Finding Two: What a Difference an "A" Makes: Warriors vs. Worriers

"Men are out there hunting with their money," one of our focus group participants said. "Women are gathering it." Her comment pointed to another gender divide reflected in our survey. Men saw themselves as warriors, women as worriers. Men were almost twice as likely as women to say they would take significant financial risks. And they were far less likely to describe themselves as worriers than women were.

Many financial advisors we spoke with thought this risk-taking was a good thing and that women should behave less conservatively—in short, be more like men. "If women don't take some risk with their money, there's a danger that they'll outlive their savings," says Mary Claire Allvine, a financial planner in Atlanta.

At the same time, women's worrying can lead to some positive results. Women are more likely to enroll in defined contribution retirement plans and make larger contributions than men. And they're more likely to buy and hold investments, rather than churn them: As a result, women's investments often do better than men's in the long run.

Again, it was no surprise to find that men take more money risks than women. It's a finding that holds true across many studies. But seeing the numbers fall out so clearly provoked new questions for me. Would traits that seem to be gender-linked change as women accumulate more wealth? Will women become warriors and leave the worry behind? Some evidence suggests women do become more confident with money as they gain more experience managing it. For instance, one study found that as a woman's contribution to family income increases, so does her financial involvement.

For Sandy Lawrence, running a business and earning money for a long period of time helped banish her "delusions of poverty." The confidence she gained with her money as a business owner continued to empower her even after the 2008 recession dealt her a major financial setback. "After the markets went bear, I thought about what I'd do if I won the lottery. I'd walk down the street and give $100 bills to homeless people. Then I realized, even if I couldn't be Bill Gates, I could make a difference. Instead of giving $25 or $50 here and there to charity, I'd get more strategic about what I supported." Instead of making lots of small donations, she started making a few larger donations, of $500 or so, and getting more involved in a few causes. "I realized I can make a difference with what little I do have in a way that is meaningful to me."

Having money and learning to use it more confidently have changed her worldview and helped her have more influence with the groups she supports.

Likewise, when women have money, they change the role they play in family investments. Where women are the primary earners, 40 percent take the lead in investing (that's *twice* the number of women who handle the family investments when women earn less than their husbands). But will women take the same risks that men do financially? Should they? After all, women are already taking significant financial risks just by being women—by living longer, by working part-time or not at all, by taking years out of the workforce for caregiving, and by disproportionately choosing careers in helping professions like health care, teaching, and the nonprofit sector, which pay less than other industries. Should women become more like men? Or is there a new model of investing that makes more sense for women? Or should each gender try to become a bit more like the other? The answers will shape the future of the financial services industry, as well as the financial future of women themselves.

Finding Three: Women Put the Financial Needs of Others Ahead of Their Own

Women's time out of the workforce, the time they spend caring for their families, their choice of helping careers—all these things point toward another gender divide that our survey confirmed. Women are more likely than men to put others' financial needs ahead of their own. In the study, both genders valued three top priorities—security, freedom, and caring for family and friends—far, far above money values like "feeling I've made it" or "gaining respect from others." But for women, caring for family was second only to security—for men, it was their third priority.

When we probed deeper, asking specifically if women were more likely than men to put family and friends' financial needs ahead of their own, about 41 percent of women agreed with this statement.

Of course, what people say and what they *do* are different things. So we also asked a group of financial advisors about men's and women's behaviors with money. Many agreed women were more likely to put others first. "If they won the lottery, most men would buy expensive toys and women would help their kids and relatives," one advisor told us. Meanwhile, economic development experts say that women are far more likely than men to invest their income in the well-being of their children and family.

The tendency to care for others before self is a double-edged sword for women. Since women live longer and are less likely to work full-time jobs throughout their careers, their retirement savings already significantly lag behind men's. A survey by Hewitt Associates found the average balance in women's retirement plans was $56,000 compared with nearly twice that for men. (Even though women are more likely to open retirement accounts and make bigger contributions, it's not enough to offset the fact that, on average, women earn less than men and spend fewer years in the workforce.) But while women may well be hurting themselves and their financial well-being, there's clearly a social benefit when women choose to use their earnings to pay for college, support their children, or help care for aging parents. Many women feel torn between the desire to do what's best for their family and what's best for their own financial future. "My child is on the verge of going to kindergarten," said Jennifer Heyman, a single mother who attended one of our San Francisco discussion groups. "Do I compromise her education so that we will survive on my income? I cannot commit to being able to afford twelve years of private school." Or should she get a new job? Or put aside her own retirement planning? "How do I make those kinds of decisions?" she asks.

In the chapters ahead, we'll see how this focus on others above self influences women's money choices at home, at work, and in the political realm, and leads them to use their economic influence differently from men. In the coming years, those differences will add up to a huge positive change for our economy (not to mention major upheavals in our families, our workplaces, and our government, as I'll explain in the chapters ahead). Until recently, women's economic influence on the world has been a tiny breeze amid the gale force of men's financial power. So any significant gender differences in money choices, feelings, or behavior had little chance to shift direction of the wind. But as women's income and wealth grow around the world, as women's control of world assets moves from $14 trillion today to $22 trillion a decade from now, you can be sure the weather will change. Whatever the cause, we worry more. We save more. We spend differently and influence differently. And these tendencies will soon create a permanent change in the economic climate.

From Alpha Females to Uncertain Searchers: Women's Five Money Profiles

Our research provoked more and more questions in my mind. I wanted to know what makes women more confident, when women's tendencies and trends help in their progress toward emancipation, and when they hurt. We focused a section of our research on women's specific behaviors around money.

FINANCIAL PERSONALITY TYPES

Percent of U.S. Women

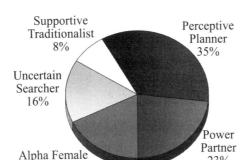

Source: Age Wave/Allianz, *Women, Money and Power,* 2006

We looked at women's responses in our survey and in the focus groups, trying to understand specific groups of women and how they fit into, and what they foretold about, the changing world. As we examined the data we'd collected, five profiles of women and money emerged. So we went back and asked women which profile fit each of them best.

We discovered that what determines a woman's financial personality is, in fact, very much how she *feels* about money, how much she *defers* to someone else to get the job done, what she *wants money to do for her,* what she *wants to do with her money,* and most important, how *confident* she is in her relationship with money. While these profiles are snapshots of one moment in time, it was immediately clear that some financial personalities will help women's economic emancipation—and others won't. And, unfortunately, those that won't are still alarmingly common.

Since conducting the study, as I've traveled about giving presentations on our findings, I've been astonished by the eagerness with which women of all stripes want to identify with one of the personalities. I've hardly been able to walk into a room where our results are known without being besieged by women who want to tell me which personality they are. This eagerness tells me that the money personalities we identified make sense to women. It also shows that women are hungry for a language with which to discuss their evolving relationships with money.

FINANCIAL CONFIDENCE INDEX

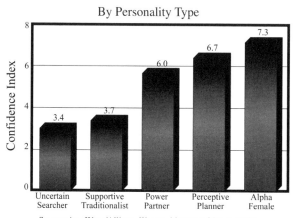

By Personality Type

Source: Age Wave/Allianz, *Women, Money and Power,* 2006

1. Alpha Female

Cheryl Fahrenholz, president of Preferred Healthcare Solutions in Bellbrook, Ohio, runs a small company advising health systems about medical records and reimbursements. She earns three times what her husband, a contractor, takes home, and manages 100 percent of the family finances. "He's on a budget," she says. "He doesn't know all the details of the finances. I have a trust for our child because I have certain things that can't go to my husband, like an ownership in my family's farm. I've arranged it so that if I die, my husband will be able to live here until he gets married, but if he remarries, they can't take half my kid's portion." Fahrenholz made it clear from the start of her marriage that she wanted to run the couple's finances. This caused some friction at first, she says, but now her husband's on board. "I'm good at it and interested in it," she says.

Fahrenholz is a perfect fit for the *Alpha Female* profile, the most confident of the five types. The Alpha Female tends to act more like society expects a confident man to behave with his money. Eighteen percent of women surveyed identified themselves in this group. The Alpha Female is the most optimistic, risk-tolerant, and aggressive of the personalities. She's a quick decision maker, self-reliant, and able to learn from her mistakes; she's far less interested in the details than in the results. She is great at delegating and uses outside help whenever possible to boost her decision making, although sometimes she's so gung ho she'll make decisions quickly before she has all the facts. Most important, the Alpha Female *feels* financially and psychologically independent and in charge. It's also worth noting that she feels financially responsible in part because she's often had to be.

2. Perceptive Planner

Naagla El Dawy, thirty-four, is head of the Human Rights Association for Community Development in Assiut, Egypt. She's been saving and budgeting since she was twelve years old. "I used to save up for Mother's Day gifts," she told me. "I see money as a source of economic security and freedom." She identified with the *Perceptive Planner* profile, the largest group in the study by far, accounting for 35 percent of all women surveyed.

The Perceptive Planner is not quite as confident as the Alpha Female, but she's highly analytical, responsible, disciplined, and optimistic. She's detail-oriented, thinks in the long term, and thoroughly researches purchases, investments, and financial commitments. The Perceptive Planner is extremely hands-on. Unlike the Alpha Female, she's motivated primarily by the desire for security and stability. Also, unlike the Alpha Female, the Perceptive Planner would never move forward without having all the facts under her belt. She's the opposite of a delegator, liking to mull things over carefully on her own before taking action. Perceptive planners can be married or single. In either case, she is insistent about doing all the research in advance and mulling things over; but, if married, she can either make final decisions with her partner or, if he's not interested, take charge for the two of them.

3. Power Partner

Linda Descano, president and chief operating officer of Women & Co., Citigroup's financial planning network for women, is the textbook example of a *Power Partner.* "My husband and I have lengthy conversations about money and clear ground rules about how we do things," she says. Some money goes into joint accounts; some money they keep separate for each partner to invest as he or she desires. "We do a formal review of all our money twice a year," she says. "It's a great partnership." Their investing styles are complementary. Hers is "more steady. I want my long-term plan," while he's more willing to chase a stock tip or sell off in a panic. The key to their financial partnership is that they understand each other's strengths and weaknesses and work together. "Every couple has to find a balance that works for them."

The Power Partner was the second most common group in our survey, scoring a 6.0 on the confidence index and accounting for 23 percent of the women we studied. A Power Partner is less interested in money for its own sake and more in what it can do for her loved ones and herself. She's collaborative and willing to strike compromises, believing that two heads are better than one. Like the Perceptive Planner, she's driven primarily by her desire for stability. Pragmatic and responsible, the Power Partner is also very concerned that her partner's needs are met as well as her own.

The Power Partner reported being the happiest of the five personalities. Also, not all Power Partnerships are between spouses or romantic partners. Sometimes Power Partners are siblings, business partners, close friends, or even a parent and child.

4. Supportive Traditionalist

Lauraine Jaeger, a lawyer originally from Montreal, had been a *Supportive Traditionalist* for decades until her husband died earlier in 2008. "I always worked, but he controlled the finances and made the decisions. He was the main earner and he did the taxes. I totally trusted his judgment. I signed tax returns without reading them. I didn't know where the money was. I knew nothing," she says. Ironically, Jaeger was always great with numbers growing up and excelled at math. But once she married, she ceded all financial decisions to her husband, for thirty-four years. In some ways, Jaeger's decision was luxurious—money was one big thing she just didn't have to worry about. But this attitude toward money also left her unprepared for life on her own. When her husband passed away, she was at sea. "There were many, many pieces of paper," she told me, shaking her head. "I spent six months literally doing nothing else but figuring it out."

Supportive Traditionalists hope that someone else will take care of everything money-related for them. Traditionally, this has been the de facto way women have behaved toward money, so it was striking to see that this was the smallest group in our survey: Only 8 percent of women self-identified with this personality. The Supportive Traditionalist scored only a 3.7 out of 10 on the confidence index. The Supportive Traditionalist is highly emotional about financial matters rather than analytical. She enjoys spending, but she's not that interested in gaining knowledge when it comes to things like saving and investing. In fact, she avoids confrontation or even discussions about money. She'd rather cede all control to someone else than engage herself. And, like Lauraine Jaeger, she is likely to find herself in deep trouble once her partner's gone.

But the Supportive Traditionalist need not stay traditional. By working to master the art of financial planning, Jaeger is actually transforming herself into an Alpha Female. "I have had to try to go from zero to one hundred in the financial-planning department and am slowly but consistently moving towards that goal. I have excellent advisors and am beginning to understand basic principles so that I can participate effectively in decision making. More importantly, I am no longer anxious about managing my financial situation."

5. The Uncertain Searcher

Least confident among the profiles, scoring a 3.4 out of 10 on the confidence index, was the *Uncertain Searcher.* About 16 percent of women identified with this group. This woman is led by her emotions when it comes to making decisions about money. She's fearful and sometimes becomes paralyzed when it's time to make financial decisions. She's an impulsive shopper who succumbs to instant gratification, and she holds few ideas about how to think about money in the long term. The Uncertain Searcher knows she's ignorant about finances, but is so fearful of long-term financial thinking that she doesn't know where to turn or whom to trust for help. She'd like to know more, but isn't sure how to educate herself.

While the Uncertain Searcher may not know where to turn for information about money and sometimes is too embarrassed by her lack of knowledge to ask, she knows she's lost and hopes to move out of this conundrum.

Power and Personality

The more research we did into the five personalities, the more surprised I was that so many women are unsure in their money skills. About a quarter of women put themselves in the least confident groups—Uncertain Searcher and Supportive Traditionalist.

After all this time, why aren't women more financially confident? This lack of confidence is a real roadblock on the path to economic influence. If women let their anxieties, fears, and lack of confidence keep them from managing money in a smart way, they'll never attain their dreams.

Women may not even be able to keep the gains they've made or hold on to their economic security as they age. Women live longer than men and earn less: If they don't save aggressively, invest wisely, and learn to control their money, they won't be able to maintain their own security—let alone continue the march toward influence. Women need financial confidence, education, and savvy to keep from slipping back—and to move ahead—for their own financial security, for the future security of their children, and to improve the collective economic power of women as a group.

Our survey provided another unpleasant surprise: I was shocked to see that younger women were almost *twice as likely* as mature women to call themselves Supportive Traditionalists—even if they weren't married. They were more likely than older women to worry about usurping the man's role, to think money might make them less attractive to men, and to say they'd see their partner as "more of a man" if he took more control of the finances.

"I'm his responsibility and he enjoys that. I married him and he wants to take care of me, so why not?" one of the younger respondents in a Chicago focus group said. "If I can have that life, I say, why not?"

Another young woman said she was joyfully anticipating her Prince Charming's praise and surprise at her great financial skills when he arrived. "I want him to be able to say he's so proud of how much money I've saved," she said.

Maybe these are just youthful fantasies about a rosy future—fantasies that our older subjects had since let go as youthful folly. Or perhaps young women are throwing up their hands and retreating from financial responsibility after witnessing the painful struggle of their own working mothers to balance life, family, and money. Maybe these younger women fear taking on the complexities of financial independence on their own. In any case, if this trend persists as this younger generation ages, it will slow women's progress toward economic emancipation.

One thing is clear: Any woman who remains an Uncertain Searcher or Supportive Traditionalist faces clear and urgent dangers to her independence and perhaps even to her very economic survival. A woman's personal financial security decreases when she's not involved in or knowledgeable about her finances—and there is no way she can reach true economic influence without understanding how money works.

The good news is, these personalities aren't fixed within us; they are not boxes drawn in concrete. More than one woman told me that sometimes she feels like an Alpha Female, sometimes like an Uncertain Searcher, and many women, like Lauraine Jaeger, have been able to educate themselves into a more confident role.

The Sleeping Giantess

The next time we do this research, I hope we'll find many more women moving up the confidence scale: far fewer Uncertain Searchers, many more Perceptive Planners and Alpha Females. To me, a growth in the number of more confident types will be a clear indicator that we're shedding internal barriers that have held women back and made us less independent and far more reluctant to take that final leap to influence.

Sooner or later, overall, that leap is inevitable. Women are on a steady upward economic course. But the speed of the journey is up to women themselves. External barriers do still block the way. Among them, as I've already mentioned, are the facts that many cultures continue to treat women as second-class citizens; that around the world, women do much more unpaid housework and childcare than men, in addition to working; and that progress on issues like the gender wage gap in the United States has stalled out. You'll read about many more barriers in the chapters ahead, but you will also read about how women, companies, and countries are overcoming them, often working together to do so. Women will need every bit of confidence and then some to clear those hurdles and gain the momentum needed to take advantage of this unique moment of economic upheaval and reinvention.

If women *can* take advantage of this moment, a sleeping giantess of collective untapped economic power will fully awaken. She's already beginning to stir. In the past few years alone, international organizations from the World Economic Forum to the United Nations have opened their eyes to the importance of women's economic equality. In 2005, the World Economic Forum began tracking an annual index of gender parity, with economic equality a key measure. The UN has embraced an ambitious goal for decreasing poverty—and a key piece of the puzzle is ending women's poverty. The World Bank is pressuring countries around the globe to keep better statistics on women and money—because what gets measured, gets done.

All these efforts suggest that the long slumber of women's economic emancipation may be ending. Women are about to rouse their full economic potential. And when they do, that power will shape the world in ways we can only begin to understand—but with results we can plainly observe in the efforts of pioneers like Deborah Szekely and Marian Wright Edelman. The influence held by women like these will soon spread in ways that will play out in our families, our offices, and our communities in every corner of the world.

In Business

THE ENTREPRENEURIAL EXODUS

Katie Rodan, a dermatologist in the San Francisco Bay area, didn't set out to break all the rules. She just wanted to treat acne. She'd been plagued by zits as a teen, so when she went to Stanford medical school in the 1980s, she headed straight into dermatology.

But the medical approach to skin problems troubled her. "The way people treated acne made absolutely no sense to me," she told me. I've known Rodan for years and still find it hard to believe she's ever had a pimple in her life. Her skin is perfect, a delicate porcelain set off by her dark hair. But her struggles with acne were long and painful. Years later, there was one thing she still couldn't understand: Why did almost all dermatologists treat breakouts like injuries—unfortunate accidents to be treated after they happened? Why weren't zits treated more like cavities, something that could be prevented by good habits and hygiene?

In 1989, two years after finishing her residency in dermatology, Rodan and her medical school friend and fellow dermatologist Kathy Fields set out to change the model, to focus on *preventing* outbreaks, not treating them afterward, and developed a new line of skin care products called Proactiv.

"Getting people to treat their whole face every day, so they could prevent breakouts to begin with—that was the real flip of the tortilla," Rodan says. But it's not easy to change entrenched ideas about what works, medically or commercially.

"When we tried to raise money, businesspeople would say, 'Well, if it's so obvious, why aren't the big companies doing it?'" Rodan recalls. The big cosmetics companies were stuck in an old paradigm: That's the way things have always been, so that must be the best way. Why change?

Since Rodan and Fields couldn't raise big money or interest major companies in developing their products, they had no choice but to break more rules. The first and biggest: "Nice doctors don't do infomercials." As an adjunct clinical professor at Stanford and a practicing dermatologist, Rodan valued the respect and esteem of her peers and knew she'd be risking her reputation by promoting Proactiv through an infomercial. But she also wanted to help more patients—and she believed the existing acne protocol was letting patients suffer needlessly.

Ultimately, it was guidance from her mother—a quiet, reserved professor of microbiology—that gave her the courage she needed. "My mother said, 'Do it. Who cares what they say?' She'd always been so quiet and proper. The encouragement to take a risk really meant a lot coming from her." Rodan and Fields made their first infomercial in 1995. "We tried to make it classy and credible," she says. The infomercial was an instant success. On camera, as off, Rodan is warm, confident, and intelligent, a refreshing combination of bubbly enthusiasm and down-to-earth smarts. Her commercials hit home.

In the years since that first act of promotional daring, Rodan and Fields have transformed the way dermatologists treat acne and the way acne sufferers self-treat it. By 2007, Rodan and Fields's company was selling $850 million worth of acne preventative products a year, to more than five million customers, 70 percent of them in the United States. Compare that revenue to the sales of all acne products sold over the counter in drugstores that same year—a mere $155 million—and you see what a massive impact Rodan's paradigm shift had on acne treatment. In 2003, Rodan and Fields shared the prestigious Cosmetic Executive Women's award for "changing the direction of the industry." Along the way, Rodan became financially independent, eventually hiring her husband, who has an MBA from Harvard and had worked with a number of start-ups, as chairman and CEO of the company.

Rodan stresses that her idea alone doesn't account for her success. Rather, a moment of cultural upheaval helped her idea succeed. "In the early nineties, medicine was going through a real transformation.

Physicians' incomes were going down and it became more acceptable to market yourself," she says. Meanwhile, infomercials were becoming more sophisticated, engaging, and well produced.

"A lot of things were changing at one time. Everything gelled at exactly the right moment to make Proactiv successful," she adds.

For Rodan, the sweetest part of it all is that her financial success didn't compromise her medical reputation, as she'd feared. Instead, it helped her become a better doctor. Because of Proactiv's success in the marketplace, she told me, "I didn't have to see ten patients an hour so I could pay my bills. I could give each patient a lot of time and attention." As a result, a panel of her own peers—the very group whose contempt she feared—chose her as one of the Bay Area's best doctors in 2008.

When I saw Rodan's face on the cover of *Oakland Magazine*'s annual best doctors issue in the fall of 2008, I thought of how far she'd come. Clearly, by breaking the rules to create a new way to treat acne sufferers, she'd found a whole new way to succeed.

Flipping the Tortilla: Changing the World's Work

To my mind, Katie Rodan's story stands for much more than just one woman's success. Women like her are succeeding in *every* industry—using their education, professional skill, and economic confidence to rewrite the rules governing how business gets done. This is nothing new: Women have been quietly transforming business for the past three decades. But as women move from financial independence to true economic influence, with the financial power to realize their visions on a big scale, the depth and breadth of their transformative potential is about to become blazingly clear. Katie Rodan's success happened at a unique moment when economic realities, industry shifts, and social mores coincided with a groundbreaking idea. The same thing is about to happen in the workplace, where new economic and demographic realities will intersect with long-term trends in women's income and employment. We're on the brink of a change that will transform entire industries, revolutionizing the way companies manage their employees and structure their businesses. We're about to see one *very* big flip of the tortilla.

Entrepreneurial Exodus

Like Katie Rodan, millions of women are breaking the rules in their industries every day. In businesses of all sizes, women are finding new ways of working that make more sense for their lives (and for the lives of their life partners and children and extended families as well). Business as usual, in a workplace designed by men, for men, with at-home spouses, just isn't working for a huge number of women. Frankly, it hasn't been working well for a lot of men either.

"The current work model is the old model," says Karen Sumberg, vice president of the Center for Work-Life Policy. "It addresses a white man with a stay-at-home wife. But that person represents an increasingly small portion of the workforce. White men are becoming the minority in the workplace, which is increasingly populated with women and men of different cultures and ethnicities." The American workforce is vastly different than it was fifty years ago, or even a decade ago. In 1950, 30 percent of the U.S. workforce was women: Today, it's about half women. In the 1950s, a minority of mothers worked. Today, 70 percent do.

But most companies are still run by men with spouses at home. In the United States, 85 percent of corporate officers at Fortune 500 companies are men. Women make up just 26.7 percent of all general and operations managers. Globally, senior male executives (75 percent of them) usually have a stay-at-home partner; while 74 percent of senior women executives have a partner who works full-time.

It's no wonder the old rules and paradigms of most workplaces don't work well for many women, especially mothers. Many workplaces are outright hostile to family needs. "My twins were born very prematurely. My son weighed less than two pounds," says Kathleen Hall, now the general manager of consumer marketing at Microsoft. Her employer at the time, an advertising agency, showed little respect for family needs. "I was on maternity leave when they said, 'You have to come back, we have a huge pitch.' I said, 'You know I have two kids in intensive care. What are you people thinking?'" Later in her career, at a financial services firm, she again encountered hostility when she had to take six weeks off to care for her eleven-year-old son's sudden severe health problems. "Even when you have a track record of high performance, you can still encounter little or no tolerance for family needs."

If a sensible response to family needs is that hard to come by for a high-power executive like Hall, just imagine how family needs are treated for the vast majority of American workers. Hall's case is just one, glaringly clear example of the mismatch between the real workforce—full of working moms, working dads, older people, and many other nontraditional workers with full lives outside the office—and the mythical corporate workforce that doesn't bat an eye at seventy-hour weeks, every week, for years on end.

When it comes to today's workforce, perception does not fit reality.

What do you do when something doesn't fit? You alter it or leave it and find something else that works better. For many women in the United States, the latter choice has been more alluring. "There's an ongoing parade of women moving out of corporations who say, 'This is too soul crushing,'" says Nell Merlino, founder, president, and CEO of Count Me In for Women's Economic Independence, a nonprofit organization that, in 2005, launched an initiative called Make Mine a Million $ Business to boost women-owned businesses over the million-dollar sales mark. Every day, more than four hundred U.S. women start their own companies—twice the rate at which men do so. The number of women-owned firms grew by 19.8 percent between 1997 and 2002, then leapt a whopping 55 percent after 2002. Today, 10.1 million firms are owned by women. These businesses employ more than 13 million people, and they generated $1.9 trillion in sales in 2008.

The growth—in numbers and in revenue—of women-owned businesses represents a massive change. But what's even more important is the way women are writing their own rules for the workplace and changing paradigms along the way—specifically, upending our ideas about when, where, and how work gets done—to fit new realities about who (men or women, parents or single people) is doing that work.

Minding Our/Their Own Businesses

As CEO of legendary ad agency N.W. Ayer in New York, Mary Lou Quinlan had it all. "A huge office, a fantastic view, my own bathroom, hundreds of people reporting to me, galas left and right. I succeeded on anybody's ranking of success in advertising," she told me. She's a cheerful redhead with a warm laugh and boundless energy. Maybe you've seen her as a judge on the reality show *American Inventor* or as a regular contributor on the CBS program *The Early Show,* or read her books on marketing and the workplace, including *Just Ask a Woman* and *Time Off for Good Behavior.*

But even this amazingly successful woman felt the traditional corporate world wasn't working for her somehow. She didn't have enough time with her husband and she spent more time at her office than in her Manhattan apartment. "Between your own fear of failure and the way your boundaries get narrower," she says, "you can narrow yourself into this version of you that has nothing to do with who you really are."

Quinlan had achieved so much, but she hadn't created a life that let her truly be herself and shape her world in her own, unique way. In the three stages of financial awareness model, I'd say she had reached independence but hadn't reached economic influence—the ability to use her financial resources to make her mark on the world.

In 1998, she stepped away from the pinnacle of corporate success to start her own company, called Just Ask a Woman, a five-person firm focused on marketing to women. Since then, she has written books and magazine articles and columns and has appeared often on television. Today, still running Just Ask a Woman, she says, "I don't have to be somebody else's version of me."

Quinlan was able to reach the stage of economic influence only because she'd moved through the earlier stages. She rose through the ranks of advertising on her own merits and used her growing financial confidence to save and invest until she had the financial freedom to break out on her own. She also approached the move cautiously, testing the waters, taking a sabbatical from her job to write and think about her next steps, then moving ahead. Ultimately, her well-established financial security and confidence gave her the freedom to launch her business.

"My resources and planning put me in a place where money did not have to be the number one driver," she says. "I see a lot of women who say they feel stuck and want to follow a dream, but they're not doing what they need to do to get into that position—putting money aside, putting their toes in the water; the dream is more likely if you don't just leap off the bridge hoping to get it. Women are great at starting their own businesses, but they need to go about it with a straight business head on their shoulders, understanding what the risks are and what they can tolerate." As her thinking here shows, Quinlan's the ultimate Perceptive Planner—a quality that helped her business thrive.

Quinlan waited until she was in her mid-forties to make the leap, but many younger women aren't waiting that long. Aliza Freud was thirty-five, a marketing executive at American Express, when she decided to start She-Speaks, a social network marketing firm. "In my last job at American Express, my responsibilities were global and there was a lot of travel. It was a dream job in many ways, but it was not a dream when I was sitting jet-lagged in Japan with my husband and two children at home," she says. Most corporate jobs today are still set up on the assumption that somebody else, like a wife, is at home taking care of the kids. Freud also felt restricted by the narrow requirements of the corporate world: They didn't fit her real self. "Senior female executives often have this feeling that somebody is going to tap them on the shoulder and say, 'We just figured out you stink and you're not talented,'" she says. "They call it the 'impostor's theory.' I felt like that was happening to me and my female colleagues at all levels." The impostor's theory, first identified by two women psychologists in 1978, argues that many high-achieving women attribute their success not to their own smarts, experience, and positive personal qualities, but to dumb luck, good timing, and other factors. As these women rack up more and more achievements and promotions, their fear of being "found out" intensifies. One possible explanation for this fear of being caught is that traditional (male) definitions of success and the trappings that come with them just don't feel quite right for women. That was certainly the case for Freud and Quinlan.

Another factor: To a certain extent and at certain companies, women *are* impostors, trying hard to play by men's rules in an environment cre-

ated by and for men. As long as she felt like an impostor, Aliza's professional and financial success wasn't enough to let her project her authentic self into the world, to make an impact in her own way.

Certainly, not all women feel this way, and many have done stunningly well in corporate positions. Being a woman at Ogilvy & Mather in the 1970s, for instance, "was fabulous," says Shelly Lazarus, who rose through the ranks to become chairman of the company. "If you can't be brilliant, be memorable. If there were fifteen people in the room, I tended to be remembered because I was the only woman there. There would come the inevitable moment when everyone turned to me and said, 'Well, Shelly, what do women think?'"

She says she always felt the freedom to manage in her style, to wear what she wanted, and to be herself. "Part of that was because David Ogilvy had an amazing instinct for putting people in positions where they would be successful. It was a true meritocracy." It certainly helped that her husband, a pediatrician, had more flexibility than she did, and that their combined earnings gave them the financial ability to hire a nanny and outsource work that would once have been done by a stay-at-home wife—giving Shelly the freedom to work "like a man."

Still, for every Shelly, there are dozens of Mary Lous and Alizas, leaving to launch their own businesses. And they're not just influencing their own careers: They're changing our economy for the better. Consider: *Nearly half* (47 percent) of all nongovernment employees work for small companies, and 60 to 80 percent of new jobs in the past decade were created by small firms. In 2008, at a time when big companies were filing for bankruptcy, closing their doors, and laying off thousands of people, small businesses were adding jobs. Example: In July 2008, medium and large companies laid off forty-one thousand people. But small companies—those with fifty workers or less—were actually hiring. Not just a few employees either. Small companies added fifty thousand new jobs that June—enough to hire all those fired by big companies that month, and then some. The trend was strong enough to prompt Nell Merlino, the founder of the Make Mine a Million initiative, to write in a blog post on the Huffington Post: "Women will lead the country out of this recession."

Entrepreneurs International

In the future, women may lead other countries out of recessions, too, especially in developing countries and fast-growing economies. In China, women are becoming entrepreneurs at a rate of 13 percent; in Brazil, at a rate of 12.7 percent. That's much higher than in Europe's more mature economies—Norwegian women start companies at a rate of just 4 percent. In Sweden, it's just 2.5 percent. In these fast-growing countries, generous work-life policies make corporate life less onerous for women. But even in Europe, entrepreneurship among women is on the rise. Although British women start their own companies at a rate of just 3.6 percent, the number of women-owned start-ups increased by 9 percent in 2008, compared with just under 1 percent for male-owned firms.

"In America, you have a long story with feminism and you have more self-made women. In Europe, no. A little more in France, a little more in Spain now," says Aude Zieseniss de Thuin, founder of the Women's Forum for the Economy and Society, a European resource organization that connects powerful businesswomen (and -men) to advance gender equity, encouraging women entrepreneurs and leaders in Europe and around the world to promote women's vision on economic and social issues. De Thuin's annual forum in Deauville, France, is so influential that it's often referred to as the "women's Davos"—a reference to the annual World Economic Forum summit in Switzerland.

A self-made woman herself, de Thuin put herself through college working as a model. "I have red hair and blue eyes and am very tall, so I could make money modeling," she says. "But I hated it. I hated the situation of women as models." A psychologist by training, she started up International Direct Marketing Week in 1981, which she sold a dozen years later, after it had become the number one event of its kind in Europe. She then launched what became the second-largest garden event in Europe, a show called L'Art du Jardin. Throughout these entrepreneurial business successes, de Thuin discovered herself increasingly interested in the situation of women in business and society.

In 2004, she decided to launch the Women's Forum. She wanted to bring business leaders together to tackle equality problems that were holding back women, companies, and entire economies. But she couldn't get a loan to launch the company. "My bankers said, 'That's a good project, but too much of a risk for us,'" she recalls. So she sold L'Art du Jardin and used the money to start the new venture.

Through her own example, she's inspiring other women to start businesses—and, through her business, giving them the tools to do it. Among other programs, the Women's Forum runs an international business plan competition, awarding a grant and a year of strategic coaching from management consulting firm McKinsey & Co. and INSEAD, the international business school.

"Because I created my first company when I was younger, mentoring younger women is a commitment for me," de Thuin told me. "It's important to advance the concept of women's vision."

Women's Game, Women's Rules

As women create new businesses, they're coming up with products and services that men wouldn't have thought of, and running companies according to different rules. In many cases, women aren't learning to play like the boys: They're teaching the boys to play by a set of rules that works for both genders.

"It's not about painting the gun pink," says Amy Millman, president of Springboard Enterprises, a nonprofit organization that helps women business owners find funding to grow their firms. "It's not about learning to play by men's rules but about creating something new." Examples are everywhere: Katie Rodan taking a new approach to acne treatment and marketing despite social disapproval from the mostly male medical establishment; Aliza Freud, whose fifteen employees at SheSpeaks work a combination of full-time and flexible hours. At Mary Lou Quinlan's firm, Just Ask a Woman, all five employees know exactly how much the firm is making, who's getting paid what, and where the money is going. "We're completely transparent," Quinlan says. "Everybody knows everything about each dollar, expense, and earnings." The firm splits the rewards equally among its three partners and is very generous with its two junior associates. "That means we're all aligned in our goals," she says. Indeed, this open, collaborative approach to finance brings many advantages. Everyone has the responsibility to understand the numbers. Everyone has equal incentive to work hard and knows she's being rewarded fairly. And every employee has a team spirit, an all-for-one attitude, which fosters mutual support.

"We're very conscious of each other's lives and objectives," Quinlan says. "Tracy's about to have her first baby, Jen just had twins, Lily ran a marathon; everybody has something, and we enable those things to happen." In Quinlan's company, the new rules—particularly new rules applying to the way money is handled, discussed, and exposed—lead to a more supportive environment where everyone can be both a great worker and a whole person with many varied interests and responsibilities.

New rules also reign at Title Nine, a multimillion-dollar women's sportswear catalog company. "I've kind of created Missy's world here," jokes founder and CEO Missy Park. A former college basketball player, Park launched the company in 1990 because she couldn't find comfortable high-performance women's athletic wear. Twenty years later, "Missy's world" isn't quite like any male-run establishment. Among Park's innovations is the annual Title Nine Big Mistake contest, where employees are asked to talk about—and celebrate—their biggest failures. "All the senior managers have to participate in a big way," Missy told me. "They have to stand up in front of the company and tell what their mistake was and what they learned from it. Me, too, I tell what mine is." The point isn't public shaming, just the reverse. "I'm trying to disempower that word 'failure' and have everyone know that failure is the way we learn."

I'm not saying only women would think of throwing a failure party (although it's pretty hard to imagine a bunch of men doing this), or of opening the books like Mary Lou Quinlan did. And I'm not saying that women-run firms are all flowers and sunshine.

But I *am* saying that a roomful of women will come up with ideas, solutions, and approaches that a roomful of men never would—and that a roomful of *both* men and women will think of a broader, more creative range of ideas than either in isolation. The point is *not* that men's rules are always wrong or women's always right. The point is that through their new economic power, women are challenging old ways of doing things, testing new ones, and leading the work world to acknowledge that new models might work very well indeed—for women *and* men. "Women are playing a different game," says Park.

For the good of the global economy, it's time to take the women's game to the big league. To do that, women are going to need to call on all of their own economic influence and then some. Women need to bet bigger on their own companies and to persuade male investors to do the same.

Women and Capital: Thinking Bigger

Ramona Capello turned down Harvard Business School. If that's not breaking the rules, I don't know what is.

She'd been accepted straight out of the University of Southern California, where she'd studied business and graduated as valedictorian. She deferred admission to Harvard and took a management job at Carnation, so she could gain work experience and save money. But the numbers still didn't add up.

"I said, 'Gosh, the education is going to cost me X, my loss of salary for two years is going to cost me Y. If I can't make up those lost dollars in ten years, I'm not sure this makes sense for me.'" Her wide, infectious smile and long, free-flowing dark hair seem completely at odds with her hard-headed business approach. "I've always been a fact-based person," she says with a grin.

She's also a farmer's daughter from Bakersfield who understands the value of a dollar. Her parents mortgaged everything to send Capello and her three brothers to college. She wasn't about to plunge deeply into debt when her career in marketing at Carnation (later bought by Nestlé) was already going well. She wrote 212 letters—typed, by hand—to potential funders, looking for grants or loans to help her pay for her MBA. Two wrote back—and both said no. "And these were places that I'd researched, where I knew I might have some chance."

In the end, she stuck with Carnation for thirteen years, rising to help manage the Coffee-Mate line, which went from a $70 million to a $250 million brand during her time there. Later, she worked at Celestial Seasonings, Kendall-Jackson Wine, and Mauna Loa Macadamia Nuts. At every company, she became a leader for a troubled brand or department and turned it around. But she never made a bid for the top job.

"I resisted being a CEO because I wanted to get married and have a family. Every time I became serious with someone, my title would get in the way," she says. But in 2004, after Hershey Foods bought Mauna Loa, Capello cashed out and finally took some time to stop and think.

"I realized then that it didn't matter what my title was," she says. "I needed to do what I do well and make myself happy." Her beloved father had passed away from heart disease in the late 1990s, and she keenly felt life's brevity. She wanted to make a difference in the world. To find a way to do that, she began lunching with people she knew and found herself talking with an old friend who was running an incubator, helping people start up new brands—specifically, new food brands. He mentioned a new patent on a natural, plant-based ingredient called plant sterols that could actually lower cholesterol and so offered hope for lowering the incidence of heart disease.

Capello latched on to the idea immediately. By 2005, she was working with the incubator, had licensed the ingredient, and become CEO of Corazonas Foods, a start-up snack company making chips that are clinically proven to reduce cholesterol. Talk about a paradigm shift.

The brand proved a success in trials at Jamba Juice, and development continued. The incubator backed development of the brand, but Capello knew she'd need more capital eventually to grow the brand. She researched potential investors and began making calls.

"I think I had forty investors or private equity firms or venture capitalists on that list," she says. Several became seriously interested. Today, she has four major venture capitalists backing her; all four came through the incubator she worked with initially, but bringing in other interested investors paid off "because it validated that other people were interested in this as well," she says.

The Misadventures of Venture Capital

As a woman-owned start-up backed by venture capital, Corazonas is in a small minority. In 2008, just 6.8 percent of U.S. venture investment went to women-owned firms, according to Dow Jones VentureSource.

Think of it. This is a staggering statistic. Just 6.8 percent. When more than half of all new companies are started by women. The venture capital community lies at the very heart of business innovation in the United States, funding the biggest, boldest business ideas—those most likely to transform industries and make a bundle along the way.

By directing almost all their funds exclusively toward male-owned companies, are venture capitalists suggesting that only men will create the winning companies of the future?

Yes, in a way, they are. If America's biggest and most visionary investors are, essentially, gamblers looking for the next big win, they're clearly giving the best odds to men, not women.

For women, this flow of money *from* men *to* men is a big red roadblock in the middle of the American economy. But if women don't play a significant role in designing, launching, and owning the companies of the future, women's economic confidence can't and won't translate into true influence. If the boys' club continues to control investment in new ventures, sending cash to other boys to finance their boys' club companies, the culture will change far more slowly than it could. Or, as the authors of a report from the Diana Project, a multiuniversity research program on women-led ventures, put it: "The substantial funding gap limits women's opportunities to grow their ventures aggressively and lead high-value firms."

This funding disparity became glaringly clear during the Internet bubble in the late 1990s. "Investment money was pouring over the transom. It was like a fire hose," recalls Kay Koplovitz, founder of cable television's USA Network, who currently serves as chairman of the board for Liz Claiborne and board member for CA, an information technology management company. She also runs a venture capital fund called Boldcap Investments. "But women couldn't get in front of the stream." That wouldn't matter so much if venture funding didn't have such a big impact on the future of business, on determining which scrappy entrepreneurs get a shot at realizing their vision and who gets to make the big money.

So what's going on? Are all venture capitalists simply sexist? Not at all. Studies suggest there are several key structural reasons for the lack of investments going to women-owned companies. For one, most venture investments result from personal connections—and for the most part, women haven't cultivated the necessary relationships with the investors (mostly men) making the deals, whether those investors are affluent early-stage "angels" or private equity firms.

"Although women excel in building social networks, their circle of contacts contains few individuals who can 'chauffeur' their deals to equity investors," concluded Candida Brush, a professor of entrepreneurship at Babson College and coauthor of the 2004 report from the Diana Project, a series of studies on women in the venture capital industry. "Women are rarely included in investors' networks and have very few points of access through referral."

Another explanation for the lack of funds flowing to women-owned firms is that women, while starting more businesses than men, are less likely to start the kinds of companies that early-stage investors are looking to fund.

The industries with the highest percentage of firms headed up by women tend to consist of services: retail (19 percent); professional, management, and educational services (16.3 percent); and health care and social assistance (7 percent). Most of the time, investors don't stand to make big returns on service or retail businesses like these. Furthermore, many of the businesses women start are very small-scale. "Seventy percent of women-owned businesses earn $50,000 or less right now," says Nell Merlino. That's barely an income for one person, let alone a thriving business that would lure investors.

Most important, many women-owned companies just don't have much growth potential; they're the kind of business Kay Koplovitz calls "cookie companies."

"There's nothing wrong with cookie companies," she's quick to point out. "But that's not the kind of company venture wants to fund." What venture does want to fund is high-risk companies that require a serious infusion of cash before they can scale up. Products like computer chips, clean fuels and technologies, medical tools or techniques. Companies like YouTube and Google. Brands like Corazonas—that take big risks and big money to launch—risks and investments that established corporations can't afford.

"The head of operations for a big food company came in and asked me, 'How can we do what you do?'" Capello recalls. "You can't," she told him. Not unless the company was willing to put 10 to 15 percent of its budget toward research and development, toward experimentation and testing. And today's competitive business climate won't permit that. "If a big, publicly traded company spent 10 to 15 percent of its dollars experimenting, the stock price would crash," she notes.

Innovation is a high-risk game: Many venture investments go bust. But for every ten that fail, one succeeds big-time. It goes public, and the investors suddenly own stock worth a fortune. Or the start-up sells to a big company, and early investors do well from the sale.

Of course, not every entrepreneur wants venture capital. Missy Park of Title Nine has avoided outside investors, preferring to grow the company based on its own revenues, so she can keep control. "We may have missed opportunities by not raising capital and scaling more quickly," she admits. "But what I got in return is a business where I have all the control, where I can make sure I'm fostering the vision and that we're focused on the long-term success of the brand, not just on quarterly earnings."

But while the venture route isn't right or necessary for every business, those venture capitalists who continue to invest little or no money in women-led start-ups may soon find themselves missing out on key opportunities.

Although the majority of women-owned companies have relatively small revenues, says Merlino, there are about 1.8 million women business owners who are already at the threshold of bigger business. Her Make Mine a Million initiative is actively seeking to push many of these ventures over a million in revenues.

"Just imagine if we could set loose those companies that already have great products and services and make those available on a wider basis. What if 50 percent of women's businesses were at $250,000 to $5 million revenue each? Every time you crunch those numbers, it puts people back to work, and in work settings that may be much more friendly to people's lives—men and women."

The Zeroes Problem

There's another barrier that keeps women from landing more venture funding. Amy Millman, president of Springboard, which connects women entrepreneurs with investors, calls it the "zeroes problem." It occurs even when women launch companies with big growth potential in technology or biotech.

"When potential investors look at a business, they're used to seeing men present the numbers. They assume the men have exaggerated and added a zero to the potential growth of the business. So if a founder says, 'My business could be worth $100 million,' the investor thinks, '$10 million.' That means when women come in and say it's going to be worth $10 million, they take off a zero and think, 'Oh, $1 million.'"

You'd think that women's tendency to underpromise and overdeliver would be an asset to an investor, not a liability. "We often tell women, 'That's a great idea, but have you thought about just how big this market could be?'" says Jen Shelby, former managing director of Astia, which coaches women business owners on obtaining capital. Women's response to the idea of presenting the big dream: "Not right now. I want to deliver what I said I would first, then think about growth."

"For a woman, the thought of not being able to do what she says she'll do, that's uncomfortable," Shelby says. "That's where you'll see women play small—not because they don't see the big vision." Women, she says, don't want to make big promises until they've fulfilled small ones—like getting the company off the ground.

Groups like Springboard and Astia, which have been around for about a decade, teach women entrepreneurs how to talk about their businesses in ways that investors will understand and respond to.

"Women don't have to learn to be men, but they need to learn what words hit a good strong chord with men, to know what language to use in presenting their ideas," says Kay Koplovitz.

Another thing to learn: Ditch the modesty at the door. Koplovitz worked with a company started by a former astronaut, developing a product derived from NASA technology. In her first presentation, she didn't mention she was an astronaut. "A guy would *never* do that," Koplovitz says.

Ramona Capello recently learned the value of being more direct and assertive in selling her vision. An important vote was coming up for her board of directors, all of whom are major investors in the company: She was seeking their green light for important new funding, so she could raise enough capital to launch a full-scale national push for Corazonas. The company had spent a year quietly, patiently building research and conserving money, but Capello was growing more and more impatient. She felt it was time to make a big move. In fact, she was ready to quit if she didn't get the go-ahead.

So she visited each board member privately and gave all the time they needed to become comfortable with her plan. "I didn't say 'Tell me what you think,'" she says. "I said, 'Look, I'm going with this. I believe in this. This is my company. This is what I want to do. Are you on board?' I didn't give them the opportunity to say, 'I think you are wrong.'"

One investor spent an hour with her; another spent eight. Then came the vote: Not only did everyone approve the new fund-raising round, but the board members themselves ponied up an additional investment representing nearly a third of what the company needed. They were so excited about Capello's big vision that they didn't want many more investors coming in and diluting their share.

"I learned that most venture capitalists invest in the CEO. At the end of the day, they want to know you're in charge. I had not realized that until I was almost at my breaking point," she says.

Who Controls the Purse Strings?

Dana Settle, a partner with the venture capital firm Greycroft, Ltd., was on a cell phone walking down a busy Manhattan street when we spoke. She's a California girl through and through, with the lean athletic build and long blond hair to prove it, but this week, she was back East to visit several institutional investors—a key source for the deep pockets of venture capital funds. "We've been out talking to pension funds and endowments, and I will tell you there are *a lot* more women in that world than in the venture world," she told me.

As a partner at Greycroft, Settle is a member of a very small club. In 2008, just 14 percent of partners at venture capital firms were women. That was twice the percentage of female venture partners in 2000, but still, the lack of women in venture capital may be one reason—although not the only one—why women-owned companies get so little venture money.

"I think the venture business would benefit from more women being involved, and I don't say that lightly," Settle says. And she doesn't say it from a sense of gender loyalty: When we talked, she'd just passed up an opportunity to work for an all-women venture capital fund. Settle believes the benefit of having more women in venture capital isn't about feminism or idealism: It's about smart business. She believes men and women bring a diversity of thought that adds up to better decisions.

In her own firm, her strength has been her instincts about people and relationships. "I tend to focus on the management team more than my partners—how the team works together, how they communicate, who defers to whom. Those sound like soft things, but it comes into play in getting products built quickly." She laughs. In her company, her instinctual feel for the warm-fuzzy aspect of management has become a running joke. "I'm the only partner in California, and I'm a woman, so I've got the 'hippie chick whammy.' But seriously, I've had a lot of success, and everyone respects that."

It's taken Settle time—years at a cell phone start-up, at Lehman Brothers in the 1990s, and at Harvard Business School—to trust her own instincts about the role relationships play in a deal. "Earlier in my career, I wouldn't raise those things," she says. She wasn't sure they counted as "real issues"—especially when the men around her weren't raising them as legitimate concerns.

Another reason women partners like Dana Settle are good for venture capital: They attract women business owners, which means a firm with women partners is likely to learn about some companies that all-male firms miss. This is why traditional venture capital firms often seek out Kay Koplovitz's venture fund, Boldcap, as a partner: The traditional firms are looking for deals via Boldcap that they would miss out on otherwise. As Koplovitz puts it, "They want to work with us because we're tapped into women's networks, and they want our deal-flow pool."

By all accounts, women excel at building networks. But those networks might be fundamentally different from men's. A study by McKinsey & Company of women leaders found that we often build a few deep relationships where men build many "weak ties"—and those weak ties may be far more effective in connecting them to the gatekeepers they need. Furthermore, venture capital is a very closed circle, and studies of social networks show that women are far more likely to network with women, not men, and women-owned companies tend to approach women investors. "It's a sort of self-selection," Dana says. Groups like Springboard and Astia are working to move women into the funding network, to train them to talk about business in a way that businesses respond to and to avoid the "zeroes problem," helping them focus on the true potential size of their business.

Meanwhile, economic and social forces are now at work that may bring more funding to women-owned companies in the future. Remember those pension funds and other institutional investors Dana Settle was visiting? The women in that industry are shopping for women venture capitalists to manage their investments.

"They are definitely trying to put money into women-managed funds," Settle reports. "They're not mandating that their money be invested in women and minorities, but there is a notion that money invested in women-managed funds will eventually go to women- and minority-owned businesses." Large corporations in general have started recognizing the value of diversity and want to reap the benefits for their own investments. Investors are realizing that a more diverse set of companies, run by a more diverse set of talent, may make better investments.

"Especially in light of the recent economic fallout, the world is seeing that men don't have a monopoly on how to do business successfully, or on morality, or on how to judge creditworthiness," says Nell Merlino.

"Particularly after what's happened in banking, in the auto industry, which are businesses run primarily by men."

If the Internet and real estate bubbles have taught us anything, it's that money needs a place to flow. During the real estate boom, that money flowed to more and more questionable mortgages. But what if more and more investment flowed to overlooked companies—those run by women and minorities? Good, solid investments that haven't been funded in years past? Women-owned firms may present the next new growth opportunity—a bubble that won't pop this time, because there's real value behind these companies.

If institutional investors continue to seek out investment funds managed by women, evidence suggests that more of their money will be invested in women- and minority-owned firms. Such a change could affect the direction of business investment in our entire nation. With more money behind them, "I think that women investors would be concentrating more on products and services that advance health care, education, and quality-of-life issues because studies show that that's how women use their money," says Koplovitz. "That's how they make decisions and personal choices when they have money—they invest it back in their communities, their schools, their hospitals. Areas that support family life. So it stands to reason that more women would invest in those fields." And firms like Corazonas, promising to make a profit while improving the health prospects of families, should only speed up the process.

FOUR

In the Workplace

REWRITING THE RULES FROM THE OUTSIDE IN

Jessica Bibliowicz is chairman, president, and CEO of National Financial Partners, a network of some five hundred financial advisory firms generating more than a billion dollars a year. Today, she can write her own rules about how business gets done at her firm. But that wasn't always the case. Back in the 1980s, when she was building her career, Wall Street was the ultimate boys' club, and heavy after-hours drinking and visits to strip clubs were considered a mandatory part of the corporate culture.

Those rules didn't work for Bibliowicz. As a married woman who wanted to be home with her husband and, later, kids, she came up with an amusing compromise. "I struck a deal with a bartender to serve me plain tomato juice instead of bloody Marys," she recalls. She got to enjoy the good parts of the party atmosphere on her own terms and, when the hijinks weren't to her taste, leave and head home to her family. Most important, "I kept the focus on who I was and on generating profits—not on being a man or a woman. I believe most of that after-hours stuff is optional. What's important is the bottom line," she told me.

Later, as head of National Financial Partners, which went public in 2004, she stopped conforming to the old boys' rules and instead wrote her own. She created a network of hundreds of independent financial advisories across the country, giving small advisors the benefits of belonging to a big firm without the big corporate structure of Merrill Lynch or Citigroup. Under her savvy management, the company nearly doubled its revenues between 2004 and 2008. When the recession of 2008 and 2009 hit, the company slashed expenses, reorganized to provide better client service, and took other initiatives to weather the storm.

"There's really nothing quite like it on any scale," said the president of one financial consulting firm about the company.

Bibliowicz clearly knows when to break the rules and when to bend them. And her bartender story, while funny, perfectly illustrates the sometimes awkward positions women have found themselves in as they gradually change the rules of the workplace. It's not yet clear whether women need to learn to play by the boys' rules or stick to their own—or create a whole new set that works for both genders.

Take negotiation. Numerous studies show that women don't earn as much as men even when they have the same education and years of experience and work the same number of hours in similar jobs. In some cases, overt discrimination plays a role. ("I know for a fact I was once paid less for a job because I was a woman," says Ellen Marram, former head of Tropicana and one of America's most successful and well-known women executives. "I fixed it.")

But another factor in the gender wage gap is the different scripts men and women follow when it comes to asking for money and credit. Many studies show that women are far less likely to ask for more when offered a job or at an annual review. And they're less likely to toot their own horn, promote their own accomplishments, and make sure everyone sees they're a star who deserves rich reward.

Here's the tricky thing. If women continue following their own rules, obeying the instinct not to ask for more or promote themselves, women will *never* make as much money as men. On the other hand, "acting like a man" here doesn't help: Some studies suggest that when women do put themselves forward in a more male way, they're viewed as abrasive, which can hurt their standing. The answer in this case isn't "act like a man" (self-promote) or continue to act "like a woman" (get underpaid), but to find a new set of rules—a way to ask for fair pay, to gain recognition, but not in the same way men do.

I think that's what's happening now in the small business arena. As literally millions of women start their own companies, they're testing different rules and new structures, and gradually finding models that work not just for women, but for everyone. As they find new ways to do business on a smaller scale, they're forcing large corporations to change, too. Women entrepreneurs have caught the swell of three key trends—just-in-time employment, cloud sourcing, and results-based work—and, by example, they've shown big corporations how to ride those waves. Companies of every size must be able to surf those trends or they will lose the coming war for talent. In the decade ahead, the smartest corporations will continue to learn from successful women entrepreneurs and find new ways to hang on to their top talent. Those that don't won't be able to compete in the new global economy.

Trend One: Just-in-Time Employees

"Being at my desk is a rarity," Cheryl Fahrenholz told me. She was driving from a client meeting in Columbus, Ohio, back to her home in Bellbrook, Ohio, about an hour away. Fahrenholz is president of Preferred Healthcare Solutions, a health care consulting company that helps doctors and hospitals with electronic medical records and insurance claims.

From the time Fahrenholz graduated from Bowling Green State University with a degree in information management, she knew that "following the so-called path like you're supposed to do won't always get you the job," she says. Advised to send résumés to the human resources departments of hospitals, she instead went to professional networking events and marched up to the people who would be doing the actual hiring—nursing directors and hospital administrators. She introduced herself, followed up with e-mails and phone calls, and landed a job at a health care system long before her other classmates.

In her new job at a big Ohio health system, she became an expert in the critical administrative side of medical records—making sure hospitals and doctors received all the claim money they were entitled to. Fahrenholz excelled at the health system and rapidly climbed the ladder to become assistant director of health information management. Eventually, she became regional manager, with responsibility for eight offices in the health system's primary care physician network. As a single woman with no kids, she could put in the long hours. Still, the big corporate system left her cold. "You go through consolidation after consolidation, and if you're lucky enough to still have your job, you're also doing the work of twenty other people."

With big employers no longer meaning lifetime security, suddenly taking a big risk wasn't really that risky. She realized she could do the same work for doctors on her own. In 1998, she started Preferred Healthcare Solutions, consulting with medical practices about how to file claims most effectively, to make sure they were being compensated and receiving all the insurance reimbursements they were entitled to.

Starting her own company felt like a risk—but her education and experience gave her the financial confidence to make the leap. "I felt like I needed six months of salary in reserve, and as a single woman with no children I could save up pretty aggressively. For the first six months after I left, I spent a lot of nervous energy worrying about where the jobs were coming from. But after that first six months, I said, okay, I'm not going to waste my energy worrying about this because I could always go get a job. Maybe it would be at a department store, but I knew I could get one if I needed it. I didn't worry about this again." Her skills and education also gave her the financial confidence she needed to grow her firm.

By 2000, Fahrenholz had doubled her salary and was bringing in more work than she could handle on her own. Rather than hiring employees, she found she could hire people on an as-needed basis. She built a network of about a dozen people, mostly women, each specializing in a different area of medical records and claims. Some took on projects at night or weekends, as a second job. Others were stay-at-home moms who'd left the workforce but wanted to keep their hand in and earn some extra money. "I never go anywhere, not even the grocery store, without my business cards, because I can spot them right away, the women in my field with the same work ethic as me, who are multitaskers," she says. Preferred Healthcare Solutions has been going strong for ten years.

Now, consultants have been bringing in extra help on a temporary basis for years. What's new and different about Preferred Healthcare, and companies like it, is that Fahrenholz makes no attempt to hide the fact that her associates don't work for her full-time. She doesn't try to make her operation look bigger than it is. She's completely transparent about the fact that her company is a loose network of professionals, available on a project-by-project basis. "Most of my clients know exactly how we work," she says. If anything, they like the fact that she has very low overhead. And clients know they'll get a team handpicked and customized to their needs.

This shift from full-time, long-term employment to a project-based employment model mirrors an important shift that happened in the business world during the late 1990s. Back then, the idea of "on-demand supply chain management" transformed entire industries. Rather than stocking up expensive inventory of parts that might or might not be needed, companies like Dell arranged to buy and receive parts only as needed, "just in time" to build the product that was ordered. Cutting inventory cut costs and decreased the risk that companies would be stuck with loads of unneeded parts. Today, Fahrenholz's firm, and many like it—often owned by women—are lowering overhead and undercutting the competition by a similar transformation in the workforce, a sort of "just in time" employment. In fact, if the assembly line was the major business revolution of the early twentieth century, and on-demand supply chain management was the transforming factor of the 1990s, just-in-time employment (or what journalist, editor, and entrepreneur Tina Brown called "the gig economy") will revolutionize the way services are provided around the world in the early part of the twenty-first century.

In a 2008 online poll of five hundred employed people, Brown found fully one-third of those surveyed were working freelance or in more than one job. These weren't low-income workers. "They're college educated Americans who earn more than $75,000 a year," Brown wrote in a piece on her Internet news site, the Daily Beast, in January 2009. Such on-demand employment brings both enormous advantages (in flexibility and independence) and disadvantages (in insecurity and lack of benefits)—and these new realities will soon reshape the way workers, companies, and ultimately, policy makers view the labor market.

Trend Two: Cloud Sourcing

In real life, Sacramento attorney Amy Pritchard looks like your prototypical mom-in-running-shoes. But on the Internet, you'll never catch her online avatar in sweats. Instead, she's usually decked out like a 1960s mod super-spy, sporting go-go boots and a mini trench coat. As founder and CEO of Metaverse Mod Squad, she wears the official virtual uniform of the fifty-five or so employees and contractors whom she hires to police and monitor corporate Web sites, Second Life spots, and other cyberspace locales.

"The virtual world is just like real life. Companies that have a virtual presence in Second Life or anywhere online need to do the same things companies need to do in the real world," Pritchard says.

Pritchard's clients—many of them large corporations—hire her company to provide "virtual staff" to host online events or provide customer service. Those staffs are largely working moms or disabled people working flexible hours from home. In 2007, the company provided a coterie of avatar agents to provide virtual "security" for Newt Gingrich when his avatar appeared on the steps of the Second Life White House.

"This thing has just grown so much faster than I expected," she says. She's been meeting with potential investors in Silicon Valley and expects to grow even faster in 2010.

Unlike Fahrenholz's ad hoc teams, assembled and employed only for one-off assignments, Pritchard's company is a true "virtual firm," employing a specific set of workers on a fairly predictable basis. She's never met most of her employees: She knows them only through the "cloud"—the virtual world—and they're linked together only by computer or phone. Even her chief operating officer is a fellow attorney she met "hanging out in a virtual sports bar," she says. The pair didn't meet live and in person until they presented the company to potential angel investors in Silicon Valley.

I met up with Pritchard at a funky artisanal coffee shop on a hot spring morning. She'd just dropped off her four-year-old daughter, Mary, with Mary's paternal grandma and was heading to the gym. That Pritchard could drop off Mary, stop for coffee, run to the gym, and manage her booming business seamlessly speaks volumes about the way her company works. Companies like hers, she says, are "great for working moms, because employees can work as little or as much as they want," she says.

Pritchard and other virtual firms are enjoying a heyday, thanks to the availability of very talented, very reliable workers who simply can't or won't work traditional hours in traditional offices. There's a wealth of available talent lying unused simply because most companies aren't thinking creatively.

What Metaverse Mod Squad is doing for virtual staffing, LiveOps, a call center provider in Santa Clara, California, is doing for customer service. To handle call center operations, the company employs educated moms, disabled people, and others who don't want to or can't work nine to five in an office. Companies that want to reduce their call center costs, but can't, for political or other reasons, outsource to India, hire LiveOps to provide educated Americans answering call center questions in a low-cost model.

"Finding people who are really smart and really well educated and really good at what they do, who want to work part-time on their own schedules, is like shooting fish in a barrel," says Garry Berger, founder of Berger Legal, a virtual law firm. Berger's firm is based at his home in Connecticut; from there, he works with ten associates scattered around New Jersey, Connecticut, suburban New York, and other East Coast locations. Each lawyer works when, where, and how he or she wants to. All are experienced attorneys, most with snazzy Ivy League degrees, a pedigree that has attracted high-profile clients including Pfizer, Thomson Reuters, and Expedia. They all work from their own home offices, putting in as many hours as they choose. They don't earn as much as they would if they became partners at one of the big law firms. But they do earn more than many attorneys—and without the stringent schedules. Plus, with no fancy marble-lobbied offices, they can charge their clients far less per hour than typical law firms. A win for everybody.

It's no coincidence that seven out of ten of Berger's associates are women—or that recently, he's found a growing number of men interested as well. Today, virtual companies, made possible largely by women's high levels of education, their intense desire to work, and the value they place on family and life outside the office, are benefiting both genders.

Trend Three: Results-Based Work

There's nothing like a good crisis to sweep in change. In many industries, the economic downturn of 2008 and 2009 forced a reevaluation of business-as-usual—at the same time that women and family's quiet transformation of the work world was gaining traction. The growing success of firms like Berger Legal, for instance, showed law firms that new models could help workers while also saving clients money. Ultimately, the hours those employees work are less important than the results they produce.

In turn, the success of the virtual workforce is calling into question the very idea of paying "per hour" in some industries.

"Clients are saying they want more value for less money," says Deborah Epstein Henry, founder and president of Flex-Time Lawyers LLC, a company dedicated to creating more flexibility in the world of corporate law. Law, like consulting, has long been based on the "billable hour": Clients are billed for each hour that lawyers put in. In law, a big firm might bill $700 to $800 an hour for a senior attorney. No wonder big law firms pressure attorneys to work sixty, seventy, eighty hours a week in the office. What's really lucrative for the law firms is that clients pay for every hour billed. In this way, law is unlike other industries: If you ask a contractor to build a house for you, or a designer to create a brochure for your business, he or she gives you a bid for the project. Theoretically, if the job takes more time, the contractor earns less per hour (at least, that's how it's supposed to work). Not so with law—you pay a hefty fee per hour.

But that's changing. The economic downturn meant corporations had to cut their costs—and legal is a major cost. In a 2008 survey of 115 corporate law departments, nearly 75 percent said they intended to slash their legal budgets by between 6 and 35 percent. More than half intended to decrease their use of outside lawyers in 2009. No wonder unemployment among U.S. lawyers jumped 66 percent to hit a ten-year high in early 2009.

Meanwhile, corporations started asking law firms for more creative billing options—like quoting a fee for the project or case. Taser International, a leading manufacturer of protective devices and weapons for U.S. law enforcement, for instance, now asks its ten regional law firms to propose a "not to exceed" fee.

What does this have to do with women's economic power? Women have been both the prosecuting attorney and exhibit A in the argument that *results* rather than time in the office are what matters. For the past two decades or more, women have been the squeaky wheel trying to convince companies to reward them on their work, not on the face-time they put in.

Now law clients want to take this a step further—paying for work product, not hours. As a first step, in 2009, the Association of Corporate Counsel, an industry group of in-house attorneys, created the "value challenge," a series of twenty meetings of small groups of clients brainstorming and testing alternative fee arrangements. If they succeed, the entire culture of law could change—an improvement for women. (And for families. And for men.)

But it's not just law firms that are changing in response to results-based work. Many industries, including consulting, accounting, and banking, are seeking ways to value and reward their workers based on output, not just hours. In 2003, electronics retailer Best Buy began experimenting with a system it called the "results-only work environment" that did away with set work schedules for some departments and measured employees only on their work product. The initial trials were so successful that the program rapidly spread throughout the company, increasing productivity by some 35 percent on average. Similarly, at Capital One, all employees can work with their managers to create their own schedules, using flextime, working from home, short workweeks, part-time schedules, and other flexibility tools.

"Hours are really a very industrial society way of looking at work," says Sally Thornton, president and cofounder of Flexperience, which connects experienced professionals—mostly women—with part-time or flexible work at large corporations and start-ups. "It's not a knowledge-economy way of looking at work." The more results count, the more flexibility workers have—and that's good for any worker, male or female, who has a life outside the office.

The War for Talent: Adapt or Die

As women have launched their own companies, they've been at the cutting edge, taking advantage of just-in-time employment, of cloud sourcing, of results-based work. They've pioneered new kinds of companies, with new ways of working that make women *and* men happier.

All this is creating a serious crisis for corporate employers. As women have fled the confines of the corporate world, big companies are losing some of their best talent—women like Ramona Capello and Mary Lou Quinlan. In 2008, the Center for Work-Life Policy dubbed this problem the female brain drain. It's a problem companies continued to wrestle with even while they were laying people off in 2008 and 2009. Because, while these companies knew the recession would end eventually, they also knew the female brain drain was coinciding with another massive demographic force—the relentless aging of the population. And that these two forces would eventually lead to what may be the most influential power shift of the coming decade: the raging war for talent. At the *exact* moment when women are becoming the most educated, most entrepreneurial segment of the labor force, companies around the world are teetering on the brink of a talent chasm, a massive shortage of skilled workers.

In the next few years, the war for top talent will become increasingly brutal. Through 2016, the workforce will grow at less than 1 percent a year. In the United States, 78 million baby boomers are just reaching traditional retirement age and will leave the workforce in droves in the coming decade. Although Age Wave studies indicate that many say they will delay retirement for up to 4.2 years, they'll be working shorter hours and seeking more rewarding jobs and different work environments and incentives than in the past. By 2012, six million more people will retire than will graduate college in the United States. By 2016, there will be three million fewer workers than the economy needs to keep growing. In Europe and Asia, the aging of the population and the rapid retirement of workers is an even bigger concern: Many countries simply won't have enough younger workers to support their aging population.

The coming shortage of workers is scary news for companies: In one recent survey of CEOs, "finding qualified managerial talent" ranked as one of the top five concerns of corporate leaders. Among the top twenty were "finding the right people to replace current managers as they retire or leave" and "finding a qualified skilled workforce." These concerns continue to haunt companies, especially those who had to lay people off in 2008 and 2009, knowing they were sacrificing talent they'll desperately need sooner, not later.

As baby boomers head toward traditional retirement age, companies battling for talent will no longer be able to ignore the stream of women of all ages heading for the exits. Because women are quickly becoming the most educated and skilled group of workers.

"If you look at college attendance and the skills women have, whether by nature or nurture, they seem to be on a winning trend," says Robert Reich. To take advantage of those skills, companies will soon be forced to play by new rules. Already, for every 100 men who graduate college in the United States, there are 133 women who graduate. There are more women than men in medical school and law school, and women have a larger share of master's degrees than men. Companies who want to keep their top talent are going to have to change, or watch their best women go start their own companies.

"The smart employers will begin to create work that works," says Ellen Galinsky of the Families and Work Institute. "A business won't get the results it wants if it doesn't have an effective workplace, if employees aren't challenged, if they can't learn, if there's not a good sense of teamwork, if there's not flexibility and if they don't get decent wages."

When Galinsky started studying the issue thirty years ago, work-family balance was seen as a personal issue. "What's changed is that people now think about the issues faced by working families as a public issue, not a private one. In polls, people are as worried about their work and family life as they are about the economy. Thirty years ago, people would say, 'It's their own fault.' Now they're saying, 'This is something we ought to be concerned with together.' It's a huge attitudinal change."

Did it happen just because it's the right thing? No. Companies and society are paying attention because the poor fit between corporate life, and the lives of half the workforce is finally hurting—or about to hurt—the bottom line. Women's economic influence—their financial ability to leave, take time out, start their own companies, or just go find a new job—is bringing the message home.

Meanwhile, that attitude change has been accelerated by public demand, by executives and workers—men and women—who care about the issue.

This cultural adjustment in attitude didn't happen because we're now a kinder, gentler world. If anything, business today is more competitive, leaner, and more global. Finding a better way to utilize women—the single most educated group of people in the United States and increasingly in other countries—"is not just an accommodation for moms who are tired," says Sally Thornton of Flexperience. "It's fierce business strategy."

That's as true for countries as it is for companies. "A nation's competitiveness depends significantly on whether and how it educates and utilizes its female talent," the World Economic Forum pronounced in its 2008 report on gender.

As the demographic shift accelerates and the global population ages, corporations are gradually waking up to the fact that they must adapt or die. The intersection of the aging of the population and the growing talent and education of women is creating new pressures to recruit and retain women, forces that are manifesting themselves in three ways: pressure for women to be included on boards, for smarter employee retention strategies, and for a wholesale reinvention of the career ladder.

The faster companies find innovative ways to fill these needs, the more likely they are to survive and thrive in the coming war for talent. Finding more creative ways of working and better ways to utilize the talents of all workers will no longer just be nice ways to get on those "best companies to work for" lists. It will become critical for business survival. Today, the smartest corporations are using three strategies to stem the female brain drain, and all stand to benefit not just women but all employees and our economy as well: They're adding women to their boards of directors, they're adopting retention strategies tailored toward women, and they're creating entirely new career models.

Women on the Board

Some twenty years ago, the CEO of General Re, the global reinsurance company, recruited Kay Koplovitz, one of the country's most successful women in business, to join the board of directors. The company was having trouble holding on to its top women and thought it might help if a few women joined the all-male board.

"When the CEO asked me to join the board, he also asked another woman. 'I don't think it would be helpful to have just one woman,' he told me. 'I think you'd stand alone on your opinions. You need at least two.'" It worked. The two women board members met periodically with small groups of women managers to talk about the challenges women faced in the company. The groups helped retention, but so did the symbolic value of having women on the board.

While the workers of America have become more and more diverse, the leaders of American business have not. They're still white men. In 2009, just 15 women led Fortune 500 companies as CEOs. Men led the other 485 companies. Those mostly male, mostly white CEOs reported to mostly male, mostly white bosses—the boards of directors, the ten to fifteen business leaders who set a company's overall vision and strategy.

Boards of directors are arguably the most important bunch of business leaders in the world. They're the ultimate insiders. In the United States in 2009, just 15.7 percent of board members of Fortune 500 companies were women.

As I write this, companies are under major pressure to transform the face of their boards. The impending war for talent is one reason. "I recently joined the board of a software company, and the senior managers who were women said it meant a lot to them to have more women represented on the board, and more voices for women," says Koplovitz. "It's almost always perceived by women in the company as a signal that women's experiences are valued. And that's great for retaining women."

Another, even more powerful force will soon drive companies to add more women. Money. It turns out that companies with more women on the board outperform those with fewer. A study by Catalyst in 2007 found that Fortune 500 companies with more women board members had a better return on equity by more than 50 percent. Another study in 2007, by consulting firm McKinsey & Company, looked at eighty-nine leading European firms. Those with more women on the board and in senior management performed better and saw their stock prices improve more.

Why? "Studies have shown there are different ways of approaching problems, so the more diversity you have, with regards to both skill sets and culture, the greater your chance of success," says Wendy Beecham, CEO of the Forum for Women Entrepreneurs & Executives, an association that supports female leaders.

For instance, Scott Page, a professor of complex systems at the University of Michigan, found that groups with greater diversity performed better when assigned complex tasks than did homogenous groups—even when the homogenous folks were, individually, better problem solvers. "The diverse group almost always outperforms the group of the best by a substantial margin," says Page. "You want diverse minds. You want people who categorize things in diverse ways."

To take advantage of this fact and stay competitive, corporate boards need more diversity of all types. We're not talking about adding a token woman. We're talking about adding two, three, or more.

"I've been saying since high school that you need two or three women, because there are so many more men. So each woman has to pick one man and win him over," says Catherine DeAngelis, M.D., the influential editor of *JAMA, the Journal of the American Medical Association.* Having a critical mass of women, not just a token, Koplovitz says, changes the whole conversation. "Men and women use different words to describe things," she says. "When you have more than one woman, it changes the dialogue. And when you have three or more women, it really takes a lot more of the work from the back room to the board room." During board meetings, she says, a lot of work, progress, new ideas, and opinions come not from the meeting itself, but from the break time chitchat—in the restroom, over coffee, at lunch. "If you're the only woman, you go to the ladies' room and talk to yourself," she says. "If you have three women, it takes that out of the background into the board room. It really does change the dynamic."

Here's something ironic. One reason women aren't on boards is that men and women often have separate networks. "For years, board members tended to pick people they knew and were comfortable with," says Ellen Marram, who serves on the boards of directors for Ford Motor Company, Eli Lilly and Company, and the New York Times Company. Even today, even among younger generations, women play a small role in the old boys' network that boards turn to when recruiting new members.

But the ironic thing is this: The fact that women are *not* part of the gang makes them even more desirable as board members, especially since the Sarbanes-Oxley Act of 2002 required more independent directors, company outsiders who are theoretically less likely to be influenced by groupthink. "Because women aren't members of the club, they're not worried about jeopardizing their club membership," says Kay Koplovitz. "I think that's one reason why women raise more questions than men. They have less to lose. They also tend to spend more time investigating issues and doing research."

The value of women on boards of directors and the importance of diversity of all types have become more urgent in recent years. Recently, CEOs have become less likely to serve on boards, partly for liability reasons and partly because demanding economic conditions mean they don't have time for extracurriculars. "For a bunch of reasons, companies are starting to go below the CEO and look for people who are running divisions," Koplovitz told me. This improves the odds for women; although female senior managers are still scarcer than they should be, they're not nearly as scarce as female CEOs.

What might happen when more women join boards of major corporations? Take a look at Norway. In 2002, Prime Minster Ansgar Gabrielsen announced to the press that if companies didn't have at least 40 percent women on their boards within five years, the government would mandate it. "What's the point in pouring a fortune into educating girls, and then watching them exceed boys at almost every level, if, when it comes to appointing business leaders in top companies, these are drawn from just half the population—friends who have been recruited on fishing and hunting trips or from within a small circle of acquaintances?" he told the *Times* of London. "It's all about tapping into valuable underutilized resources." Within a year, the percentage of women on boards in Norway skyrocketed, from 6 percent to 24 percent. But not enough to forestall the threatened legislation. In 2005, a 40 percent female quota for boards passed. Five hundred to six hundred women joined boards of directors. It's too early to tell the financial results. But it's interesting that this new group of women has more education and better professional qualifications than many of their male board peers. They're also a younger, fresher group, bringing new energy to the companies they're helping to lead.

Now other countries are following suit. In 2007, Spain passed a law mandating that women hold 40 percent of board positions within eight years. And Germany and the Netherlands are also looking at ways to increase women at the top.

One thing is clear. If U.S. companies don't do as the rest of the world is doing and start moving women into board positions and other top slots, we won't be able to keep up.

Winning the Retention Game

Forget the myth of corporate bureaucracy. When companies commit to solving a problem, they can move very, very swiftly. That's what we're starting to see in the technology industry, where you can practically hear the female brain drain happening. On the lower rungs of science and tech firms, about 41 percent of highly qualified scientists, engineers, and technologists are women. But their drop-out rates are astounding—more than half quit their jobs over time, especially when they reach their mid-thirties, according to a study by the Center for Work-Life Policy. The report cited machismo and hostility, a "dispiriting sense of isolation" that comes from being the only woman on a team or at a certain rank, the culture of crisis and endless hours, punishing travel schedules, and a lack of a clear path to promotion.

To address the problem, Cisco created its Executive Talent Insertion Program in 2007, seeking out and rapidly grooming high-potential women to add to its senior management team members. As of July 2008,

Cisco's female hires were at 25 percent, up 18 percent from 2007. In that year, 22 percent of in-house promotions went to women, up 15 percent from 2007. Impressive short-term progress on a long-term problem.

Other science and tech companies, including Johnson & Johnson and Microsoft, are hoping to win the talent wars by grooming their future women leaders. Intel's Women's Engineering Forum supports female engineers by showcasing their research, fostering solidarity, and mentoring. And Alcoa has instituted a rotation program to let high-potential women take on "line" roles for a temporary period as part of an overall career plan. At the time of this writing, the programs were relatively new, but they all suggest the urgency with which smart companies are now approaching the female brain drain.

At the same time, companies are trying to keep their women by adding more sophisticated flexibility arrangements—often turning to small women-owned firms to guide them. In the San Francisco Bay area, Sally Thornton launched Flexperience to consult with big companies on restructuring work. In addition to staffing companies with experienced women who want to work part-time or in flexible jobs, Thornton consults with companies in creating tools to help workers assess whether they're good candidates for flexible work arrangements. Her clients include Pixar, Levi Strauss & Co., and Genentech.

"A lot of these engagements start around the retention of key people," she says. "Even though we think there's an overwhelming amount of talent out there that got laid off in 2008 or 2009, there are actually little specific niches where it's very difficult to find and retain people." By coaching companies on flexible and alternative work arrangements, she says, she's helping everybody. "It's good for big businesses that want to retain senior women," she says. But flexibility and alternative work hours are also "good for start-ups that can't afford this high-level talent full-time."

Flexible work arrangements have been around for decades, but they're becoming more specific, more targeted, and more sophisticated. Global consulting form Accenture, for example, recognized that many parents would like to take more time off but hadn't saved—so the company started a sort of Christmas club, letting would-be parents set aside part of their salary for an extra three months of maternity leave. The company also initiated a program to let consultants choose to notch down their constant travel for a time, while still keeping strategic jobs. PricewaterhouseCoopers has a Mentor Moms initiative, which helps new moms before and after their maternity leave. Globally, companies of all sizes are also making an effort. In Sweden, some firms make up the difference between governmental maternity leave payments and a woman's actual salary. General Electric in Bangalore launched a "restart" program to help women engineers and technologists return to the company after taking a career break.

In Argentina, Fundación Compromiso, a nonprofit that trains other nonprofits in better management, is too small to offer lots of maternity benefits or hire replacements for workers out on maternity leave. But they've developed an informal buddy system, so mothers out on maternity leave can stay in touch and help keep projects moving without feeling pressured to come back before they're ready. "If I have a baby, I want my boss to do that, and I want my sister-in-law's boss to do that," Mariana Lomé, executive director of Fundación Compromiso, told me. And it pays off. "When these moms come back to the office, they have a very high commitment to work. They use their time better, because they want to finish and go home to their babies. It's a very valuable decision to take care of women."

Beyond Flex: Reinventing the Career Track

Once upon a time, Deloitte's Cathy Benko was as big a fan of flexibility programs as anyone. After all, the vice chairman and chief talent officer of Deloitte is a mom herself. And the company clearly had to do better by women. Although about as many women as men started their careers at Deloitte, only a small percentage became partner—just 12 percent in 1999.

That was a business problem, since many of the company's clients were women and didn't like the lack of diversity they saw. Deloitte had added flexibility programs and a groundbreaking initiative called Personal Pursuits that let men or women take several years off for personal projects, while staying in touch with Deloitte. The programs seemed to be working. By 2009, 21 percent of partners were women.

Still, Benko was troubled. "It's not that flexible work arrangements are bad. But they're not the solution," she says. "It's kind of a Band-Aid for those people who can't fit the expected ladder norm." The solution, she concluded, wasn't putting a Band-Aid on the ladder: It was throwing out the ladder. "What organizations haven't figured out is that the norms are wrong." The ladder wasn't working for women—and it wasn't working for most men either.

In fact, in some ways, the ladder doesn't exist at all anymore. There's no more lifetime employment at one company, allowing slow, steady, upward career progress. Hardly anyone will work at a single company for fifty-plus hours a week, fifty weeks a year, for forty-five years, like they did in the past. And the ladder itself has become a lot shorter thanks to corporate reengineering. "Organizations are much flatter than they used to be, largely because of corporate reengineering," says Benko. Real careers for both men and women today look more like a sine wave, with peaks and valleys, times of more productivity and intensity, and times when work takes a backseat.

To adjust to the new reality of career paths, Deloitte reinvented the entire idea of career trajectory for *all* its employees, men and women.

After running a pilot program for several years, Deloitte rolled out its Mass Career Customization program over several years: By 2009, more than 90 percent of its U.S. employees were using it, and many overseas offices were also adopting the idea.

The idea is simple. Instead of offering an auxiliary work-life balance program as if balance were an occasional, exceptional problem, the company simply treats its employees of both genders as people who will naturally want to ramp up or ramp down their work at different stages of their lives. At every performance review or other formal meeting about careers, supervisors or HR counselors pull out a grid, mapping four dimensions of a person's career at any given time: Pace, Workload, Location/Schedule, and Role.

At least twice a year, employees are asked about how intense they want their work to be in all four career aspects now, and in years ahead. At any point, they can ask to ratchet up or ratchet down their pace, the intensity of their work, where they work and what hours, and whether they play an "individual contributor" or "leader" role in their job. Ratcheting down might include telecommuting, flexible hours, or other flexible work arrangements. But they're a subset of the overall career-planning process.

It's an innovative approach, one directly inspired by Benko's experiences with her kids. "I'll tell you what else has informed my thinking," she confides. "Buying toys with my kids. You can go to a Web site and say, 'I want the truck, I want it blue, I want four doors,' and you get your own self-designed car. Build-A-Bear Workshop is another great example." Raised with that degree of choice, she says, "I look at my kids and think, what can their expectations of their future workplace be?" Building a career where you can pick your workplace, pick your role, isn't all that different.

So far the "build-a-career-path" plan seems to be working, boosting current career satisfaction of employees by 25 percent and anticipated satisfaction with future careers by 28 percent. Over time, the company has found, about 10 percent of its workforce wants to dial up or down at any given time—and that it's an equal split of men and women who choose to do either (interestingly, two out of three people who want to make a change ask to dial up their work—which is helping the company identify a new pool of ambitious employees). Companies like Deloitte are finding entirely new ways to define careers and create happier, more productive employees—and people.

The Perfect Storm

All these shifts, within corporations and outside of them, are driven in part by women, an example of the domino effect triggered by the rise in women's economic and workplace power. They're shifts that benefit women and men, that help any worker seeking flexibility and opportunity to succeed outside traditional corporate limits. When the workplace moves toward valuing the quality of the work produced over the number of hours it took to produce it, companies become meritocracies. It's better for the firm, better for the employee, ultimately better for our economy. We all win.

It's the perfect storm: an intersection of economic pressure, technology, the shift to a digital information economy, and increasing workforce demand for more creative ways of working. Women are perfectly positioned to exploit this convergence of forces—since we're far less invested in, and often alienated by, the old establishment. Look for women to lead the way, followed by younger men—Gen X and Millennials—whose values and expectations have been shaped by a growing desire for the flexibility and full life that women have pioneered.

What does all this mean? We believe these power shifts—to just-in-time employees, cloud sourcing, and results-based work; in venture capital, on boards, in career paths—will separate the winners from the losers in an increasingly competitive business environment. Those companies that adapt to the changing workforce in these specific ways will gain a competitive edge as the battle for talent heats up, and those countries that encourage the shift—by changing tax laws and treating part-time workers and "nontraditional" workers more fairly, making it easier and less punishing for companies to employ people in these ways, providing more healthcare options, for example—will emerge as winners in the global economy. Those that don't will fade away.

FIVE

In the Marketplace

WOMEN *ARE* THE MARKET

As college basketball players at Yale in 1981, Missy Park and her teammates had to wear men's basketball shoes and uniforms. Even though girls and women had flooded into this arena since the passage of Title IX in 1972, a federal statute guaranteeing girls and boys equal access to sports, the companies that made athletic wear hadn't caught on. High-performance sports clothes for women athletes didn't exist.

"I was lucky my feet were a women's size ten. That's a size they offer in men's shoes," Park says. Another teammate wasn't so fortunate. She had to scour the boys' department to find the right fit.

Grumbling to one another, the players vowed to change things some day. "We all said we wanted to graduate and create the women's Nike," Park recalls. After college, she moved to Berkeley and worked for outdoor gear company The North Face, and then Gary Fisher Mountain Bicycles. But even in the heart of Northern California's active outdoor culture, Missy couldn't find workout clothes she loved, so in 1990, at age twenty-six, she launched Title Nine, a catalog company selling attractive, functional athletic wear for girls and women.

"I just saw this hole in the marketplace. Not because I did a lot of market research, but because I was there at the start of this," she says. She dug into her savings, bought a two-line phone from RadioShack, put up a merchandise rack in her garage, and started talking to apparel makers. As head of a tiny start-up, she had a hard time convincing big suppliers to ship merchandise to her. One company asked her to fill out a credit application. "I didn't even have a credit card," she recalls.

But she soon found a handful of suppliers who had no choice but to deal with Title Nine—like-minded women who were launching women's sports lines, like Jogbra. "They were on the leading edge and were looking for people who got it," Park says. "They were still trying to sell to old-school sporting goods stores. I came along and they figured I was as good a bet as anybody . . . because they really didn't have anybody else to bet on." These women agreed to ship her relatively small quantities and Park launched her catalog. That was 1990. By 1997, the company's revenues were $10 million a year. In the past decade, her revenues have quadrupled.

At age forty-seven, Park still looks like the long, lean athlete she was in college. But today she has no problem finding sports clothes she loves. She and most of her two hundred employees test all the products that they carry in their catalog and in their twenty retail stores. That's one reason why Title Nine's 1.2 million customers are fanatically loyal: Any employee who deals with customers wears the products and therefore knows them intimately. That loyal audience has helped the company grow even while big corporations, including Nike and Gap Inc.'s Athleta, have caught on to the women's sports market. By understanding women's needs early and jumping in, Missy Park built herself a powerful lead.

"I could see the market," she says, "because I *was* the market."

A Lucrative Reality Check

Title Nine is a shining example of a basic fact that much of the business world has been missing. Women *are* the market. Not just in apparel, but in virtually every sector.

"Women have been the primary buyers for just about everything for a long time," says Marti Barletta, author of *Marketing to Women: How to Understand, Reach, and Increase Your Share of the World's Largest Market Segment.*

Consider: Women are responsible for 83 percent of consumer purchases in the United States, including:

- 62% of new cars
- 92% of vacations

- 90% of food
- 55% of consumer electronics
- 93% of over-the-counter pharmaceuticals
- 80% of health-care spending
- 94% of home furnishings

In addition, women hold 89 percent of bank accounts and 51.3 percent of personal wealth in the United States and have a purchasing power of about $5 trillion in consumer spending, which, as I mentioned in Chapter One, is larger than the entire economy of Japan.

"Anybody who has any brains should be focusing primarily on women," Barletta told me. "And they're not."

I caught up with Barletta recently in Chicago at a conference focused on marketing to women. When I'd walked into the ballroom, I'd been shocked to find only about two hundred people in attendance, mostly women. With American women representing the third largest market in the world, how could a conference like this draw so few people? And where were the men?

To me, the absence of men was visible evidence of something another attendee at the conference pointed out to me. Except for a few industries, most of American business seems to think their prototypical customer is a man, and that women are a niche market.

"We have not gotten to a place where it is second nature to assume that when we talk about 'marketing' or reaching 'consumers,' we're *really* talking about reaching women," journalist Fara Warner told me. She's the author of *The Power of the Purse: How Smart Businesses Are Adapting to the World's Most Important Consumers—Women.*

No wonder so many industries are missing the boat when it comes to pleasing women customers.

- 84% of women feel misunderstood by investment marketers
- 74% of women feel misunderstood by auto marketers
- 66% of women feel misunderstood by health-care marketers
- 59% of women feel misunderstood by food marketers

In an increasingly competitive world, *not* taking that leg up will leave companies stuck in the mud while their competitors thunder off over the horizon.

Need proof? Goldman Sachs tracks a stock index of thirty global companies poised to profit based on women's growing global economic power. Many sell cosmetics, apparel, and accessories; most are luxury brands. If you'd bought stock in that Women 30 index ten years ago, you'd now look like a financial genius: The index did much better than global equities as a whole in the same period.

Some of the growth in that index comes from the new hunger for luxury goods from the burgeoning middle classes in Brazil, Russia, India, and China. In addition, Goldman Sachs reported, "We believe a significant portion of this growth is also due to higher female incomes," a trend that should continue "over the next 10 years," according to the company's analysts. It's clear that, as women move from financial confidence to influence, and as they finally begin to catch up with men in income, their spending power will be impossible to ignore.

This is not a matter of companies learning to "market to women" with the cleverest ad campaign. It's nothing less than the reinvention of businesses around the needs of the very best customers—who, in just about all cases, in just about all countries, happen to be women.

Women's Spending Power: Swift, Strong, and Startling

Pretend, for a moment, that you're a large grocery chain. You do lots of customer research, as do the big food manufacturing companies you work with, who want you to stock your shelves with their products. Between you and those food manufacturing companies, you know everything about grocery shoppers—and you know that 70 percent of households' principal grocery shoppers are women.

But a few years ago, something surprised you: Milk sales appeared to be dropping in certain categories. Why? Because millions of shoppers— who were predominantly women—switched to organic milk. In the latter category, sales were skyrocketing—and continued to grow, increasing by

Until now, companies could afford—sort of, I guess—to miss oppo
tunities like women's athletic wear (now a $25 to $30 billion market, a
cording to Park). But we're rapidly nearing a time when ignoring wome
spending power and market influence will be not just foolish but dev
tating to any company that wants to stay competitive in the global ec
omy, because the worldwide rise in women's income and econor
influence coincides with a massive, long-term shift in the business
mate, making it more difficult than ever for companies to gain and h
on to a competitive edge.

A whole set of forces is destabilizing business as usual, making it h
for leaders to stay on top, especially if they neglect an essential segme
the market. Among these seismic shifts: Consumers are increasingly
picious of brands and corporations; technology is lowering the barrie
entering any business, making it easier to knock off products and le
global competitors spring up overnight; and almost all products ar
coming more and more "commoditized"—less and less unique and
cial, chosen less for brand name and more for price. At the same tim
number of middle-class consumers worldwide is skyrocketing, rapid
ping spending power away from Western consumers and toward eme
nations.

This rocky new reality is anything but business as usual, and v
utterly unforgiving of companies that overlook the most powerfu
sumers in the world. We've already started to see the evidence. I
the economic meltdown of 2008 and 2009, auto companies, finan
stitutions, the real estate market—industries that have traditiona
geted men—collapsed.

"It's a battle for share, a battle for profits," says Mary Lou Q
founder of Just Ask a Woman and author of *What She's Not Telli
Why Women Hide the Whole Truth and What Marketers Can Do A*

In every industry, Quinlan says, "there are some who think
getting the money without trying, so why make a change? But a
keter, I would look at my most successful competitor and wonder
not getting that money. Intelligence about women customers '
you a leg up."

22.5 percent in 2008. The same thing was happening in baby foods—sales of natural, organic, and specialty baby foods grew a whopping 70 percent between 2006 and 2008.

Milk and baby food were the bellwethers for a dramatic shift of values, primarily among women shoppers. For the past few years, sales of all natural and organic foods have been on a rapid upward trajectory. What was a $1 billion market for organic foods back in 1990 reached a whopping $23 billion in 2008. And the market for all organic products, including food, organic cotton, etc., grew from $28.2 billion in 2002 to $36 billion just two years later.

That's 28 percent growth in *two years,* a huge change by any standard—and it's women who are driving the change. "Women make 80 to 90 percent of consumer decisions, so they've fostered the success of Whole Foods and this entire movement," observes Nell Merlino, founder, president, and CEO of Count Me In for Women's Economic Independence. "They are helping create a whole new way of eating."

This rapid shift of dollars to natural and organic products is literally changing the landscape of America. Farmers are converting tens of thousands of acres to more organic methods. The amount of land dedicated to organic livestock in California, for instance, increased by 27 percent in 2005, and five thousand additional acres were added to organic vegetable production, a 12 percent increase.

Still, it would be easy to dismiss the shift. After all, organic food sales are still only around 3 percent of the total market. It might be awfully tempting to write the change off as a temporary blip caused by elite, educated, granola-eating white folks who read Michael Pollan or saw *Super Size Me.* In a way, it would be comforting to believe that. If it's a trend that's already peaked, you don't have to make any deep-rooted changes in your business.

But if you're really a visionary company, you look at the fundamental values of your shoppers and realize that women's spending on organics and healthy foods isn't a whim—it's related to basic spending priorities, including the tendency of women to put others' needs ahead of their own financial well-being (even if it means shelling out $6 a gallon for organic milk during a recession). Knowing your best customers as well as you do, you'll put in the research and find this isn't just a niche phenomenon. Turns out it's not just affluent white women driving the trend. African-Americans, Asian-Americans, and Hispanics are more likely to buy organic products than the general population. More than half of "heavy" organic buyers—purchasing an average of nine products a month—earn less than $50,000 a year.

So you might break the rules and invent a whole new line of business based on the spending of your female shoppers. That's what Safeway did. In 2005, the company launched a private label brand of organics, called O. In 2007, it launched another brand, called Eating Right, which stressed nutritional value. These weren't just two more store brands. Instead, Safeway actually spun those lines off into new, stand-alone brands in 2009, persuading U.S. competitors, including Albertson's and Price Chopper, to sell them. In 2009, international chains including Shoprite in South Africa and Exito in Colombia, began to sell the O and Eating Right brands, too.

Persuading your competitors to sell products for you? *That's* a radical new way of capturing market share. And it's only possible because Safeway moved faster than the competition to respond to changes in the demands and preferences of its most valuable customers—women.

Sometimes women's market influence is so glaringly evident that people don't even notice it. Sure, we all see more and more organic farms, and notice organic Purely O's (bearing a suspicious resemblance to Cheerios) in the aisle. But it's so obvious it needs to be pointed out—that's the impact of women's dollars. Failing to anticipate changes in women's tastes can result in rapid failure.

Remember the low-carb craze? In 2003 and 2004, one in eleven adults in North America (where most dieters are women) were on the Atkins diet, and sales of carb-heavy foods plummeted. Pasta sales dropped 8.2 percent, rice sales 4.6 percent. Companies suddenly boasted new low-carb sodas, snacks, even beer. But by July 2005, only 2 percent of U.S. adults were on Atkins and the Atkins company filed Chapter 11. Clearly, staying ahead of women's tastes and choices has an urgent bottom line effect.

The Global Middle Class

In 2005, Junphen Juntana, a corporate communications manager at Siam Commercial Bank, bought a lovely, cream-colored two-story house in Bangkok, with four bedrooms and three baths. Juntana's home is in an up-and-coming neighborhood, near a planned spur of the city's sky-train—a nice perk, given Bangkok's brutal traffic.

Juntana's life is very different from that of her parents, who sold fruit, rice, and fish from their two-bedroom wooden house in the rural province of Chonburi in eastern Thailand. When Juntana was growing up, her family had no car and relied mostly on bicycles to get around.

The youngest of five siblings, Juntana excelled in school and landed a scholarship to Chulalongkorn University, Thailand's top university. In person, she is soft-spoken and charming, a graceful thirtysomething with a radiant smile. But it would be a mistake to let her gentle ways mislead you about her influence. She's translated her smarts, hard work, and outstanding education into financial confidence and serious purchasing power.

"Women are not just housewives and mothers anymore," she says of Thai women. "We take a role in working, earning money, and showing our ability."

If you think the spending power of Western women is impressive, just wait. In the coming decade, the growing economic power of global middle-class consumers like Junphen Juntana will skyrocket. By the year 2030, the number of global middle-class consumers is expected to increase more than two and a half times, from 430 million in 2000 to 1.15 billion. And many of these new middle-class consumers will be women. A whopping 93 percent of the global middle class will likely be living in developing countries. China and India alone will account for two-thirds of the increase.

Look at what's happening in China: In 2002, China bought just 1 percent of the world's luxury goods. By 2015, it will buy 29 percent of them, unseating Japan as the world's largest luxury goods market. The jump corresponds with a leap in urban wages, especially for younger women:

Average monthly wages for urbanites in China ages twenty to twenty-nine jumped 34 percent in 2006, compared with average urban income, which grew 18 percent.

"Young women who move from rural to urban centers in China often make more money than young men who do the same," says Fara Warner. "Young men, what do they become? Construction workers. Young women become office workers with the possibility of more advancement. They tend to learn English. You have this shift very ironically in a culture that has traditions of believing that women are property."

As these young women feel their earning power, they're using it. "The spending for big-ticket items has shifted more toward women as women have gained economic power," Warner continues. "This is true throughout the world. As women gain economic power, they begin to purchase things that mostly men bought before. You see it in China. You see it India. You see it in Thailand. You see it throughout Latin America. When you have access to capital, you buy things that are representative of that capital."

Changes in global economics mean that companies simply can't continue to ignore women's spending power, abroad and at home. Not if they want to survive. How will businesses rise to the challenge? The answer is different in every industry. To give you a taste of how some sectors are meeting the challenge, I'll explore three areas made ripe for transformation by the rise in women's economic influence. Bear in mind that these same forces are at work in *every* industry, and around the globe. As you read, ask yourself how they might affect your industry—and what impact your own dollars are having.

Financial Services:
Discovering Women's Money Lives

My family never had a lot of money when I was growing up. My father was young and restless, never really finding his true career path or a solid financial footing. My mom sometimes worked secretarial or bookkeeping jobs. We moved every three years or so, and not just down the block, either. From New Jersey to Arizona, from California back to New Jersey, never staying one place long enough to feel like it was home. I attended nine schools before college.

When my husband, Ken, and I got married, we broke the cycle. After our youngest, my son, Zak, was born, we settled down to live in one house while raising our kids. Zak and our daughter, Casey, lived in the same house and attended school with the same group of friends until they went off to college. Our house feels like home.

So when Ken and I sat down with our financial advisor a few years ago to talk about possible investments, I knew exactly what I wanted to do.

"Let's pay off the house," I said.

Our financial advisor looked at Ken and rolled his eyes. "I wouldn't recommend that, Maddy," he said. "That would be incredibly conservative and shortsighted. There's better use of that money. If you want to increase your net worth, that's not how to do it."

By all conventional financial planning rules, he was right and I knew it. But I wanted the security of knowing our home was paid for. That made sense to Ken, too, so that's what we decided to do.

Paying off our mortgage turned out to be a smart financial decision. When the economy turned south in 2008, it hurt our business for a while, but we didn't lose nearly what we would have had we put more of our money into the stock market. And when the credit crunch brought on the foreclosure debacle of '08 and '09, we didn't have to worry about paying our mortgage. We didn't have one. There's no way we could have had financial peace of mind if I'd listened to our financial advisor.

In fact, *he's* the one who should have listened to *me*. After all, women like me are his future. Women control 51.3 percent of the country's wealth and represent 50 percent of investors in the stock market.

But the sad truth is, the financial services market is still aimed mostly at men. Eighty percent of financial advisors are men. And they're not listening well to women's needs and preferences. They're playing by outdated financial rules. They're designing and marketing their products the same way they have for eons, targeted primarily to men. Financial services companies still assume that women who buy financial products have the same values, needs, and product interests as men, that they speak the same language of bulls and bears, and that they want the same kinds of relationships that male clients seek.

Not so. First, women's financial needs are very different from men's. Women follow career paths that tend to be more cyclic than linear. Women have times when they're in the work force full-time and times when they're not. Times when their energies go to raising kids, caring for aging parents, and times when they go toward starting their own businesses. That creates more ups and downs in their money lives than in the traditional male money lives on which most financial services are based. Also, women outlive men and need their money to last longer. Women seek financial strategies that fit the realities of their financial lives.

Meanwhile, women also want financial relationships that are centered around their needs, values, and goals. They want long-term relationships, not one-off, product-driven purchases. Women need to balance the right long-term risk with investments that make them feel safe. And women don't necessarily speak, or want to speak, the language of bulls and bears.

I'm not the only woman to get the eye-roll from a male financial advisor. In early 2000, Citigroup sponsored a conference for senior women executives, some of whom struck up a conversation about their own experiences. The more they talked, the more they agreed that they'd never found financial advisors who really understood and listened to them— even though these were all senior-level women working in financial services, with easy access to the best planners.

"We discovered this group wanted to talk about all things money. But they didn't feel like anyone in financial services was talking back in a way that mattered," says Linda Descano, president and chief operating officer of Women & Co., Citigroup's network helping women with financial planning and education. No wonder so many women simply check out when it comes to money management.

That's exactly what Descano herself had done. During her first marriage, she left all the finances to her husband while she worked long hours building her career, then in environmental consulting. "I figured he knew what he was doing," she says ruefully. "I discovered we had amassed significant credit card debt, and as the breadwinner, I absorbed the responsibility to repay that as part of the divorce settlement."

Descano didn't want that to happen to other women. Eventually, she became so involved and excited about financial planning that she changed careers and joined Citigroup Asset Management as a portfolio manager. Today, she leads Women & Co., as it radically redesigns financial services around women's needs.

Citigroup didn't launch Women & Co. to be nice. The company did it to save its business. In the course of researching women's income and financial power, Citigroup realized that most of its financial-advising relationships were actually with men—even when advisors *thought* they had a relationship with both partners in a couple. The men's wives might come to the meetings, but they weren't feeling engaged or included. Across the industry, when women were widowed, a shocking 70 percent of them moved their assets to another financial services firm.

"We realized the relationships we now form with couples are eventually going to be relationships with just the woman of the house, because women live longer. And the fact is, in most cases, she doesn't know us or trust us," Descano says. "It's less expensive for us to retain those customers than try to get them back."

Meanwhile, the company was exploring the demographic data. "We saw the amount of wealth that women are generating today—not through marriage but as executives and business owners. We looked at educational trends, with more women getting undergraduate and advanced degrees and professional degrees than men, and entering higher paid careers. We looked at the fact that women live longer and will control more than two-thirds of private wealth over the next decade or two," says Descano.

Everywhere they looked, the evidence supported women's rise to economic influence. One recent survey showed that 74 percent of women have some sort of retirement savings. Another showed that, after married couples, single women were the second largest group of home buyers, responsible for buying one out of five homes in the United States.

Citigroup's research added up to one compelling business need—the company needed to find a way to form lasting relationships with women. Fast. "The pure, hard economics of the situation were that women are redefining the landscape and making more and more of the financial decisions," Descano says. "If we can't understand their priorities, how to work with them, and what they expect from a financial partner, we're going to have to work much harder to keep them." Other financial services companies were also trying to crack the women's market, but they didn't seem to be taking the right tack. Some of them "sort of 'wrapped it in pink' and dumbed it down," Descano recalls.

To meet those needs, Citigroup launched Women & Co., a financial services division of Citibank, entirely devoted to servicing the needs of women, in 2000. Citigroup designed Women & Co. as a network to promote things that women said they wanted from financial advisors: an ongoing relationship with financial advisors and institutions, and a holistic understanding of how financial products and services fit into each woman's personal financial picture.

Citigroup's findings and the company's reaction to those findings fit with our own research at Age Wave, where we found that most women fall into the Perceptive Planner or Power Partner groups: They want to analyze decisions, educate themselves, and reach out for help and resources.

"We created Women & Co. as a membership community, and that model has really resonated with women," Descano says. "They like the idea of belonging to something, and having a structure and network to share experiences with and come together with. They also liked a process that wasn't all about talking about the product or hearing a sales pitch from Citi." A membership fee of $125 (waived for Citigold members) gets women access to a wealth of financial education resources: live seminars, podcasts, articles, newsletters, and quick answers to questions about taxes, retirement, educational savings, buying a home, hiring a contractor, and related items. Overall, it's a long-term play for the consumer's trust.

If Women & Co. wins that trust, Citi is likely to keep these customers for life. "Statistics say that women are hard judges at the start, but if you win them over, they're more loyal and stay longer with brands," says Mary Lou Quinlan.

"This is enlightened self-interest," Descano admits. Although Descano won't divulge the size of membership or financial results of Women & Co., she will say, "We have really been embraced by women in this country. We have grown significantly since our national launch in 2003. And women don't just get engaged, they stay engaged. Otherwise, we wouldn't still be around six years later, especially in this economic environment."

Best of all, Citigroup overall is learning more about a group that could well become its very best clients. "Our big take-away has been that women want to be involved in a very collaborative experience and that we can be very transparent in the way we do that. We can say, yes, we're part of Citi, but we respect that you work with other financial advisors, too, and we have a product-neutral stance."

Banks around the globe are also realizing that women could be—if they're not already—their very best customers. Micro-lending pioneer Grameen Bank in Bangladesh makes 97 percent of its seven and a half million loans to women, and almost all are paid back. In Austria, Raiffeisenbank opened a women's branch in the town of Bad Gastein in 2006 that includes services aimed at women, more female staff devoting extra time to women customers, and helpful conveniences like a place for kids to play. A year after opening its women's branch, the company saw double-digit growth in its female customer base.

Even in countries where cultural norms restrict women's movements, women's money speaks loud and clear. In the Middle East, the Dubai Islamic Bank created the Johara Banking line to serve women. In the United Arab Emirates in 2007, a government holding company launched Forsa, an investment company run by women to "invest the capital of sophisticated women investors."

One study suggested that Gulf women controlled some $246 billion but had little or no access to investment banks where they can grow that cash. Although women in Saudi Arabia lack the right to vote or drive a car, they do have financial freedom. In fact, they own a third of all Saudi brokerage accounts and 40 percent of all family-run farms. For the cultural comfort of women, Saudi banks have created separate entrances and banks staffed entirely by women, to cater to their needs more effectively. Some of those needs include borrowing plans and credit cards, Internet access, and even brokerage services.

Note that these banks and financial services companies aren't just repackaging existing services in "pink," so to speak. They're offering new services, in new ways—which sometimes involves reinventing their entire companies. "We were one of the first to take advantage of all the different areas of experience at Citi. We cut across credit cards to retail banking to wealth management," says Descano.

In the past, she says, financial services at Citigroup—and in the financial services industry in general—were presented as separate products. "You could go to a credit card site, which would have a lot of information about credit cards. You could go to an investment site that talked about investments," she says. Women & Co. moved Citigroup as a whole toward a more holistic approach. "Women told us they want to understand the whole picture. So Women & Co. does not push products. Our value is in helping people understand the implications of their decisions about their money." This approach sounds simple, but it's a sea change for a company that had always looked at credit cards, mutual funds, life insurance, savings accounts, and other tools as separate products.

To reframe the picture, Women & Co. built tools and an educational framework emphasizing overall financial goals and choices. For instance, dozens of investment companies offer "retirement calculators" that compute how much a person needs to save to support their retirement. But Women & Co. took a different track, creating a document with a series of questions helping women visualize retirement. "It helps you think through what a day in the life of retirement would look like. Do you see yourself on the tennis court five days a week? On a cruise? Will you relocate? How much vacation will you take?" Similarly, Women & Co. created a "document finder" tool for its clients, helping them list where all their important financial documents and records are kept. A simple tool, but one that a business focused just on credit cards or investments might not think of. Women & Co. tools like the document finder and the retirement vision process are now used widely throughout Citigroup's divisions, including in its sales training programs.

"Before Women & Co., much of the [banker-client] conversation was around products," Descano says. The focus on women's financial needs in Citigroup "has shifted conversations away from a product or single issue. 'Wealth management' was not in the lexicon five or ten years ago. Today, I'm amused when I see how many conversations are about life transitions and family dynamics, using the same language we've used since the start."

By bringing a new vocabulary and a more holistic framework to its clients and to its parent company, Women & Co. is giving its customers a more satisfying, big-picture overview of their finances, available services, and how they all fit together. At the same time, it's developing a more sophisticated way to build relationships with customers of both genders.

Start Your Engines:
Transforming the Automotive Industry

You don't have to look far to find women who have had a bad car-buying experience. "One of my colleagues was buying a car recently, and she became more and more irritated because the car salesman was talking only to her husband," says Mary Lou Quinlan of Just Ask a Woman. "So she said, 'You know, I feel like you're not paying any attention to what I say.'" The car salesman, surprised, insisted he was paying attention to her. "Oh yeah?" replied the buyer. "What's my name?" The dealer—who had made a point of using her husband's name repeatedly—was speechless.

It's true. Women buy 62 percent of all new cars sold in the United States and influence more than 85 percent of all car purchases, and they're the fastest-growing segment of buyers for both new and used cars. All told, women have full or partial say over a staggering $80 billion worth of spending on cars.

But car dealerships do a terrible job communicating with women. Seventy-four percent of women say they feel misunderstood by car marketers.

"The auto industry today is in trouble, and automakers are struggling so hard," says Jody DeVere, president and CEO of Ask Patty, a site staffed by women car experts who advise other women on car purchases and service. "Yet they're only doing lip service to women in terms of marketing and selling. When what they need to do is change, and create an environment where women don't equate buying a car or getting it serviced with going to the dentist."

It's an industry that's owned and operated by men. Some 95 percent of the country's twenty thousand auto dealers belonging to the National Automobile Dealers Association are male. And it shows.

"It's a very male culture. They're family businesses, and they've been owned by men for a long time, so that's part of the culture," says DeVere. As part of her job, she travels around the country training car salesmen to build better relationships with women. She's used to the boys' club vibe—she worked in the male-dominated technology industry for years before moving to the automotive industry in 2000. She became president of the Women's Automotive Association International, and later launched AskPatty.com.

Still, she wasn't prepared for the locker-room antics of car salesmen. During one training presentation to a large group of salesmen recently, she explained the importance of careful listening with women customers. "Men and women communicate differently and can misunderstand cues and signals," she said. "Men need to learn how to listen, and why. It makes women trust you and creates a relationship." Meanwhile, a group of salesmen in the back was whispering, shuffling papers, and giggling.

"When the Q and A time came, they asked me inappropriate questions, which I'm used to. I used humor to deal with it." At the end, she cleaned up the literature and found that the men, all in their forties, had drawn crude cartoons of her with labels like "Manhater.com."

She was angry at first, but then thought, "At least the management is smart enough to know they have a problem and they need me." Two weeks later, she received a surprise gift—a $275 Mercedes-Benz branded handbag she'd mentioned during the speech. The note read, "Dear Patty. Just wanted you to know that some of us were really listening."

Isn't it nice to know that the day is coming when the guys in the front of the room—the ones who sent DeVere the handbag, the ones who sincerely *want* to listen to women with respect—will get their reward? The market's already changing in ways that the cavemen in the back will never keep up with. The industry's so out of touch that GM, after struggling for years, sought bankruptcy protection in 2009, shutting down some twenty-four hundred dealerships around the country and laying off tens of thousands of people. Although the company emerged from bankruptcy later that year, their struggles, and those of other U.S. car manufacturers, show how poorly the auto industry has kept up with the times—perhaps nowhere more clearly than in its failure to acknowledge the power of women buyers.

One obvious solution to the auto industry's women's problem would be more women car salespeople and dealers, which some manufacturers are trying to promote. In 2001, GM launched its Women's Retail Initiative to support and encourage female dealers. In 2008, it morphed the initiative into a deeper, more far-reaching network of women dealers, encouraging them to connect, meet, and support one another. The company continued these efforts even while it was closing dealerships and filing for bankruptcy.

"The current struggles in our industry are actually helping us fortify our women's network by rationalizing for women dealers why it's important to get and stay connected with each other," says Marina Shoemaker, director of General Motors' Women's Retail Network. "From my vantage point, this also gives us the opportunity to mobilize and marshal these women dealers to do great things for their individual dealerships and GM overall. We're exploring strategic ways to have women dealers help us grow their market share among women vehicle buyers." Today, GM has about 250 women dealers in its network. They contribute more than $6 billion (yep, billion with a B) in sales revenue to GM. The company expects its network of women to grow, partly because more dealer parents are tapping their daughters to take control of the business.

Other solutions to the rift between the auto industry and its primary—yet unhappy—consumer could include designing cars around women's needs. I'm not talking about more purse hooks or adding a hole in the headrest for ponytails. I'm talking about more attention to women's core values, making cars safer, practical, affordable, and stylish. Look at GMC's Acadia, a seven-seater crossover between a station wagon and a minivan. Introduced in 2006, the Acadia was designed for moms, by a mom: Chief engineer Grace Lieblein, mother of a teenage daughter, headed an all-female design team to dream up a car that's been lauded for such family-friendly conveniences as seats that slide around with one hand instead of two, interior space that's easily reconfigured for people, car seats, and cargo, and more than two dozen storage compartments. In its first year on the market, 53 percent of the Acadia's primary drivers were women (compared to 40 percent for crossover vehicles overall). GMC had to cut TV advertising in the car's first year because demand exceeded supply. Clearly, if GM's salespeople still don't quite get the female market, it's apparent that its engineers (at least the female ones) *do*.

Simpler, quicker solutions could also make a big difference. When Cheri and Don Fleming opened Valencia Acura in 1997, the dealership ranked last among national Acura dealers in sales and customer satisfaction. Cheri Fleming quickly turned that around, adding personal touches to the showroom including freshly baked cookies and gourmet coffee, manicures on Mondays, massages on Wednesdays, and shoeshines on Fridays.

Think Manicure Mondays sound annoyingly pink? The results have been nothing but green. Today, the company's customer satisfaction scores are above Acura's national average, and more than 75 percent of its business is repeat and referral.

But car dealers don't have to offer cookies and manicures to improve the buying experience. The most important thing they can do is change the way they listen, DeVere says. "Women like to tell stories. We don't talk in bullet points. When I come in to get my car serviced, I want to tell you the whole history. But men tend to interrupt and cut to the chase, and that makes me feel bad, like they're not respecting me. Men need to learn how to listen," she says. Not because it's polite, but because real listening will sell more cars.

Can small changes, like better listening, really help? Marti Barletta thinks so. "When you're starting from zero, doing even a little bit to appeal to women in general can make a huge impact. That first 20 percent of your effort will get you 80 percent of your value. Most companies are not even in the beginning of the curve."

Reinventing Media: Women and Social Networking

On Mother's Day last year, I laughed out loud at a video my daughter, Casey, e-mailed me. It was a clip from MomsRising, an advocacy group lobbying for better treatment of mothers and families in the workplace and at home. The cause is serious, but the video was anything but. It featured a fake newscast about the newly announced Mother of the Year . . . in this case, me! The video seamlessly incorporated my name into text, signs, and a tattoo. Between marveling at the technology and laughing at the hilarious script, I thought about what a dead-on hit that video was for moms. The "fake news" format was classic Jon Stewart style; the cool technology was mind-blowing; the mom jokes rang true ("A new study confirms that pulling your hair back into a ponytail is not the same thing as taking a shower"). As the video trickled from mother to daughter, from sister to sister, from friend to friend, it eventually spread to a staggering 10 million moms in the first two weeks of May 2009. That's the jaw-dropping, game-changing power of social media at work.

"In the United States, each individual receives more than three thousand media messages or marketing points per day," says MomsRising cofounder Kristin Rowe-Finkbeiner. "We live in a marketing culture, and in order to be heard, there has to be some literacy about how people are hearing things." MomsRising has drawn more than a million members through its savvy use of social media and, along the way, has breathed new life into the women's rights movement.

Perhaps more than any industry in the past, the emerging field of social media is being invented, evolved, and shaped by women, both as users and as developers. It's already changing the way women interact with messages and brands, and what companies have to do to reach women. And we're just starting to feel the impact.

"Women have been all over this space, as much as men, as users but also in technology development. That wasn't the case with Web 1.0," says Charlene Li, coauthor of the book *Groundswell: Winning in a World Transformed by Social Technologies.*

In other words, women are *inventing* social media as well as using it. Caterina Fake founded Flickr, the photo-sharing site, in 2004 with her husband; two years later, 3 million users had posted 130 million photos. (Yahoo! bought Flickr in 2005 for a reported $30 million.) Lisa Stone, Elisa Camahort Page, and Jory Des Jardins founded BlogHer, a networking site for women bloggers that sponsors conferences and an ad network, and scored their third round of financing in May 2009, for a total of $15.5

million in venture funding. (Remember, less than 4 percent of venture capital goes to women, so you know this was a hot idea.) Former Goldman Sachs advisor Gina Bianchini launched Ning in 2004, which lets users start up their own social networks. Five years later, some 33 million registered users had launched an astonishing 1.5 million networks of their own.

The success of these women depends on other women—the 42 million women a week who use social media—blogging, reading or posting to blogs, weighing in on message boards, updating Facebook, Twitter, etc. In 2009, 63 percent of Facebook users were women, 63 percent of MySpace users were women, 58 percent of Friendster users were women, and 55 percent of Twitter members were women. The women-driven trend shows no sign of slowing. In the fall of 2009, more women joined Facebook than did men in every age bracket. *Twice* as many women aged twenty-six to thirty-four signed up. As for social media overall, 75 percent of women who use social media reported that they were more active in 2009 than 2008. Women's interest in social networking seems to be on a steep rise.

All this has created "radical changes in how women communicate and share information," says Kelley Skoloda, director of global brand marketing practice at public relations firm Ketchum and author of *Too Busy to Shop: Marketing to "Multi-Minding" Women*.

Consider "mommy blogs" like ParentTalkToday.com, by Southern California mom and writer Kathy Sena, and Metropolitan Mama by Stephanie Sheaffer. The mothers who write these blogs are doing what moms have always done—sharing insider tips, networking, making information more available to other mothers, and laughing while they do it. By bringing these old-fashioned activities to social media, they've taken the single most powerful marketing method—word of mouth—and added a megaphone. "They're talking from a very authentic, candid point of view that women have not experienced before except in personal conversations with their finite circle of friends," says Skoloda. Increasingly, bloggers serve as trusted advisors recommending products and services to their faithful audience. Bloggers offer a combination of media and marketing, of conversation and commerce, that's shifting paradigms and forcing companies to reinvent the way they interact with women.

"Social media is transforming and will continue to transform how companies market," says Skoloda. "Women always want to connect. They have a natural ability and capability to connect. Now the digital tools are enabling them to connect with virtual friends and family who may be in the same life situation but they've never met."

That provides a whole new pool of trusted advisors for women to turn to when making their buying decisions. Suddenly, brands can't rely on the one-way monologue created by TV ads, magazine spreads, and other traditional advertising. Instead, brand messaging has abruptly become a conversation—one that marketers can't control as completely as they used to.

In this way, Skoloda says, "female consumers are taking over brands."

The smartest companies are finding ways to make social media work for them, not against them. Many are sending their products to bloggers and inviting bloggers into the product development process, asking for input. "If you engage bloggers along the way, and take their advice and make changes, it's not like it used to be, where there was this secret room where you did your research and created this new product and ta-da!" says Skoloda. "Before you even get it out there, they'll think it's awesome."

Some companies are also creating their own social networks. After several false starts, for instance, Walmart launched a blog called Check Out, where people wrote about what they were buying and why. "That's been a huge hit," says Charlene Li.

Some women are turning the marketing power of social media into a business. Aliza Freud, for example, whom you met in Chapter Three, launched the social network marketing firm called SheSpeaks, a company that helps clients reach women in new ways, largely by creating a large online network of women willing to sample new products. The SheSpeaks panel is used by clients for research and for spreading the word about new offerings. For instance, SheSpeaks worked with client Häagen-Dazs to create "house parties" around the country to introduce the new ice cream line, five. (By the way, five, which contains just five ingredients, was created in response to the natural food movement driven by women consumers.) "At the end of the day in this environment, brands don't have as much control. We're helping companies figure out how to deal with that," says Freud.

The recession of 2008–2009 accelerated the power of social media, as marketers cut their advertising budgets and shifted money to far less expensive online efforts. Social media has the advantage of being cheap and easy to measure—both attractive qualities during a recession when companies want to get the most out of every dollar.

Amazingly, all this is only a beginning. In just a few years, "social networks will be like air. They'll be everywhere you need them or want them," says Li. Instead of logging on to Facebook to ask friends what movie to see or book to read, you'll be able to access your friends and their buying information and reviews wherever you're shopping. As social networks and shopping sites like Amazon.com become increasingly interconnected, new opportunities for marketers will open up. With women shaping so much of the social networking world, the expansion of new media may help unleash women's true market influence at last.

What Women Want

In every field, women's market influence offers enormous opportunities, but also fearsome perils. As it turns out, it's tremendously easy to strike the *wrong* note with women, particularly by relying too much on tired stereotypes. That's what Dell learned in spring 2009, when it launched a Web site called Della to promote the new lightweight netbook to women. With women buying 66 percent of computers, the strategy seemed wise. Alas, the initial execution was anything *but*.

Instead of stressing the computer's size, weight, and convenience for travel, the site featured tips about using the laptop to count calories, find recipes, and watch cooking videos. Women, understandably, trashed the site online, and the company quickly revamped its content in an attempt to better appeal to women customers, but eventually Dell simply shut the site down.

To strike the right tone with women consumers, the smartest companies are finding new ways to get closer to women, to learn what they truly think, need, and want. Traditional ways of tracking, researching, and talking to their customers simply aren't working. Focus groups, for instance, don't always get beyond the superficial. "We found that women often tell marketers half truths, for a lot of reasons," says Mary Lou Quinlan of Just Ask a Woman. "A lot of marketers are buying half truths and creating programs that flop. Women will say, 'I try to be healthy,' when we're really an obese nation, and Mom is going to McDonald's three times a week."

To get a better handle on women customers, companies are reinventing the way they do research. Some companies with women-focused products are using new tools like the "girlfriend group"—a group of women who know one another and gather at a friend's house to talk with researchers. "It's a lot harder to lie in front of a friend who knows the real answer," says Quinlan. Her firm also pioneered another new idea—talk show–format research, where they put research participants onstage and interview them Oprah-style. "It's lots of fun, and somehow using the microphone as an empowering tool helps get better comments. The format also keeps one person from monopolizing the conversation," Quinlan says. For these and other research efforts, she insists that marketers be in the room, taking part, instead of sitting behind one-way glass eating potato chips.

Other companies send trained ethnologists into the field with actual customers. Best Buy, for instance, sent ethnographers to ride along with customers considering an electronics decision. Big food companies send anthropologists to talk to women in their kitchens.

"Consumer packaged goods companies have done a lot of ethnography and digging into how women actually consume the product," says Quinlan. "The one-hundred-calorie snack packs are a perfect example," she says, of something marketers wouldn't have thought of without watching women consumers.

"The problem is, when you open a box of crackers or cookies, it's hard just to go in one time once you rip it open." As a result, snackers end up eating more than they really want to and don't feel good about the experience. "That's the kind of thing you only really get from watching women snack," Quinlain says.

The Triumph of Good Design

When the economic upheaval of 2008 and 2009 affected every industry, why didn't more companies wake up to the need to reinvent themselves—not just their marketing but the way they develop products and align their own internal divisions—to serve their very best customers, who happen to be women?

"There's still a stigma out there; there's still the idea that marketing to women is somehow a niche activity," says Marti Barletta. There's also an idea that, while women have always bought products designed for men, men will never buy products designed for women.

But, it turns out, that's not true at all.

Look at Best Buy. The company overhauled some of its stores—called, internally, the "Jill" stores—around the tastes and needs of women customers, specifically young moms who buy a lot of technology. "We worked on the Jill stores, and had a lot of conversations about what wasn't working for moms," says Quinlan. "If you have kids, they'd run away and you could never find them. You'd search for a salesperson, and they'd say, 'This isn't my department.' You'd call ahead to know if something was in stock, then get there and find out they didn't have what you came for on that trip you didn't have time to make in the first place." The Jill stores created wider aisles, lower racks, and a concierge service to help customers find what they needed ahead of time.

"Not only was it successful for women, but for men, too. You can't really tell what's different, other than 'Hey, this is a nice store laid out in an appealing, clear way,'" says Quinlan. "The solutions are never to make a female-only store, just to come up with better logic that works well for everyone."

Personally, I believe that when products are redesigned to work for women, they're often good for men, too. It's like the "universal design" phenomenon—when architects and designers started creating homes and public spaces with the elderly and disabled in mind, they discovered that pretty much everyone liked wider doorways, bright lights, lever handles on doors. When housewares entrepreneur Sam Farber decided to create gadgets that were easier for his wife Betsey to use when her slight arthritis made gripping difficult, OXO Good Grips peelers, can openers, and utensils became hugely popular with consumers of all ages and abilities.

As the primacy of women's market power becomes recognized and even continues to increase, the products and services thoughtfully designed for women may prove better for everyone. To reach this new stage of gender-friendly design, marketers will need to move way beyond "pink" and consider their consumers in a far more sophisticated way. Ultimately, as women's economic influence grows, the companies that direct that level of care and attention to their very best customers will win. The others simply won't be able to compete.

SIX

At Home

THE FUTURE OF MEN

Until 2001, Garry Berger of Ridgefield, Connecticut, followed the classic script for a successful law career. Step One: Ivy League law degree. Step Two: Summer associate gig with big New York law firm. Step Three: Clerk for federal judge. Step Four: Join big New York law firm as an associate. But he balked at Step Five: Work eighty hours a week to become partner.

In 2001, Berger's son Max, then two, was diagnosed with autism. Berger and his wife knew something would have to change. "We both wanted to be able to give Max whatever he needed," he says. So he quit Big Law and went into business for himself, launching Berger Legal, the "virtual" law firm we mentioned in Chapter Three.

Within a year, Garry Berger was working from home, spending more time with his family, and earning as much as he had before. Soon he had more work than he could handle, so he hired a group of other attorneys—mostly women—who also wanted flexibility, freedom, and challenging, well-paid work. Eventually, he was earning a steady enough income that his wife quit her job, also in law, and opened a clothing store near their home.

Does Berger regret jumping the track? "You're joking me, right?" he responds with a laugh. "Having a good work-life balance, having control of my schedule, fitting everything in among all my obligations to clients, my wife, my kids, playing golf? All that together, that's what I call successful."

If Berger's story sounds familiar—with its conflict between the fast track and family and its new definition of success—it's because women have been writing their own version of this tale for decades.

"Men are where women were twenty years ago," says Michael Kimmel, a sociology professor at the State University of New York at Stony Brook, and author of *Guyland: The Perilous World Where Boys Become Men*. Back then, he says, women were adding *career* to their repertoire; today, men are adding *care*—for children, for aging parents, for communities. And while some (okay, many) might call men's engagement on the home front belated, this overdue participation may, in fact, be setting the stage for the final, deciding battle in the war for gender equality. A battle that men, more than women, will fight. Ultimately, of all the power shifts created by women's economic emancipation, the most monumental may prove to be its impact on men—their values, their expectations, and their very definition of manhood.

Don't get me wrong. I'm *not* talking about some revolutionary "feminization" of men, where they simply swap roles with women, putting on aprons while women wear suits. What's happening isn't role reversal: It's role reinvention. It's a full-blown paradigm shift, one that gives both men *and* women more options when it comes to providing for their families and expressing their own talents and strengths. In this new social order, both genders are less shackled by a narrow vision of career success. Men in this new world have more social and workplace support for becoming involved fathers, equal partners in their homes and communities, and more complete people.

This change in the way we live is going on right now, in ways that are so obvious and self-evident that it's easy to miss just how groundbreaking they really are. Men are reimagining their life just as women shifted theirs twenty or thirty years ago, hoping to create lives that include important responsibilities at home as well as at work. Case in point: When Myra Strober, a labor economist who teaches at Stanford's Graduate School of Business, offered a course about work and family in the early 2000s, only a handful of men signed up. (At the time, it was called "Women and Work.") Today, the course is titled "Work and Family," and men represent 40 percent of her class. Why? "More and more men are interested in being good dads," she says of her students. "They also want to be good husbands and be supportive of their wives."

This redefinition of fatherhood is happening in millions of families around the country, where fathers are spending many more hours with their children every week than their fathers spent with them. It's happening in small ways, as even the most high-flying, type-A dads drop their kids off at day care and duck out for soccer games. It's happening in bigger ways, as growing numbers of dads take paternity leaves, telecommute, or use flex-time.

These changes are sweeping through families at every income level. In middle-class homes, moms are pulling equal economic weight; in lower-income homes, dads like Adrian Zamarripas, a warehouse worker in Phoenix, Arizona, who works nights and watches his kids during the day, are more likely than higher-income fathers to split child care with their wives (because day care or babysitters are too expensive). This change is happening through the thousands of daily arrangements men make because they love their wives and their kids and want happy families. "The solution isn't a broad political movement toward a new fatherhood," Kimmel says. "It's the day-to-day accommodations that men are making, where they're compromising and adopting new family arrangements that demand more from them at home. And they're finding they're actually enjoying it."

Shifting to this new model of fatherhood can be acutely uncomfortable, even painful. Often, men feel caught between a rock and a hard place, expected to fill the old-time breadwinner role and the new superdad model at the same time. Are they supposed to be the breadwinner? Will their wives think less of them if they step off the fast track? If work-family pressure is taking a toll on the kids or the marriage, who steps back? And how do they support their partner best?

"Men want to be supportive of their wives, and they don't know whether being supportive means they should agree with her if she says she wants to be a full-time mom, or whether they should challenge her on that," notes Myra Strober.

While men in general, and fathers in particular, are going through a time of ambiguity, the shift in roles is already bringing tremendous benefits to both genders. The more our communities and employers can acknowledge, recognize, and support these changes, already well under way, the more concerns like closing the gender wage gap, making sure families can afford great day care, making good education affordable, enacting child-friendly laws and policies, and advancing work-life balance will become *family* issues, not just women's issues. As the genders work together to redefine womanhood, manhood, and the family, our children will thrive and our society and economy grow stronger.

"My hope is that in ten years, our culture and the workplace will understand that caregiving is part of every human life," says Jeremy Adam Smith, author of *The Daddy Shift: How Stay-at-Home Dads, Breadwinning Moms and Shared Parenting Are Transforming the American Family.* "If our society can get to a place where it respects that in men, it will also respect that in women."

The Rise and Stumble of the Male Breadwinner

Next time you watch a blundering dad in a movie like *Daddy Day Care* or *Cheaper by the Dozen,* try to remember that our society didn't always view dads as befuddled dimwits, doling out Twinkies for breakfast. As Smith reminds us in *The Daddy Shift,* the late-twentieth-century Distant Dad was a post–Industrial Revolution invention. While colonial American moms were playing a key role in providing economically for their kids, their husbands were taking an active, involved role in child-raising. Fathers taught their kids to read, to work in the fields or the family business, and many Civil War dads wrote home to their wives about their acute guilt at not being physically present to take an active role in parenting. (Of course, African-American slave families were often broken up by their owners, preventing many parents of either gender from knowing or raising their children.) From the mid-nineteenth century until World War II, as factory work and office jobs replaced agricultural work, families divvied up the labor, often (though not always) sending dad to work and keeping mom at home. (Again, this differed for African-American families: Since emancipation, black mothers have been more likely to work outside the home than white mothers.)

Along the way, traits that seemed more useful in the workplace or at home became more and more identified with one gender or the other—until the idea of an involved dad fell from an expected given to a silly sit-com premise. "We've been living with a model of what's masculine and what's feminine that basically assigns half of human traits to men and half to women. Society said to both women and men, 'You can only be half a person,'" says Kimmel. When women began entering the workforce in large numbers, "[women] were saying, 'We don't want to be half people. We want to be whole people.'" That is, people who work for wages *and* care for their families and communities. "Men are finally realizing, 'Hey, we don't want to be half people either,'" says Kimmel. "Talk about a win-win: It's about being a complete person."

Because women were the first of the genders to take back both halves of themselves—work and family—they became the pioneers of work-place change. "Women were the canary in the corporate coal mine," says Cathy Benko, vice chair and chief talent officer at Deloitte, the international accounting and consulting firm, and author, with Anne Weisberg, of the book *Mass Career Customization*. As newcomers to a corporate world designed expressly for workers with wives at home, women were the first to feel the painful squeeze when social expectations, economic necessities, and workplace traditions collided. So it was women who broke ground on many of the work-world innovations we talked about in Chapter Four, and the family changes we'll examine in Chapter Seven.

Today, however, says Jeremy Adam Smith, the baton of work-family balance has passed to men.

"From the 1950s to today, women experienced incredibly rapid and unprecedented change," says Smith. But starting around 2000, "the change for women leveled off, but for men it seemed to accelerate in a lot of ways." As we move into the future, men may run the next leg of the relay in pursuit of a balanced life.

A Sea Change for Men

In 2008, the Families and Work Institute conducted a major study of men's and women's attitudes about work-life balance—and found, in many cases, that men's attitude toward parenting, dual-career families, and work-life balance had changed more radically and more rapidly than women's. For instance, back in 1977, a whopping 74 percent of men agreed with the statement "It is better for all involved if the man earns the money and the woman takes care of the home and children." Far fewer women (58%) concurred. But in 2008, just 42 percent of men agreed with that statement—nearly the same percentage as women who agreed (39 percent). The Families and Work Institute called this convergence of opinions *"a striking and seminal change in attitudes."* Women had also become less likely to endorse traditional gender roles during the previous two decades, but the change (a drop from 52 percent to 39 percent) wasn't as dramatic. What's most striking here is that for the first time since the 1970s, the genders have similar attitudes about their roles in the family.

True, more than a third of men and women still think it's better if women stay home and men earn the money. But when we look toward the future through the lens of trends, it's the change that counts—and the change in men's attitudes has been rapid and consistent and shows no signs of stopping. Furthermore, the recession of 2008 and 2009 may have accelerated this trend, as men lost more jobs than women and, in many cases, the wife's wages saved the day.

Men are also now much less likely to worry about a working mother's bond with her children. In 1977, less than half of men surveyed agreed with the statement "A mother who works outside the home can have just as good a relationship with her child as a mother who doesn't work." Today, just over two-thirds of men (67 percent) agree with that statement. Again, women's attitudes have also changed but less dramatically, since they never really doubted the bond between a working mother and her children; in 1977, 71 percent of women agreed that the mother-child relationship was equally strong whether mothers worked or not, and in 2008, 80 percent did.

As men's attitudes toward dual-career families were changing, so were their job descriptions as husbands and fathers. According to the same Families and Work Institute study, employed fathers today spend much more time with their kids—3 hours per workday, up from 2 hours in 1977. (Women's 3.8 hours has stayed fairly constant, so the gap is closing.) Younger dads spend even more time with their kids: Dads under age twenty-nine now spend 4.3 hours a day with their kids, up from 1.9 hours a day in 1997, and compared with 3.1 hours a day for dads ages twenty-nine to forty-two.

Regardless of how much time they actually spend with their children and on the home front, dads are acutely aware that they now shoulder heavier responsibilities in child care, cooking, and housekeeping. Only 48 percent of dads say their partners take more responsibility for child care (down from 58 percent in 1992). Forty-nine percent of employed men say they take on as much or more child-care responsibility as their partners (up from 41 percent in 1992). Meanwhile, 56 percent of men say they do more cooking than their partners, up from 34 percent in 1992, and 53 percent of men say they do as much or more cleaning as their partners.

By these measures, it's clear dads feel they're doing their fair share and more at home. Still, moms aren't ready to hand over the superhero cape just yet: Only 31 percent of wives say child care is shared evenly, and just 20 percent agree that their spouse shares equally in cleaning duties. But regardless of who's really scrubbing the toilets, men *perceive* their roles differently than they used to.

"It has clearly become more socially acceptable for men to be and to say they are involved in child care, cooking and cleaning over the past three decades," according to the Families and Work Institute authors. We're moving into an era where both men and women are working what sociologist Arlie Hochschild famously dubbed "the second shift."

Global Conversations: Blazing the Trail to a New Model

In Myra Strober's classroom at Stanford, some of the top business students in the United States—men and women who will lead large companies and launch small ones—are focusing on far more than the bottom line. They're learning about earnings discrimination, the economic value of stay-at-home parents, the economics of child care, the role of public policy, and other ingredients in the time-management, work-life soup. These students—increasingly men—sign up for Strober's "Work and Family" class because they know that down the line, understanding and resolving work-life conflicts will be as critical to their success as mastering PowerPoint and Excel.

Few of Strober's students of either gender are parents. Most aren't even married. But many of her male students *are* in a relationship—often with a classmate or someone at another business school. Sometimes couples take the class together; sometimes they take different sections of the same class. "It makes for interesting conversations," Strober says. Consider lofty questions like this: How much is a stay-at-home spouse worth? How do you value her or his contributions to the other partner's career? Or less lofty ones like this: Who stays home when Benjamin is sick?

Many, though by no means all, of these men are what you might call junior masters of the universe. But even these high flyers (perhaps especially these high flyers, since they're likely to meet and marry high-flying women) want a head start on the work-family conversation. "They want to know how they can meet their career goals and still meet their family obligations," Strober says.

These early conversations—about who does what, how to handle child care, what trade-offs are acceptable—aren't just happening in Palo Alto. They're happening in Europe and in South America. They're happening in North Africa and the Middle East, which the World Economic Forum ranks last among eight global regions in closing the economic, political, education, and health and survival gender gap. They're even happening in Morocco, which ranked 125th of 130 countries in the size of its gender gap.

"My fiancé and I think about building a family as a shared responsibility with shared rights," says Kawtar Chyraa, a twenty-two-year-old college senior in Ifrane, Morocco. When we spoke, she'd recently become engaged. Her fiancé was studying finance and getting ready to work for his family's business. Although this young couple won't marry until they finish their studies, they're already talking about work-family balance.

"We're both planning to have a career and children, so if any adjustments need to be made, they will be made in both our careers, not only mine. We're discussing this whenever we talk about our careers. It's definitely on our minds."

If these conversations are happening among young Moroccans, you can bet they're happening in the Nordic countries—where women's economic power has long been established, accepted, and encouraged. In these countries, women earn much more than in other countries, compared to men. (In Sweden, women's earned income is about 81 percent of men's; in Norway, it's 77 percent.) And many studies suggest that when women earn more money, couples share housework more equally.

"Internationally, the more money women earn, the more likely men are to be participating at home," says Jeremy Adam Smith. And now that women around the world spend more hours at the office than they used to, men are picking up the slack (or the socks) at home: Data on time use in twenty countries shows that men contributing to housework, child care, and shopping went from less than one-fifth of all men in 1965 to more than one-third today.

All this data suggests that when women work and earn money, the family changes. Men's lives become more like women's, with more equal sharing of breadwinning and bread-baking, so to speak.

That's the situation for Gunnar and Eva-Maj Mühlenbock of Stockholm, Sweden. Both work long hours for good salaries—she as a law firm partner, he as an accountant. They share housekeeping and parenting duties for their two sons, Peder, sixteen, and Markus, eight.

"I'm not doing most of the work at home," Eva-Maj Mühlenbock says. Twice a week, a housekeeper comes to help with cleaning and meal preparation. Gunnar does the cooking, as well as his share of the housekeeping. "He's a much better cook than I am. I've been really lucky with that," Mühlenbock admits.

She and Gunnar have also been lucky with child care. By law, they were each able to take a significantly long parental leave after the birth of each child. "Our women are usually home for a year and come back, and then their husbands are home for six months," she says. To encourage both men and women to take parental leave, part of that paid time is reserved specifically for dads. If they don't use it, they lose it.

"I think the system with parental pay sends a signal to employers here," says Mühlenbock. "It says, we want a future where both men and women are educated, go to universities, and have their own careers, but also as a society, we want couples to have children."

When Eva-Maj and Gunnar went back to work, their children went to the high-quality, affordable day care available to all families. Swedish policy ensures that child care won't cost families more than 1 to 3 percent of their income and offers at least three free hours a day of preschool for four- and five-year-olds. Meanwhile, Eva Maj's mother- and father-in-law had recently retired when Peder was born, and they provide lots of extra help. Eva-Maj had just made partner at her firm, and the help was very welcome.

To cover the inevitable sick days and emergencies, Gunnar and Eva-Maj found a simple solution. He scheduled all his client meetings after lunch; she set all of hers before. "If something should happen, we knew how to share those days," she says.

Gunnar and Eva-Maj's efforts to create an equal balance in their home has let both of them rise to the top of their careers, while spending lots of time with their sons. While Sweden is far from perfect—"women still do more than men at home" says Eva-Maj—it does come much closer to true gender equality than many other countries. With a long history of laws and policies that assume men and women alike want to work and have families, the country consistently ranks at or near the top of the World Economic Forum's Global Gender Gap list. Since Sweden makes combining work and family relatively easy, it's not surprising to hear that nearly as many women as men work, and that as far back as the early eighties, Swedish men were spending 30 percent more time on housework than U.S. men.

In countries such as Sweden—and Norway, Finland, Iceland, New Zealand, and other high scorers on the Global Gender Gap list—the conversation about who does what, a conversation taking place in tens of millions of homes around the world, isn't confined to the house. In Sweden, the fair division of labor is seen as a matter of public policy—one that both women and men have a say in.

These policy discussions, in which both genders participate, are setting an example for women's rights activists in developing countries: The idea is to include men, not alienate them. "Let us reason together and see what makes a better world for both of us," explains Mahnaz Afkhami, founder and president of Women's Learning Partnership for Rights, Development, and Peace, which works with organizations in eighteen countries in Africa, Asia, the Middle East, and Latin America. In Iran, for example, when women launched a petition to reform family laws and gathered a million signatures, fully a third of those signatures came from young men. In Lebanon, an advocacy campaign to give women equal citizenship rights for their children drew heavily on support from men.

In many other countries across the globe, supportive men are helping make women's economic emancipation a gain for the family, not a stress. "In Argentina, we have very sensitive men who admire women, and we now have two generations of men educated by women that work outside the home," says Mariana Lomé, forty-one, executive director of the nonprofit Fundación Compromiso in Buenos Aires. Lomé's father didn't want Mariana to go to college and especially not to study journalism; given the military government that ruled Argentina when Mariana was growing up, her father felt she'd be safer at home, raising a family, in a less confrontational role. So Mariana studied in secret; she and her mother didn't tell her father Mariana was attending college. Today, her father's proud of her accomplishments. "He tells everybody I have a university degree." She understood her father's position, but as head of her own organization, she's working with the women and men on her staff to create an open, equal environment. "Working together can improve all these things," she says of the barriers women still face to having a job and a family. She recently helped improve things in her own family, joining forces with her sister-in-law, who wanted to work after having her first baby. "We were very surprised when my brother said he wanted his wife to stay home. So both of us—my sister-in-law and I—told him he was crazy. This is the twenty-first century." He came around: Now both he and his wife work.

All these stories—from one couple's kitchen to national policies—have something in common: "This is about moving toward a shared vision," says Mahnaz Afkhami, "not necessarily a world where men and women split every duty fifty-fifty, but where people interact with each other in different ways. This movement is changing the architecture of human relationships." Of course, some countries still have a very long way to go: In some countries, it is illegal for women to drive, attend school, or vote. But in much of the world, in small ways and large, we're inexorably inching toward a "his and hers" society where men and women can make the best use of their own talents and strengths.

The Price of Fatherhood

In Sacramento, Richard Rojo is heading out to pick up his four-year-old twins at day care. His wife (who happens to be my coauthor on this book) is traveling on business, so he's arranged to leave early every day this week. His boss doesn't mind: She knows he'll work late at night to make up the hours. Today, he's wrapping up a conference call on his Bluetooth headset as he unlocks the bright green gate that opens into the garden at his sons' preschool. Entering his sons' classroom, he finds twenty-four preschoolers sitting in a circle, listening to their teacher reading a picture book called *The Napping House*. Zach runs to hug his father. Alex keeps his seat, but a huge grin steals over his face when he realizes his daddy's watching. "I love picking them up," says Rojo, gathering their Lightning McQueen lunch boxes and their naptime blankets. "I used to do it a lot more, but now I have a longer commute, so my wife does most of the drop-off and pick-up."

For Rojo, life is a daily marathon. He leaves for his job as a university administrator at six-thirty in the morning and comes home twelve or thirteen hours later. Then he's on child-care duty until bedtime, after which he makes lunches and washes the dishes. His day doesn't really end until ten or eleven at night (after he's checked his e-mail one more time and responded to any late night requests).

"There's never enough time to get it all done, and we're both exhausted," he admits. Once upon a time, men worried that women would take their jobs and salary. As it turns out, the real social turmoil wrought by women's employment wasn't caused by what men *lost* in terms of jobs and salary, but by what they *gained*—much more responsibility at home.

It's not an easy transition, as harried dads like Rojo can attest. While men on average still aren't putting in as much time on child care and housework as women, they're clocking far more hours than ever before. They have to. In most married couples today (57 percent), both partners work. Dual-income families are now the norm. In two-thirds of families, wives are the primary or co-breadwinner. In the United States "the 'traditional' family structure includes only about 15 percent of people," says Cathy Benko. But, she adds, most offices act like their employees are what economists call "unencumbered workers," free to put in long hours with no other obligations, and someone else at home to do the laundry, cook the meals, and check the homework. "Established norms are predicated on a family infrastructure to support them that by and large doesn't exist today."

The new norm leaves far fewer hours for cooking, cleaning, trips to the dentist, or for dropping off a forgotten lunch box.

"It's hard," says Adrian Zamarripas, twenty-five, who works the night shift at a distribution warehouse in Phoenix. He and his wife, Sharice, a medical assistant, have worked opposite shifts for nearly six years. Even just finding time to interview them was a challenge, since they're almost never around at the same time.

"I get home at five in the morning, make sure my daughter and son have breakfast, and drop my son off at school at eight," Adrian told me. Sharice's mom then comes over later so Adrian can get his "night's" sleep in the afternoon. Then he gets up and makes dinner—his barbecued steak is a big hit with the kids. Then he heads out again, usually before Sharice gets home from her job as a medical assistant (and, again, her mother usually covers the gaps in their schedule). "We don't get to see each other that much. Sharice will be going to work in the morning and I'll say, 'Hi, I love you.' We really don't see each other until Saturday."

With men and women sharing home and income-producing responsibilities this way, it's no surprise that men in dual-income couples (which is, again, the majority of families) are now feeling more work-life conflict than women. These men report the most work-life conflict of any group of adults. In 2008, a survey by the Families and Work Institute found that 45 percent of men felt serious conflict between their work and their family life, compared with 39 percent of women. For the first time, men feel more conflicted than women. Back in 1977, only 34 percent of dads in two-income families reported "some or a lot of conflict."

Of course men are more stressed: They're finally being asked to do much, much more at home, with little to no give at work. Men like Adrian Zamarripas and Richard Rojo are feeling pressures unthinkable to their fathers as they try to ease some of the work-life burden that wives have been bearing, increasingly, since the 1970s. And I believe soon these enormous pressures will cause a seismic shift, reshaping the world for both genders.

That Awkward In-Between Phase

In August 2006, Jeremy Adam Smith, the author of *The Daddy Shift*, went back to work after spending a year as a stay-at-home dad for his son, Liko. Going back home wasn't in his plans—until he was laid off from his magazine job in 2009.

"When I found out I was getting laid off, I was really thrown for a loop," he told me. As we talked, Liko was perched on Smith's lap, waiting for Dad to take him to the beach. "The financial aspect is important, but psychologically," he says, staying home "was still a struggle."

Smith had been happy to return to his role contributing economically to the family and to resume his professional identity. Giving those things up wasn't easy—even though he'd written an entire book about caregiving dads, breadwinning moms, and the value that comes from shared responsibility. Adjusting psychologically to new roles isn't easy. For generations, men's self-worth has come, in part, from their breadwinner status. Take that away, Smith found, and even the most enlightened of fathers can feel adrift.

"Since the Industrial Revolution, men were good fathers by bringing home the bacon. That was their central identity," says Joshua Coleman, a psychologist and author who focuses on parenting, couples, and relationships. "With women entering the workforce in record numbers, and in a high percentage of homes earning as much as or more than men, how do men now define themselves, when the traditional idea of being a provider and protector is not as appealing?" This tension between traditional and evolving male roles can create stress and conflict for men and their families. "Often, there are tensions between the family you're in and what you grew up with, which does influence us at conscious and largely unconscious levels." These strains may have been heightened by the economic crisis of 2008 and 2009, when layoffs sent family finances reeling, and more men lost their jobs than women.

For those of us who have agonized over the work-family question for years, it may be tempting to brush these psychological tensions aside, saying, "Welcome to our world. Now, do the dishes." But that would ignore the very real distress felt by the men we love. And, especially in the wake of the recent economic meltdown, dismissing men's efforts, instead of helping them feel valued, could doom us to repeat the mistakes of the past.

"The recession has been accelerating change, which happened in the Great Depression, too," Smith observes. Back then, huge numbers of men were laid off, while women's employment climbed. "The difference was that there were no possibilities—none, zero—on a cultural level for men to take on roles at home or taking care of the children. This created a lot of conflict. The divorce rate was extremely high, and there wasn't any sense that men could still be valuable to the family if their employment went away."

When roles, values, and expectations change for women or men, family stability can suffer. That's what happened in the United States in the mid-1960s and the 1970s; at the same time women added "career woman" to their existing roles of wife and mother, divorce rates climbed. The social fabric tore.

Today, in other ways, American women continue to pay for tearing the social fabric: Their happiness levels are at an all-time low, according to researchers at the Wharton School at the University of Pennsylvania. "The increased opportunity to succeed in many dimensions may have led to an increased likelihood of believing that one's life is not measuring up," the authors write. "Or women may simply find the complexity and increased pressure in their modern lives to have come at the cost of happiness." Meanwhile, in Europe, where public policies often provide ample support for working families/parents, happiness has *risen* over time for both men and women (with men experiencing the greater increase).

The Cost of Change

The hard truth may be that change, especially changes in gender roles, always comes at a price, whether it's in an American kitchen or an African bakery, as Acumen Fund founder and CEO Jacqueline Novogratz found out when she set up a micro-lending program for women in Rwanda. "Men would literally come up to me in restaurants and say, 'You're ruining our women, you're disrupting our families, what are you doing?'" To Western ears, that sounds unbearably sexist. But men and women both want to protect family and the parts of their life and culture they value. As gender roles shift, we need to ask what men, women, children, and communities are gaining and losing. Then we need to decide, as a society, what price we're willing to pay for those changes. We all need to pay attention to the trade-offs we're making, and that's a job that can only be done fairly when both genders work together as partners for the good of our families.

These kinds of partnership discussions are now taking place around the world.

In expanding economies from Latin America to the Middle East, from countries that are predominantly Catholic to those that are Muslim-majority, nations are examining the gains and losses that may come from changing opportunities for men and women. Developing nations are looking closely at ways to improve their economies and the well-being of their communities, which almost always includes opportunities for women's economic empowerment, and they're finding the answer isn't exclusively women's rights, but family rights. "Almost across the board in Muslim-majority countries, women are working, making money and participating," says Afkhami. "The question is, 'How do you negotiate rights amid culture, religion, and tradition?'"

Often, the answer is recognizing that any power shift involving women and girls necessarily involves men and boys, too. "Whenever possible we include men" in the leadership training, she says. She recalls a workshop in Morocco: "The men who came in at the beginning said they were concerned because in their opinion, women could not be leaders. They were rather smug about it and even some of the women agreed with them." By the end of the workshop, when the group discussed case studies about leadership challenges, "the men had completely changed their position. It became a different conversation." The simple process of talking through ideas and listening to one another began shifting the expectations of both genders—and generating creative solutions.

That's happening around the world. In some Muslim-majority countries, women's ability to work is restricted not because their fathers or husbands don't want them to work but because of cultural concerns about the safety of traveling as a woman.

"I can understand, being from Pakistan myself, why parents or families may not want their female daughters or daughters-in-law or wives to travel to work alone," says Saadia Zahidi, head of constituents for the World Economic Forum. "Even if they trust that the workplace is completely safe, they're not comfortable with having their daughter travel back and forth." Rather than trying to change the way fathers and families feel about their daughters' safety, many companies have started providing company van rides. "Providing safe transportation has made a huge difference for companies. Their numbers of women completely changed," Zahidi says.

In some countries, safer travel for women is necessary. Closer to home, listening and talking may provide the solutions to helping men and women accept, value, and work well within their changing roles. Having written *The Daddy Shift* before his layoff, Jeremy Adam Smith had a head start on salving his wounded pride. "I had to remind myself consciously to draw on my book research and remember that something could be gained" by losing his job and becoming a stay-at-home dad again. "The message is that guys have to talk about this stuff, and hear about this stuff, because when they are faced with sudden unemployment, the cultural template is not established enough, not ubiquitous enough, that guys can just click into it."

Smith believes that if men can talk about their own experiences and what's happening to fathers and fatherhood in general—especially as more dads spend more time at home due to the recession—we'll see that "we're creating new roles for these guys, something that has its own dignity and its own kind of power." In that case, men's ability to switch between career and caring roles becomes a tremendous asset, making families more flexible during hard times. That flexibility becomes "a strength we're bringing to the crisis." Smith hopes that ten years from now, the template of father as chief at-home parent "will be more viable, so guys can just step into it when confronted with change," whether they've been laid off or are making room for their wife's high-powered career.

That template is already supported by evidence that involved fathers improve the lives of their families and children. In the United Kingdom, a study of more than eleven thousand people born in 1958 showed that children whose fathers spent more time with them had a higher IQ than those with less paternal attention. Girls with involved fathers are less likely to have mental health problems later, and boys are less likely to tangle with the police. Children who do housework with their fathers get along better with their peers and are less likely to disobey teachers, have school trouble, or become depressed. Anecdotally, in the course of my interviews for this book, one woman after another credited her success to her father's attention and involvement.

"My father, he was my first love," says Kawtar Chyraa, who's finishing her last semester at Al Akhawayn University in Ifrane while working at Toyota of Morocco. "I wanted to be worthy of his love and respect, and for him it was education that mattered. So I showed that at school I could beat the boys and be first in the class."

Wives, too, appreciate the contributions of their supportive spouses. Some studies suggest wives are more attracted to mates who help out around the house and that relationships are more fulfilling when both partners pitch in.

Reverse Sexism in Work-Life Programs

While individuals and families win out when dads get involved, most workplaces in the United States seem oblivious to these advantages. Today, only 13 percent of companies offer men paid parental leave. And while about a third of U.S. employees work at companies that offer flexible work arrangements, very few men feel comfortable taking advantage of them.

"It's not that men want different things," says Benko, the chief talent officer at Deloitte. "It's that they've felt hostage. They haven't felt like they had permission, as women do, to play the kid card." Making use of flexibility policies and taking paternity leave are still, in many cases, considered career suicide.

This may be because most CEOs and other top managers are men whose careers were made possible by having a wife at home. Most of them never experienced the levels of work-life stress that men routinely shoulder today. And for those older fathers who did, once upon a time, try to get more involved at home, the workplace was even less forgiving than it is today. Perhaps because of that, these men see a bigger role at home as something that is impossible for career-minded men: Whenever *they* tried shifting gender roles a little, it didn't work.

"I pity that generation of dad," says Smith. "Their role expanded to include caregiving; however, the economic structures and social structures were still designed for the sole male breadwinner. There was zero support for the male caregiving role. This created a lot of conflict in marriages. Men were confused and that created a huge spike in the divorce rate."

As the difficulties of work-life stress for men become more and more evident, Smith thinks senior managers—especially the men—will come around. "I think there's a sense of guilt among today's CEOs and senior managers. They look at the younger generation trying to be better fathers and more equitable partners and think, 'Good. You should do this.' "

Deloitte's Benko agrees that change is in the air. "From the boomer male perspective, their attitude has changed quite a bit," she told me. "A number have said, 'I missed my kids' soccer games when they were growing up, and I don't want to miss my grandkids', so I'm not willing to make the same choices I made the first time around. Although, by the way, when I made those choices, I didn't know they were choices. They were the established norms.' "

As white male gatekeepers have started to come around, so have smart companies and communities. In 2002, California added paid family leave, providing men and women up to six weeks of paid leave per year to bond with new babies or care for sick family members. So far, many more women than men have taken the leave, but male participation rates are climbing rapidly. In 2004, 17 percent of the parents who used a paid family leave to bond with a new baby were men; by 2008, 22 percent were. And nearly a third of the people taking paid family leave for any reason were men, a percentage that grew from 30 to 32 percent. In June 2008, the U.S. House of Representatives passed the Paid Parental Leave Act for federal employees, ensuring that federal government workers, men and women, could take a maximum of six weeks partially paid time off each year to bond with a new baby or adopted or foster child, or to care for a seriously ill parent. (As we write this, the Senate has not yet passed this act.)

Corporations are realizing the value of personal leaves as well. "When I started consulting on work-life balance issues ten years ago, I spent a lot of time on women's issues," says Deborah Epstein Henry, founder of Flex-Time Lawyers LLC. "What has changed over those ten years is that, for my clients, the work-life focus has become more gender-neutral and reason-neutral." Companies are finding that both men and women have lives outside of work and that sometimes those lives need more space. At law firms around the country, Deborah Henry says, "men are speaking up on this issue. The voices mostly come from those in their twenties who are saying, 'We don't want to live this life our parents live, we want a more integrated life. We're dual-centric.'" Having men embrace and champion the idea of a dual-centric life, she says, is a "real change." In her research, Henry has seen men's usage of paternity leaves at law firms rise steadily.

Managers—men and women—are seeing the benefits for dads and their work. "A guy working for me just came back from paternity leave and I have another one going out," Kathleen Hall told me. She'd just moved to the Seattle area to become general manager of consumer marketing at Microsoft and found the corporate culture tremendously accommodating for dads. "It's not like they're taking a couple of weeks. They take three months. They wait until their wives go back to work, and then the dad takes his time. It's kind of cool. In some ways, I think the company views this as a positive." She feels it's evidence of a corporate culture that encourages a rich, well-rounded life.

The more that men take paternity leave and use flex schedules and other corporate work-life supports, the more acceptable, even routine, such arrangements become for other men, and for everyone. "People keep asking me if I had to go in and negotiate my flexible work arrangement," says Richard Rojo, who recently arranged to work from home two days a week while his wife takes a traveling assignment. "I didn't, really. I just said, 'Here's what I'm going to do.'" For Rojo and increasingly for men and women in their thirties and forties, flexibility is a given, an assumption, not something to negotiate or ask for as a special privilege. Rojo assumed he could get the job done wherever he worked from, and his boss trusted him. Certainly, he may have faced more objections in a more old-fashioned, traditional office culture where face time still counts more than output. But Rojo works at a university, in a flexible, creative culture. "My boss and my boss's boss are both mothers. And everyone in the office seems to like the idea that I'm doing this to support my wife's career."

Throwing Out the Ladder: The New Shape of Careers for Men as Well as Women

Deloitte, a global firm that provides tax, accounting, and risk management consulting as well as other services, has realized that men as well as women are unlikely to be able, or willing, to climb the career ladder the old-fashioned way—working forty-plus hours a week, fifty weeks a year, for forty years. "Tacking flexible work arrangements onto that ladder as a special accommodation for moms didn't begin to solve the problem," says Cathy Benko. That's why Deloitte reinvented the entire idea of career trajectory for all its employees, not just for a handful of women or special cases, adopting the "mass career customization" program I described in Chapter Four. The system works for men as well as women, and allows almost all the company's U.S. employees to ratchet the intensity demands of their work up or down, depending on their personal needs.

Incorporating a formal check-in on an employee's desires regarding pace, location, and role, at every performance review, transformed conversations about performance and careers, Benko says. "Both managers and employees felt the robustness of the career conversations became much richer," she says. "Men and women said, 'The visual gave me permission to talk about things I wanted to talk about but didn't know how to bring up.'

"The solution is not one-off flexible work arrangements. It's for companies to expect that and plan for it." That's what Deloitte's mass career customization effort is all about—a major paradigm shift, a completely new way to think about careers for all employees regardless of gender.

Partners for Life

Today, the pressures, demands, and ambitions of men and women may be closer to each other than ever before. More and more women and men are seeking work-life balance, to succeed at home and at work. In America, we're gradually becoming a partnership society, where both men and women have similar levels of education, opportunity, ambition, and responsibilities.

"It's like thirty years ago, women learned to paddle both sides of the canoe, but men just stayed on one side," says Warren Farrell, author of *Why Men Earn More* and *Father and Child Reunion.* "Now men are learning to paddle on both sides of the canoe, too."

And that gives families and society more options for moving ahead. If Dad loses his job, Mom can ramp up her work while he takes over on the home front. If a child is sick, one or both parents can dial back on the workload.

"We're creating new roles for guys, roles that have dignity and their own kind of power," says Jeremy Adam Smith. Many men are enjoying the new options for work and private-life engagement and satisfaction. Having a wife with a good, steady job certainly helped Jeremy Adam Smith retool his career, from nonprofit manager to author, journalist, and editor. Richard Rojo's job flexibility will help his wife advance her career; Adrian and Sharice Zamarripas's creativity in working split shifts saved them child care and gave their kids the equivalent of a stay-at-home parent without the associated cost. And already, the new roles these men have taken up, as more hands-on fathers, are bringing them closer to their children and providing their children that special leg up on life that engaged fathers offer.

Much can go wrong, especially if companies, the government, and families are slow to recognize and embrace the fact that the "nontraditional" workforce is now the norm. But when countries and communities embrace the partnership society, they offer their citizens and their children the best hope for equality, prosperity, and happiness. (Remember those Scandinavian statistics!)

In countries around the world, but particularly the United States, the next steps toward an equal future may depend less on women than on men. When men ask for and embrace flexibility, paternity leave, and other work-life balance measures, when they become bosses who encourage men's family ambitions as well as work ambitions, when they enact or support policies and laws that help two-income families, they're working toward a better future for both genders.

· SEVEN ·

In the Family

MUTINY ON NOAH'S ARK

fam·i·ly *n, pl* fam·i·lies
1 : a group of individuals living under one roof and usually under one head : HOUSEHOLD. 2a : a group of persons of common ancestry: . . . 5 : the basic unit in society traditionally consisting of two parents rearing their children

—WEBSTER'S NEW WORLD COLLEGE DICTIONARY,
4TH EDITION

Social worker Megan Koehler, age forty-eight, didn't want her seven-year-old daughter, Lexie, to grow up as an only child. Their family was small enough as it was: Megan, who wanted children but wasn't married by her late thirties, had conceived Lexie using an anonymous sperm donor. By the time Lexie was a toddler, Megan was in her early forties and her attempts to conceive again (using the same sperm donor) were unsuccessful.

So Koehler found another way to expand the family. She joined the Sibling Donor Registry, a database of parents who used sperm donors and who wanted contact with their children's biological relatives. Within an hour of entering her sperm donor's number, Koehler found three other families who collectively had six kids sharing Lexie's birth father. One of the families, a same-sex couple in Fort Collins, Colorado, had three children, who were all Lexie's half siblings (Emily, a year older than Lexie, and twin boys, Ian and Aidan, three years younger).

In the past two years, Lexie and her mother have been to Colorado three times, and her sibling family has come to Los Angeles twice. The kids love being together and the half siblings began to feel like family from their earliest visits. "It's an amazing bond," says Koehler.

Lexie and her half siblings show how fluid the definition of family has become in recent years. Sure, Lexie's case might seem like an unusual family arrangement, but in the United States, at least, the most basic unit of society—the family, traditionally two parents plus kids—has been replaced by a wide and colorful palette of choices: same-sex couples, single parents by choice, blended families, traditional families, four or even five generations living together and caring for one another—and every imaginable permutation of these options.

All these forms are part of a radical shift in family structure that's happened in the United States since the late 1960s, largely as a result of women's growing economic influence. As large numbers of women, for the first time in history, became able to support themselves and their children without help from a man, they became free to leave unhappy or abusive relationships and create family situations where they had more power. At the same time, traditional roles within marriages that did remain intact were turned on their heads by women's new responsibilities at work. Meanwhile, since the mid-twentieth century, legal changes had begun giving women equal power and rights within marriages. All these forces combined to create a proliferation of family patterns where women had far more say than ever before in decisions and roles.

But while family patterns have changed radically in the United States, most workplaces, communities, and government bodies still make policy as if every family had a full-time wife at home. Compared to other industrialized nations, America falls flat on its face in terms of supporting families as they really exist. The United States ranks last in maternity leave, ranks twenty-seventh of thirty-seven countries in public expenditures on child care, and provides astonishingly little assistance for families caring for aging parents. The nation's failure to recognize that 70 percent of children grow up in families where both parents work, that affordable day care is as necessary and important as affordable health care, and that men and women in the workforce both have far more responsibilities outside work than ever before, threatens America's continued economic competitiveness.

Throughout the industrialized world, women's mass move from dependence to independence has played a major role in reshaping the family, both in traditional two-parent families and in newer family models. And throughout the industrialized world—except in the United States—communities and governments have responded to this sea change with smart supports for families.

What becomes clear when you compare the actions of other nations with America's nonresponse is that right now the United States stands at a crossroads. American communities, employers, and lawmakers can continue to behave as if all families have a stay-at-home spouse devoted full-time to the house and family, and can continue to make policies, set work and school schedules, and tax workers in ways that presume it's unreasonable and undesirable to have two partners pursuing fulfilling careers and happy family lives. If America stays on this road, the country's ability to tap women's full economic potential will falter, and the nation will fall endlessly behind those countries that remove obstacles to work-family balance.

Fortunately, another, smoother road beckons: American communities, employers, and state, local, and federal governments can simply recognize today's families in all their forms and treat them as a rich source of creativity, energy, and fulfillment that should be supported for economic as well as for moral reasons. This smoother road is the one that countries like Sweden, Norway, and France have already taken successfully. It's a route that makes sense for the United States, too—a path that will accelerate women's economic rise to influence and will allow Americans to enjoy the benefits that rise will bring. Women's move from survival to independence has brought American women far. But they won't make a mass leap from independence to influence until the United States recognizes the new realities of family life.

Working Women to the Rescue

Changes in family structure don't happen overnight, and they're not caused by just one force. But looking back across the past three decades, it's easy to see that women's move from economic survival to independence has had a massive, positive impact on the well-being of the American family: In the past three decades, the *only* families in the United States that have seen a real increase in family income have been those with a working wife, according to a 2008 study by the Joint Economic Committee, the U.S. congressional body that reviews economic conditions.

Take note of this for just a moment: It is *the wife's income alone* that has boosted families to new levels of prosperity. Between about 1970 and 2006, the real household income of married couples in the United States where the wife worked grew by 43 percent (from a real income of $60,746 in 1970 to $86,621 in 2008), according to the U.S. Census Bureau. But this income increase *did not occur* in families where the wife did not work outside the home: During the same period, the real income of married couples where the wife did *not* work stayed nearly flat, growing by a meager 5 percent, from $46,040 in 1970 to $48,502 in 2008. In fact, when the Joint Economic Committee reviewed this data in 2008, it declared that "over the past three decades, only those families who have a working wife have seen real increases in family income."

MEDIAN HOUSEHOLD INCOME GROWTH

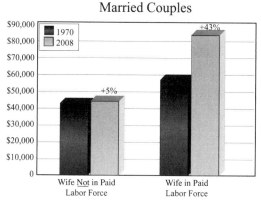

Source: U.S. Census Bureau, Historical Income Table—Families, adjusted for inflation

You can see the economic rise of the two-income family in the United States right before your eyes on the chart. See that 43 percent increase? You know who created it? Wives. Moms. Women. The impact of these working women is astounding. In the past several decades, "most married couples with two working parents have moved out of poverty," says Heidi Hartmann, president of the Institute for Women's Policy Research. It's not just that women are working, it's that they're pursuing more training and higher-income jobs, which benefits their whole family. "By going to college and getting more education, women have been more able to support children," says Hartmann.

Without a doubt, the most powerful change brought about by women's increased earning power is the lifting of families out of poverty. As I discussed in Chapters One and Two, once basic survival needs are met, humans move on to their next set of needs in Maslow's hierarchy. For women, the first thing after food and shelter is usually providing economic security for their families; that's the first thing they do when they climb from survival to the beginnings of independence.

This isn't only happening in America: Around the world, when women become economically empowered, they immediately use their money to help their families. Look at women workers like those at A to Z Textile Mills, a manufacturer in Tanzania that makes mosquito nets for beds. "When you're sitting talking with women workers in the bed net factory, the first thing they say they want to do, if they have children—and most of them are single moms—is send their children to school," says Jacqueline Novogratz, CEO and founder of the Acumen Fund, a philanthropic venture that invested in A to Z. "Then, with great pride they will talk about how they will get eye surgery or heart surgery for their fathers. Typically," Novogratz told me, "60 percent of women's income goes to taking care of family needs, while 30 percent of men's income moves in that direction."

That's one reason microcredit pioneer and Nobel Peace Prize–winner Muhammed Yunus changed the Grameen Bank's policy. The bank's borrowers were only about half women at first; now 97 percent of the bank's borrowers are women, because women are the people helping their communities. "Money going to the family through women brought so much more benefit to the family compared to the same amount of money going to the family through men," Yunus has said.

"Children become the immediate beneficiary if the mother is the borrower."

Finally, Having a Say

In America over the past thirty years, working wives and mothers have essentially provided a bailout plan for the American family: By going to work, they've let their families keep growing economically. That was already a notable contribution before the economic meltdown of 2008. But during and after the meltdown, women's earning power often became even more critical—men lost more jobs than women, and working wives emerged as the financial heroines of their families.

Along the way, as women's incomes have made them crucial financial contributors to the family, women have also risen to become equal decision makers within the family.

That doesn't sound like a radical idea, does it? Yet, until the late twentieth century, a wife's promise to "love, honor, and *obey*" her husband was a critical element in most wedding ceremonies. As that's changed in America, so has the entire structure of the family.

"What's totally new in families is not that women are earning their own way, but now, when they do, they have their say," says Professor Stephanie Coontz, author of *Marriage, a History.* Until recently, she says, "everyone knew that women were essential to the family's survival. But no one thought that should give them equal say in family situations until the mid to late twentieth century. As late as the 1970s, final decisions about family matters belonged to the husband. It was the man's right to determine where the couple lived, if the wife could take a job, how to dispose of property, and how it should be utilized." Before the twentieth century, husbands usually got custody of children, since children were regarded as property and married women had limited property rights. That changed in the twentieth century, as society began to regard women as more appropriate or natural caregivers for young children.

Today, women in the United States have as much, if not more, influence on family decisions as men. A 2008 Pew Research Center survey found that in 43 percent of American families, women had the final say in most decisions, including financial management, purchases for the home, what to watch on television, and weekend activities. Thirty-one percent of couples shared responsibility for the final decision. In just 26 percent of families, men had the last word in most decisions.

The growing influence of wives and mothers on their families has resulted in a full-scale social revolution. Within traditional marriage, gender roles are moving toward more equal sharing of earning and caregiving. Outside traditional marriage, economically independent women are choosing extended singlehood, blended families, gay marriage, and a galaxy of other family constellations. At the same time, changes in longevity and other demographic factors are creating new economic pressures even on traditionally structured families and placing women at the center of new, increasingly complex family structures. Women today are not in a sandwich: They're the center of a Rubik's Cube.

Portrait of the Twenty-first-Century Family

In the United States, nearly one in three children grows up in a one-parent household. Only 30 percent of children have a stay-at-home parent. In 2007, a whopping one out of four American babies was born to parents who weren't married.

But many communities have been slow to recognize that the family of today—and tomorrow—doesn't look *anything* like the family of the 1950s or earlier. Quality child care *and* elder care in the United States are still staggeringly expensive and hard to find. Wait lists for high-quality child care can stretch for years. Attempting to hire and legally pay taxes on a nanny is so complex that it practically takes a Ph.D. in tax law to do the forms. In the United States, employers, the government, and society in general seem to believe dependent care is a private problem for families—mostly women—to solve.

The United States is one of only four out of 173 countries to offer no national paid parental leave (the others are Liberia, Papua New Guinea, and Swaziland), and ninety-eight of those countries offer at least fourteen weeks of paid leave. In a 2009 "report card," Save the Children evaluated support for early childhood development in the world's twenty-five wealthiest countries, and the United States came in fourth to last (Australia, Canada, and Ireland fell below American scores). The total U.S. public expenditure on child care or preschool education adds up to less than 1 percent (.06 percent, to be precise) of the nation's GDP—that's about a third of what Iceland (second only to Sweden in the Save the Children report card) spends. Fifteen of the world's wealthiest countries subsidize regulated child care for at least 25 percent of all children under age three. The United States is not one of those countries. Given that early childhood education and development have been linked to professional and economic success later in life, it's more than likely the United States will pay a steep price in economic competitiveness in years to come unless the country adjusts—and soon—to the new needs of the modern family.

But there is good news in the United States: America's families see what's needed, even if the vast majority of the country's communities, employers, and lawmakers don't. Whatever individual battles, setbacks, and trade-offs lie ahead, make no mistake: In the coming decade, the voices of America's evolving families will be heard on an unprecedented scale. The inexorable rise of women's economic power and family position will make the true needs of families known. The growing chorus of families insisting on better, fairer treatment for mothers, fathers, and children is about to awaken lawmakers and business leaders to the new realities of family life. The United States can't afford the alternative. Within a generation, the countries that understand and respect new models of family will emerge as economic winners, by making it easier for men *and* women, mothers *and* fathers, to put their talents, education, and skills to work.

I'm not saying this because it's the way I want the world to be (which, by the way, it is). This is not a list of idealistic demands. This inevitable change is a fact—the voting patterns, the policies, the rising tide of the changing family lapping at the shore of the modern world.

Mothers Rise Up

When Kristin Rowe-Finkbeiner's infant son, Connor, was diagnosed with an immune deficiency in 1995, Kristin had no idea she was about to become a five-star general in a full-scale mothers' revolt. At the time, she just wanted to keep her son healthy. Kristin, then twenty-seven, quit her job with a Washington State environmental advocacy group to stay home full-time. Meanwhile, her husband, Bill Finkbeiner, then a Republican state senator, switched to a four-day week. "Thankfully, my husband had job-linked health care, or we would have been in deep trouble quickly," Rowe-Finkbeiner says. Under his parents' watchful care, Connor stayed healthy and built up his immune system over time: Today he's a healthy preteen.

During the two years she spent as a stay-at-home mom with Connor and her second child, Anna, Rowe-Finkbeiner became ever more aware of the importance of health care, work flexibility, and family leave. During naps and after bedtimes, she turned her professional skills as a political advocate toward the issues, researching motherhood and family legislation. One day, she called the Census Bureau to find out how many stay-at-home moms there were. No luck: "Try the Bureau of Labor Statistics," they said. Nothing there either: The BLS didn't track stay-at-home moms because their labor was "unremunerated."

Those invisible moms alarmed Rowe-Finkbeiner. Counting at-home parents, she told me, "matters in a big way, because Census figures are used as the basis for major urban planning decisions, like transportation." How could millions of mothers just not count? "It was my first step in understanding how invisible mothers are," she says.

As she continued her research, she quickly found it wasn't just stay-at-home moms who were invisible, but working moms, too, in other ways. She learned how few families received any day-care assistance. She learned that 80 percent of low-wage workers—many of them moms—had not one single day of sick leave. She found that the gender wage gap was much wider for mothers than non-mothers: Women without children earned 90 cents for every dollar a man earned, but mothers earned only 73 cents—and single moms, just 60 cents. "The more I researched, the more I found, my goodness, it's even worse than I thought," she says.

Rowe-Finkbeiner was discovering a simple truth: Although the shape of families had changed radically, laws, social policy, community support, and school schedules and policies were set up for a bygone world, one where mothers stayed home and fathers worked. Kristin Rowe-Finkbeiner was shocked into action.

"My great-grandmother was the first president of Planned Parenthood, my grandmother followed her in that presidency, and my mom was a strong feminist. I thought they'd done all this work already," she jokes. "Turned out, they hadn't."

Rowe-Finkbeiner teamed up with Joan Blades, cofounder of political advocacy group MoveOn.org, to write *The Motherhood Manifesto: What America's Moms Want—and What to Do About It.* Then the pair launched MomsRising, a grassroots advocacy group lobbying for better treatment of all mothers and families.

MomsRising's compelling message: It doesn't have to be this hard for working parents. And it's not your fault that it is. The dilemma of working families, Rowe-Finkbeiner says, "has been talked about as a balancing problem, an epidemic of personal failures. But when this many people have the exact same problem at the same time, this is not an epidemic of personal failings. This is a structural failing that needs to be addressed."

Take Matt and Jaida Stone of Hoboken. (They asked me to change their names and professions for privacy reasons.) She's a high school guidance counselor; he's a freelance writer and part-time writing teacher. When their second child was born in 2008, they realized they couldn't afford day care for two kids, which would cost them $40,000 a year—more than 20 percent of their total income. Tax laws let them set aside some pre-tax dollars for day care, but in the end, that saves them roughly $1500—less than 4 percent of their total day-care costs. Ultimately, these costs drove Matt out of the workforce for a year.

"Pragmatically, there really was only one choice that made sense," says Matt. "I'd take the year off work and take care of Olivia, and Jaida would keep working. Jaida's the one with the steady income and the health benefits." So Matt became a stay-at-home dad, toting Olivia to music classes and playdates, taking her to collect her younger brother, Tyler, at day care, and making most of the meals. When Tyler turns three and qualifies for Hoboken's free early-learning preschool program, Matt will start working again.

If Matt had his own health benefits, if health insurance weren't so expensive, if tax breaks were better for day care, would he have stayed in the workforce? "Definitely. There's no question that I love taking care of Olivia. She's a great baby. And I get a kick out of being the only dad at music class. But there are other things I want to do, too," he says. Among them: continue to earn money for the family, to build his writing business, and to improve his teaching skills—in short, to develop his own talents and increase his market value.

Fortunately, Matt and Jaida live in a community, if not a country, that's starting to respect the needs of today's families. If it weren't for Hoboken's free preschool program for three- and four-year-olds, Matt would likely have to take two years off instead of one. He'd lose another year of experience, another year of building his career skills, another year of contributing to his Social Security benefits and retirement savings, another year of realizing his full economic potential.

I don't mean to downplay the value of Matt staying at home—or of mothers who make the same choice. Matt loves the extra time with the baby, and many families feel an at-home parent is an important choice they're willing to sacrifice for. But for Matt and Jaida, improving their family's economic security is a priority. They grew up in comfortable middle-class families, went to good colleges, and earned master's degrees: They want to be able to afford the same quality of life for their children. They also want to save for retirement so they won't burden Tyler and Olivia later.

Statistically speaking, their chances of meeting these goals are much better if both of them work. That's not ideology. It's economic fact. As we've already seen, in the last three decades, on average, *only* two-income families have enjoyed steady economic growth.

Yet, even though for decades it's been *essential* to have two working parents to improve a family's economic status, public policy and most employers make it very, very hard to have two parents working full-time outside the home. As Kristin Rowe-Finkbeiner discovered, this reality and other facts of modern family life have remained almost invisible in the United States. But no longer.

Consider the impact MomsRising has already had. The group played a key role in rallying support for the reauthorization of the State Children's Health Insurance Program—which provides the matching funds for states offering health insurance to poor children and was the second bill President Obama signed into law. MomsRising also played a leading role in the passage of paid family leave in several states. And it mobilized its members to lobby for the Lilly Ledbetter Fair Pay Act (the very first bill President Obama signed into law), which made it easier to sue companies for gender pay discrimination.

And consider this: MomsRising achieved most of those policy changes in 2008, when its membership was just 160,000. Today, MomsRising has more than a million members. Just think what they'll be able to do with those numbers, numbers that only continue to rise.

MomsRising is a good example, but far from the only one, of parents and other advocates working to ease the burden on working parents. Gradually, communities and even some states are taking actions, small and large, that will ease the undue burdens on these families. Georgia, Florida, Illinois, and Oklahoma have adopted universal preschool measures, making at least a few hours of free preschool for four-year-olds available, giving parents a big break in the cost of child care and providing kids with a valuable jump start on school. In smaller ways, other communities are also recognizing changes in family structure and gender roles. In 2009, Colorado's state legislature passed a measure guaranteeing time off to attend parent-teacher conferences and educational activities to all employees in the state who work for companies with more than ten employees. This time off may be unpaid, but it's a symbolic recognition that parents of both genders must be allowed to take part in their children's educations.

These legal changes are signs of things to come, of a day when parenting, education, caregiving, and work-life balance are no longer considered "women's issues" but family issues—and economic and political issues that affect everyone. Women's growing economic clout and social and political influence are bringing attention and focus to family-friendly policies. There's a steady hum of discontent on blogs and in columns dedicated to work-life balance. When I checked Blog Catalog, a vast online listing of blogs, in June 2009, there were eighteen hundred mom blogs listed and about three hundred dad blogs. By October 2009, just four months later, there were more than two thousand moms and four hundred dads blogging about their adventures in parenthood. The voice of parents' networks is growing louder, quite literally as I write this.

Meanwhile, with the rise of women's economic power, other unprecedented demographic shifts are converging to reshape the family—and the combined pressures of these forces will soon make the work of Moms-Rising and other family-centered groups more urgent than ever.

The Evacuation of Noah's Ark: Couplehood Is Temporary

When Jennifer Heyman was growing up in Chicago, she never thought twice about whether she could combine work and family: Her mother was an urban planner in Chicago, so Heyman assumed she, too, would combine career and motherhood. She just didn't expect to do it without a husband.

"My mother used to say that while my friends were out looking for their next boyfriend, I was out planning my next trip overseas," she says. After business school at the University of Chicago, Heyman traveled around the world, worked abroad, and launched a career in marketing. She loved her life. In her late thirties, she was living in San Francisco when she broke up with a long-term boyfriend. She thought about what she wanted from her future and realized her biological clock was ticking—loudly. She wanted kids, but with no new relationship on the horizon, her choices were limited. An acquaintance had had a child on her own. Heyman was intrigued with the idea. "I thought, 'If she can do it, so can I,'" she says. After looking at the pros and cons of adoption and biological single motherhood, she chose to use a sperm donor. Today, she lives in San Francisco with her four-year-old daughter and works as a freelance marketing director for large companies. It's not easy to do it all herself, but she's never doubted her choice and feels well supported by an active network of family, friends, and other single moms. "The Bay Area is such a home to alternative families. Anything you can think about exists," she told me. She's considered expanding her alternative family by sharing her spacious home with another single mom and child. "If it were the right person, it could be economically beneficial and beneficial for having a pseudo-family relationship and support system. The commune of a generation ago is the community of today. It's about reaching out and building that community," she says.

Heyman is part of a phenomenal shift in demographics that suddenly became clear in 2007. That year, for the first time in American history, there were more single than married women in the United States. That's an astounding change. In its simplest terms, what it means is that *most women will spend more of their lives single than married.*

Much as many women want a life partner, the stark reality is that in this age of later marriages and longer lives for women than men, like it or not, life partnership is a temporary arrangement for most women. We're likely to never marry, or to divorce if we do, or to outlive our partners if they're male.

The implications of this change are breathtaking. For most of recorded history, the "Noah's Ark" model—one man, one woman—dominated society. But that boat's been leaking steadily for the past few decades.

Two main cultural explosions have blown holes in the hull. First, women's economic freedom to not marry: As women have earned more, they've married less and later. In the United States, the median age of first marriage jumped from twenty-one in 1972 to an all-time high of nearly twenty-six today. Educated women marry even later—college grads marry around age twenty-seven; women with a graduate degree marry at around thirty. In 1970, 62 percent of women over age fifteen were married; today, just 53 percent are. The percentage of women ages forty-five to fifty-four who have never been married doubled in that time, from 5 percent to 10 percent.

You don't have to be an economist to understand why educated women are delaying marriage or skipping it altogether. The more educated you are, the more you can earn; the more you can earn, the less economic need you have to marry at an earlier age. The change in divorce laws has also helped. In the United States, we're no longer subject to divorce laws that automatically award custody of children and property to husbands, so it's easier to leave unhappy marriages.

The other explosion that's sinking Noah's Ark is women's longevity: Females of all species tend to live longer than males, and women outlive men by about five years.

As women age, their increasing tendency toward singlehood will have a staggering economic impact on their lives and on the overall economy. On the plus side, many working women will have more disposable income to spend, invest, and, in general, influence their lives, their families, their communities, and the world. On the downside, women will need to make more conscious efforts to manage their money wisely for the long lives they are likely to be living.

A Leak in the Ark: The Rise of Single Moms, by Choice and Otherwise

In the last chapter, we talked about the changing roles for men, particularly the role of father. There's no question that dads are playing a far bigger role in their children's lives. But that change is taking place only in families that have a dad—something that's true for fewer and fewer families. The number of unmarried mothers has skyrocketed in recent decades and shows no sign of slowing. In 1960, only about 5 percent of babies in the United States were born to unmarried mothers. Today, unmarried moms give birth to just under 40 percent of all American babies. About half of those new mothers are living with a male partner at the time of the baby's birth. Today, 23 percent of all children live in a mother-only household, up from 18 percent in 1980.

More and more of those mothers are like Jennifer Heyman—well-educated women in their thirties who choose to give birth to a child regardless of whether they're married. This group of mothers was only about 7 percent of the total of single mothers in 2005, but as *New York Times Magazine* writer Emily Bazelon pointed out in May 2009, that represented a *145 percent rise* since 1980 in the percentage of women who choose single motherhood. Add to that the number of single women who adopt—thirteen thousand a year adopt children from the U.S. welfare system alone, and that's not counting the thousands of women who adopt from China, Guatemala, and other countries. Clearly, one result of women's economic emancipation is the rise of single mothers by choice.

Of course, many single mothers in the United States didn't choose singlehood—they were widowed or abandoned by their partners. And regardless of how mothers become single—by choice or otherwise—the unfortunate truth is that in the United States "single mothers are still the poorest family group in society," according to Heidi Hartmann of the Institute for Women's Policy Research. Thanks to women's greater education and earning power, she adds, this group is less poor than in the past. But with nearly a quarter of kids living only with their mother, the high poverty rates of single moms is a terrible threat to the well-being of American children.

Having a single parent should not doom a child to poverty, and in other industrialized nations it doesn't. In Sweden, about 55 percent of children are born to unmarried mothers, but the availability of ample government support for children and for affordable day care means single mothers and their children don't suffer the ill effects they suffer in single-parent American homes. "In Sweden, you see very little variation in the outcome of children based on marital status. Everybody does fairly well," Wendy Manning, a professor of sociology at Bowling Green State University in Ohio, told the *New York Times*. "In the U.S., there's much more disparity." The unequal treatment of American children with single parents is a product of U.S. laws. By making life easier for *all* parents, married and single, Sweden makes sure all children benefit. In Save the Children's 2009 report card on wealthy nations and early childhood support, Sweden ranked first among all twenty-five and was the only country to have achieved all ten benchmarks counted by the report (which included things like paid parental leave, subsidized or regulated care for at least 25 percent of all children under three, and public spending on child care equal to at least 1 percent of GDP).

Facing a lack of social support, single moms in the United States often turn to one another for help. "Our generation is very used to building networks and creating community in our professional lives, so we do the same thing in our personal lives," says Jennifer Heyman. Heyman's parenting network includes friends, other single moms, and an au pair who lives with her to help out. She's also very careful in her budgeting—both of money and time. "I approach everything from the standpoint of what's going to be meaningful to my daughter," she says. "I could work more and earn more, but if I have to spend less time with her because I'm working, then I have to make the time somewhere else—less time with my friends, or myself. So I'll make the financial trade-off for more time."

As networks of single mothers expand, so will their influence. In the coming decade, expect the voices of single mothers to swell and join the growing chorus of families demanding with more and more urgency that American institutions adjust to their changing shapes, creating a more robust future for us all.

Vertical Families and the Rubik's Cube

Another new reality for families hit me right between the eyes some years ago, when I was reading the *New York Times* and spotted this chilling line: "On average, women today spend 17 years of their lives caring for children and 18 years assisting aged parents." Think about it—most women will spend *more time taking care of parents than they will children*. Already more than 44 million people in the United States provide care for a chronically ill, disabled, or aged family member or friend every year, and 61 percent of family caregivers are women. Most of that care is uncompensated; often, it leads to caregiver burnout.

Lucy Carrico, a San Francisco Bay Area mom of two young boys who works full-time, describes her situation this way: "I had a new baby, I was commuting to Austin every other week from San Francisco, and we were doing a major remodel on the home we just bought. My mother was ill, my dad wasn't well. It was just the classic case: everything going on at once. You call this the sandwich generation? We were grilled cheese with a burned crust." Ultimately, her husband, Tod, quit his job to become full-time caregiver to their two sons.

Situations like Lucy's are becoming increasingly common, and they're just one manifestation of the impact of our longer lives. I've spent more than twenty years studying the longevity boom, and the enormity of the change still takes my breath away. Back in 1900, average life expectancy was 47 for men, with women living about two years longer. By 2005, life expectancy in the United States skyrocketed to 80.4 for women and 75.2 for men. That's an unbelievable increase in one hundred years.

LIFE EXPECTANCY

Male vs. Female

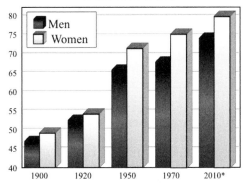

Source: Centers for Disease Control, U.S. Census Bureau, "Expectation of Life at Birth," 2009
*projected

At Age Wave, the demographic research company I cofounded with my husband, Ken, we call the dramatic rise in life expectancy a "longevity bonus"—not just extra years, but extra decades of life to enjoy, as long as you stay physically, mentally, and fiscally healthy. This longevity bonus has brought new challenges, like those that Lucy Carrico faces, but also new opportunities. Grandparents, for instance, are playing an important role in caring for grandchildren and relieving some of the pressure felt by working families. In Phoenix, Sharice and Adrian Zamarripas, whom you met in Chapter Six, work split shifts so they can avoid the expense of child care for their two children: At night, Adrian works in a warehouse; during the day, Sharice is a medical assistant. But the whole arrangement wouldn't

be possible without Sharice's mother, who still works as an assistant in a pathology lab. When not at work, she spends several hours every day watching the kids, often at her home. "The kids think of her and my dad like a second set of parents," says Sharice. "The kids love to go over there. My dad shows them how to drive the tractor, and they feed the goats."

In some ways, this daily involvement of grandparents in the lives of grandchildren is a throwback to agricultural societies and communities where many generations lived and worked together. What's different today is that those older adults are often healthy and vital, often still working, and sometimes playing a big financial role in their children's and grandchildren's lives. Today, about 28 percent of preschoolers with employed mothers stay with their grandparents part or all of the time while their parents are working. Nearly six million grandparents have grandkids under eighteen living with them.

Meanwhile, many families have adult children living with them. Nearly half of college students now move home after graduation. I call this stacking of generations the rise of the vertical family, and it's one more trend that makes today's family more like the complexity of a Rubik's Cube than just a sandwich.

For an idea of just how complex this Rubik's Cube can get, take a look at the family of my coauthor, Christine, the forty-one-year-old mother of twins, Alex and Zach. A petite brunette with brown eyes and a sprinkling of freckles, Christine lives in Sacramento with her husband, Richard. Her parents divorced when she was thirteen, and each remarried. Her father, now in his mid-sixties, later divorced again, married a third time, and now has two sons, eight and ten—just a few years older than their nephews Alex and Zach. In total, Christine has one full brother, two half siblings from her father's second marriage (a boy and a girl, both in college), the two half siblings from his third marriage, and three stepsisters from her mother's second marriage. Her children have six grandparents (Christine's birth parents; their new spouses; her father's ex-wife, whom Christine keeps in touch with; plus her husband's mom).

"Not even I know what some of these relations are called," Christine says with a laugh. "Is there such a thing as a half-step-cousin twice

removed?" Just last spring, she found herself going to a half brother's high school graduation, her full brother's business school graduation, and her stepsister's wedding all in the same month. At the same time, her sixty-five-year-old mother caught pneumonia and couldn't fly in from Los Angeles to watch the boys, so Christine and her husband canceled a long-planned weekend getaway. Meanwhile, her mother, stepdad, and father all retired in 2008—only to see the stock market crash and put them in financial discomfort.

"There are a lot of people to worry about already," Christine says. "And that's only going to get more intense as my parents and stepparents enter their seventies and eighties."

Christine's family may seem dense and tangled—but it's hardly unusual. In fact, it's a perfect example of what I call the Rubik's Cube family, the logical result of shifting family patterns combined with the longevity boom. The rise of same-sex couples, remarriages, and blended families has only made the puzzle richer and more complex.

Today's Rubik's Cube family is made up of many moving parts, creating a constantly shifting pattern of connection, dependency, love, concern, and, sometimes, conflict. When one of the pieces moves—a baby is born, an older parent needs care, a working mom or dad takes a new job—it affects the entire puzzle. And women, because of both their historic caregiving role and their growing earning power, are squarely at the center of this cube, the gear in the middle connected to everyone and affected by every twist of the cube.

Minding the Family Business

The longevity boom and the Rubik's Cube family combined have serious financial implications for women. First and foremost, women's financial security in retirement faces serious and growing threats. In fact, the very concept of retirement, at least as we know it, may not be around much longer. Back in 1935, when Social Security was adopted in the United States and the retirement age was set at sixty-five, life expectancy was only 62.5 years—in other words, chances were good that you'd die before you retired.

You certainly wouldn't expect to live another twenty to twenty-five years, like most retirees do now. Today, with most of us living so much longer, retirement itself desperately needs reinvention.

That's especially true for women. Not only do we outlive men and, thus, need to save more for a longer retirement, but, as women—especially single ones—we're far more likely to be poor than men.

Being an older single woman is still a leading indicator of poverty. That's not surprising, since we tend to work less and earn less than men and take more years out of the workforce, caring for family. Add to that the fact that the burden of caregiving lands on women, typically without additional pay. The net result is that even though women live longer than men, they tend to save less for retirement. A study of pension and annuity income conducted by the Employee Benefit Research Institute during 2007 revealed that about 43 percent of retirement-age men received benefits, at an average of $18,293 a year. Only 28 percent of women received benefits, and the benefits they did receive were far lower—an average of $11,895 per year.

"Women's financial life cycles are different than men's, and unless we all start realizing it and making plans accordingly, we'll have a huge financial crisis on our hands," says Mary Claire Allvine, a financial planner in Atlanta. "With women spending more time single and outliving men, they need to start saving more aggressively."

Women's poverty patterns are very different from men's, and so far, the social safety net has been more suited to addressing male poverty cycles. The result: More older women are poor.

"Men are the most poor when they're children, and the line goes straight down as they age," says Heidi Hartmann. "For women, poverty goes up from childhood. It's tremendous in their twenties, probably because that's when they're having children, it drops as children age, but bounces up again at sixty-five and above, as men die off." The difference between men's and women's cycles of poverty, she says, "is stunning."

To live out quality lives, women must now start saving as soon as they can and take advantage of those extra years of life to both work and save longer. In general, women must plan for a longer life, and one that includes periods of working and not working, of higher and lower income, and, above all, a life in which they're solely responsible for their financial well-being.

And younger women need to understand just how complex their family role is likely to be—and start preparing for it early, through good financial planning and education. In our Age Wave study of women and money, we found that older women (those in their mid-sixties and up) felt more confident than young women about their ability to manage their money and make good financial decisions. Older women were much less likely to want to be rescued from financial distress by a handsome prince. When we asked older women what advice they would pass on to their daughters or granddaughters about money, they thought it was ten times more important to start planning early, gain financial knowledge, and remain financially independent than to marry someone who was financially stable. This is advice today's young women need to take seriously.

Foreign Exchange: Ideas from Overseas

As families become increasingly complex, every business and every nation has a choice: It can embrace the real, vast variety of family structures and provide better support for parents, children, and whichever sort of Rubik's Cube they populate. Or it can continue to do nothing—which is, itself, a choice.

To glimpse what it looks like when a society supports working parents, look at Europe. There, some countries, including Norway, Sweden, and France, bend over backward (compared to the United States, at least) to make things easier for working parents. When Marie Clemence (one of the four interview subjects in this book who asked us to change her name), a Paris-based design consultant who works with the government and large companies to predict future trends, had her son, she was able to stay home for sixteen weeks with full pay. After that, she says, "I put him in day care sponsored by the government of France. It's a very good day-care system. I can work and know my child is taken care of very well from nine A.M. to six P.M." The French child-care system provides subsidized care, either for at-home nannies or for child-care centers, for children ages two-and-a-half months to three years, while the French Ministry of Education also provides nursery schools for children ages two to six, with rates based on a sliding scale so families can choose the type of care that's best for their child—and know they can afford it. With this kind of support, it comes as no surprise that 80 percent of French women ages twenty-five to fifty work, the vast majority of them full-time. That's the highest rate of working women in all of Europe.

In Sweden, when Eva-Maj Mühlenbock, a law partner, had her children, the state provided her and her husband, Gunnar, a combined total of sixteen months of parental leave. Most of that time is paid at 80 percent of the parent's income. The laws have changed over time, but today, two months of that time is reserved for dads (if they don't use it, they lose it). In Norway, mothers enjoy forty-three weeks of new-baby leave at 100 percent of income or fifty-three weeks at 80 percent, and the father gets five weeks of leave.

Those kinds of policies send a signal to families that society wants men and women to work *and* to have children, if they choose. Raising children well is a complex job, and these countries try to make it easier. Not only does the financial support help, but so does the social climate, the idea that of course both genders want to work and have healthy, happy families—and shouldn't have to choose between the two. France has one of the highest birthrates in Europe (only Ireland and Iceland have higher), at 1.98 in 2007, followed by Norway, at 1.9, and Sweden, 1.88. When it's easier for parents to work and have kids, they choose to have families.

And when countries don't make it easy? Adults don't have children. Thus the recent front-page headline on a popular German tabloid: "Baby Shock: Germans Are Dying Out." Until recently, the country offered far less generous support for parents than other European countries; child care is both expensive and difficult to find, and the workplace is reputed to be notoriously family-*un*friendly. The result: Germany has had one of the lowest birthrates in Europe. Also near the bottom is Italy, where child care is expensive, affordable housing is in short supply, and the work culture makes it difficult for women to interrupt their careers. The result? Italian women are choosing work over family.

"Many women want to combine family and work, but if society doesn't permit that, then women opt for their career," Steffen Kroehnert, of the Berlin Institute for Population and Development, told the BBC. "When you compare Germany with other European countries, you have a higher birthrate in, for example, Sweden or Denmark, where there is higher gender equality on the labor market."

In Europe, the plunging rate of birth and the aging of the population have become sources of political anxiety. In most European countries, couples aren't having enough kids to "replace" themselves when they die. That's a big deal, because it means they won't have enough workers paying into the social security system to support older people when they retire. Out of the twenty-seven countries in the European Union in 2007 (the latest year for which figures are available), only Iceland and Ireland met or passed the replacement level of 2.01 children per family.

This anxiety is leading countries like Germany to rethink their policies. There, the population is expected to plummet from 82 million to as low as 69 million by 2050. The government is scrambling to develop family-friendly policies. In 2007, the country adopted a generous paid parental leave policy. One parent can stay home for a year and receive 67 percent of his or her full salary. Even better, if a second parent wants to take a turn staying home, the family gets an extra two months of paid leave, for a total of fourteen months. It's great for kids, great for families, and a huge incentive for dads to take time off, too. And guess what? Birthrates started to rise after the law went into effect.

The evidence seems clear: Adults in developed nations should not have to accept things as they are. Mothers shouldn't have to choose work over family, and neither should fathers. Governments and communities can do a lot to make work-family balance easier. Unfortunately, policy makers in the United States have been slow to respond to this information, so Americans are stuck in an outdated paradigm. The United States, for instance, is one of just two developed countries that doesn't offer national paid parental leave (the other is Australia—which offers a substantial financial "baby bonus" to all parents whether they take leave or not).

"Our society is just not supportive of mothers. It's an uphill battle," says Andrea Steele, founder and president of Emerge America, a group seeking to get more Democratic women into office. She's speaking of her own experiences as a mother of three—but also of the women she trains to run for office. "When we ask women to run for office, a lot of them who are mothers just say, 'Are you crazy?'" That reaction is understandable, but it creates a self-perpetuating problem—when women are too busy to run for office, that means fewer female legislators, which means fewer family-friendly policies—and thus, few women with the time to run for office.

Lack of support from the government, as well as companies, is one reason why so many women opt for alternative work arrangements—flextime, part-time, or launching their own businesses. The United States is definitely *not* sending the signal that it's all right, natural, even positive, for women to want to work and have children. No wonder only 21 percent of working moms say that full-time work is the ideal situation for them. (The rest say part-time work or not working would be preferable.) It's just too hard.

Solving the Rubik's Cube

But change is coming. Despite the lack of national incentives or support, some 70 percent of mothers in the United States work. The staying-single trend is only accelerating, while the financial impact of the longevity bonus is just beginning to hit, and it, too, will accelerate changes in family structure. The United States has a history of doing the right thing—eventually. Think of the civil rights movement, think of women's suffrage. The entrepreneurial, can-do ethos of the American people won't allow the nation to inhibit the rights and ambitions of so many for too long. So it's probably only a matter of time until U.S. citizens and legislators fully understand that families—families that will include many single parents, many homes full of multiple generations, and many two-parent partnerships in which both parents work—need child care and elder care and other obvious supports and opportunities if they are going to be able to fulfill their work potential, and if the nation is going to survive as a successful one into the coming decades.

Already, you can see the beginnings of real change. Pressure is increasing on communities and institutions to adapt to the new family.

Around the country, the very definition of "family" has become a fierce battleground, partly because of the struggle to legalize gay marriage. In the 2008 election, family issues were a huge vote driver. More than 60 percent of voters said they were more likely to support a candidate who they thought would help parents balance work and family, with policies such as fair pay, health care, and paid sick days. Another post-election poll found that both men and women were less concerned with the national economy than they were about work-family balance issues—and this at a time when the national economy was entering a full-blown crisis. Slowly, quietly, the buzz heard at mothers' groups, on mommy blogs and daddy blogs, at playdates and in day-care parking lots, is beginning to swell into a chorus of voices calling for communities and for the country to support the family as it exists today, in all its forms.

The stakes of these power shifts in the family are incredibly high. As families change, state and national government policies and corporate policies need new ways to respond to new questions. How should new kinds of families be taxed? What benefits should they receive? What policies will best ensure the safety, happiness, and success of children in every type of family? As we live longer, will we be able to afford to have people retire at age sixty-five? And as we require longer periods of care, who will bear that burden? Are today's schools, day cares, retirement homes, and legal policies designed for today's changing family? Behind all of these issues lies one fundamental question: Does our society value and support today's working families? Families the way they really are and not how they *used to be* or ought to be?

When the answer is yes, then everyone will have more freedom to fully utilize his or her talents. When the answer is no—no to cheaper, better day care, no to family-friendly policies, no to sick leave, no to affordable health care—then families will continue to feel stressed, frustrated, and confused. Often women, and increasingly men, choose to keep their valuable talents on the sidelines. As writer Lisa Belkin pointed out in her seminal *New York Times Magazine* piece, "The Opt-Out Revolution," only 38 percent of women graduates from Harvard Business School's classes of 1981, 1985, and 1991 were working full-time and a quarter to a third of professional women in a variety of industries were out of the workforce.

Figures like these don't begin to account for the number of women and men who don't pursue more education, additional training, or better careers because of the cost or difficulty of finding good child care or elder care, and the lack of other work-life supports.

Ultimately, those governments, communities, and families that develop creative ways to solve the Rubik's Cube will thrive; those that remain focused on the past won't. The future of each country—and the people in it—is as simple as that.

EIGHT

In Politics

CLOSING THE LEADERSHIP GAP

Ann Lininger, forty-one, grew up in the gently rolling golden hills of southern Oregon, a largely rural part of that state that has never fully recovered from the fall of the timber industry in the early 1990s. As a teenager, she worked in the office at her father's construction company, staring out the window in envy at her brother, who drove the heavy equipment. So one day she asked her father if she could quit working in the office and drive the front-end loader instead.

"To his credit, he said, 'If you think you can do it, give it a try,'" she recalls. She didn't have the first clue about driving the machines, but, she says cheerfully, "there's nothing like on-the-job training."

Today, as a mother of two in Portland, she's engaged in a very different kind of on-the-job training. In early 2009, she left her job as a transactional lawyer specializing in project finance and real estate development, and entered local politics.

If Hillary Clinton hadn't lost the 2008 Democratic primary, Lininger might not be a county commissioner today. "I was really hoping that Hillary Clinton would get the presidential nomination," Ann told me. She's an attractive mother of two with shoulder-length hair and a wide smile. When Clinton didn't get the nomination, Ann looked around at her own community and wondered, "Is a woman *ever* going to get the top job?" She saw many women in mid-level jobs at law firms, companies, nonprofits, and in community leadership. A few in the number two spot. But hardly any at the very top.

"I decided I could either be cranky and bitter or try to do something positive. So I called up some friends and said, 'Let's help each other make that final sprint,'" she recalls. One evening in December 2008, about thirty Portland-area women met to confide to one another their biggest dreams and help one another achieve them. The group included lawyers, professors, an IT system designer, and women from the energy sector and other industries. Most of the women were ages thirty-five to fifty, married and mothers.

At that initial meeting, Lininger admitted for the first time her secret political aspirations. With her law degree from New York University and years of work experience with community organizations, she felt that she was "born for this work."

That very night, after the meeting, she sat down at her computer and began looking for a way into local politics. As it turned out, the Clackamas County board of commissioners was about to appoint an interim commissioner until the fall elections.

For Lininger, it was the front-end-loader story all over again. She had no experience, but she knew she wanted to be in the driver's seat. She called friends for advice. She reached out to her network and her friends' networks. She lobbied the commission and made her case, thinking, "You can't control the exit outcome, but you can control having the gumption to go after your dreams." So she went for it. She didn't get the appointment, but her confidence and credentials impressed the right people. When another spot came open later, she easily won the job.

Today, as county commissioner, she's immersed in decision making for her community, mastering the intricacies of land use and zoning, all while raising her family and preparing for the general election in May 2010 to keep her seat. "It's not easy to run for office with little kids," she admits. Her husband, David White, a lawyer, has stepped up, spending more time with their daughter, Julia, a first grader, and son, Adam, in fourth grade, and taking on extra chores at home. Lininger's mother is pitching in, too: She drives the five hours from her home in southern Oregon one week every month to help make it all work and will continue to do so until the election.

Lininger earns much less as a county commissioner than at her old job as a lawyer. Her house is far from perfect these days, and life is even crazier than it used to be. "But if you want to have a representative democracy, you have to have *all* the people represented—working moms, working dads, people with little kids," she says. When we spoke, the enthusiasm in her voice was unmistakable. "We want the very best, most capable, most passionate people in leadership, so we have to look at *everybody* to figure out who those best, most capable, most passionate people are. If I think I'm one of them, and I rule myself out because I'm a woman, that would be a shame."

Around the world, it's becoming clear that women *have* been ruled out of political roles—and leadership roles in general. As we'll see, women are only a small proportion of leaders in almost every field. Fortunately, in the United States and elsewhere, women and men are working together for change—creating and adapting systems that draw on a richer set of skills, experiences, and points of view when making decisions that affect all of society.

Where Are the Women?

When Ann Lininger looked to see who was at the top of companies and political bodies in her community, she saw men. That's true across the United States in business, politics, law, academia, even in nonprofits, which employ and promote more women than most fields. Nationally, 80 percent of top corporate leaders are male. Ninety-seven percent of Fortune 500 CEOs are men; 88 percent of U.S. governors are men; 83 percent of U.S. members of Congress are men; 76 percent of state legislators are men.

"Women are 52 percent of voters," says U.S. congresswoman Cathy McMorris Rodgers, a Republican representative from eastern Washington State. "But we're 17 percent of Congress." Not only are we not leading the world in political equality, but we're far behind many other countries. The United States ranks fifty-sixth in the world for political empowerment of women, according to the World Economic Forum

(WEF)'s *Global Gender Gap Report*, which measures women's political empowerment by several standards (the ratio of women to men in elected office, senior cabinet or ministerial positions, and leading the country). By WEF's count, the United States is behind Mexico, China, and Pakistan. Behind Germany, Uganda, and Peru. If you look *only* at the percentage of women elected to Congress, compared to the percentage of women in other parliamentary bodies, the United States ranks seventieth in the world. Yet this glaring truth seems to be the best-kept secret in America.

"People *think* that women are in power," says Marie Wilson, founder and president of the White House Project, a nonpartisan, nonprofit organization advancing women in politics and business, "but that's not really the case in any field." The White House Project's 2009 *Benchmark Report* looked at women holding top jobs in ten fields; they counted the percentage of women who were college presidents, Fortune 500 corporate officers, members of Congress, law partners, heads of nonprofits, newspaper publishers, radio and TV news directors, and in other top jobs. Across all ten fields, women on average held just 18 percent of the leadership positions (ranging from 7 percent in the military to 39 percent in nonprofits). Note that in all these fields except the military, women make up half or more of the workers.

TOP LEADERSHIP POSITIONS

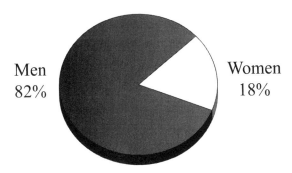

Men
82%

Women
18%

Source: *Benchmark Report* (The White House Project, 2009)

WOMEN IN TOP LEADERSHIP POSITIONS

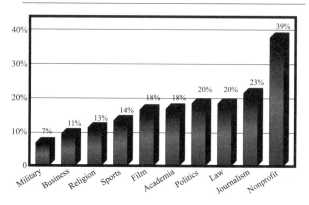

Source: *Benchmark Report* (The White House Project, 2009)

Women have done a remarkable job of moving into that "middle place"—moving from survival to independence on the scale of economic power, moving from entry level to middle management. Senior leadership positions in every field, however, from politics to finance, from health care to film, are still held overwhelmingly by men.

That's especially damaging in the realm of policy making. As our country emerges from economic turmoil, almost all the critical conversations about the fate of our nation—about the economy, the environment, national security, the health of our families—are taking place without equal input, guidance, and influence from *half* our population. Could this possibly be good for our country?

Common sense says no. Yet the halls of power continue to echo with male voices, only occasionally tempered by a female note.

"It's clear from our report that the political dimension is where the world as a whole is performing extremely poorly," says Saadia Zahidi, a coauthor of the World Economic Forum's *Global Gender Gap Report.*

We've already seen what happens to corporations when they fail to take a his-and-hers view of the world: Companies with a lot of women at the top thrive. Companies without don't perform as well. Similarly, the world is beginning to see the dangers of a unisex approach to politics.

In 2008, three key global forces suddenly converged to make glaringly clear the folly of excluding women (and anyone who's not white or wealthy) from leadership in the United States and elsewhere. First, the global financial meltdown threw into abrupt, stark relief huge failings of status quo leadership in the highest echelons of power in the United States. The meltdown also made the need for transparency at every level of U.S. companies and governing bodies entirely clear. Then, at virtually the same moment, the U.S. elections blew a breath of fresh air into the political arena, as powerful, high-profile women helped shape the race and reminded voters of the truth before their eyes: Women had previously been left out of the power game, for the most part, particularly in presidential elections. And finally, these two American events coincided with an international upsurge in women's power, a backdrop in which women increasingly held the highest political offices. In 2008 and 2009, women were serving as presidents of Argentina, Chile, Finland, Gabon, India, Ireland, Liberia, and the Philippines, as chancellor of Germany, and as prime ministers of Bangladesh, Bosnia, Haiti, Iceland, Moldova, Mozambique, and Ukraine. At the same time, women held increasing numbers of key cabinet and ministry posts and were being elected to more parliamentary positions in every region of the world except the United States. By 2009, women made up almost half of Sweden's lower parliamentary house, *more* than half of Rwanda's, and 43 percent of Cuba's.

"Men have the money, they have businesses, they have everything. But women, we don't have that," says Tharwat Al Amro, thirty-eight, who was elected to the lower house of Jordan's National Assembly in 2007. "Now we are starting to talk about what women need, how we can help women with the law and how to involve women in politics, in education, in health." Since 2003, Jordan's electoral system has reserved 6 seats (out of 110) specifically for women, and women's groups are calling for a 20 percent quota. It's a small step, but it's bringing women into the spotlight. "Everybody here is looking to the women," Al Amro told me.

In America and around the world, women stepped into the political spotlight at the very moment when status quo leadership created spectacular failures. In 2008 and 2009, economic, political, and international forces converged to show clearly and abruptly that the United States and the world at large can no longer afford to neglect the leadership talent pool of 50 percent of the population.

It isn't just women who've been waking up to the need for women's leadership. Men see it, too. Men like those in the U.S. House of Representatives who helped elect Nancy Pelosi as speaker of the House in 2007. Men like José Luis Rodriguez Zapatero, the prime minster of Spain, who appointed women to half his cabinet positions. Men like the thousands of men in Iran who added their names to the controversial Million Signatures petition to improve family rights. Men like King Mohammed VI of Morocco, a champion of women's equality and proponent of women's election to office. What's new about this nascent political movement is that *both* genders are uniting to take down the "no girls allowed" sign. The men aren't joining in just because they're nice guys (although many, many are), but because they understand that their nations can't afford to do otherwise.

In Rwanda, the nation is looking to women policy makers to steward the long healing process after war and genocide, by adopting a quota that insists on women having at least 30 percent of the votes in all national decision-making bodies. In Kuwait, women finally got the vote in 2005. In Europe, over the last decade eight countries have instituted national or regional quotas to get more women into office, and in twenty-seven countries, political parties have voluntarily adopted measures to make sure that many more women candidates run for office.

Ultimately, many of these countries are realizing the same thing that Ann Lininger did: Effective leadership requires that the *best* talent be tapped, regardless of gender, and that *both* genders have a voice. As the world gets smaller and our local, national, and international policy challenges become more complex and daunting, those nations and communities that enlist women as well as men to lead them into the future will find new political and economic opportunities blossoming around them. Those that fail will fall further and further behind.

"Five years ago, the conversation about getting more women into leadership roles was about it being the *right* thing to do," says Beth Brooke, chair of the White House Project and global vice chair of public policy, sustainability, and stakeholder engagement at Ernst & Young. "Now it's not just the right thing to do, but the *bright* thing to do." Following the international economic meltdown of 2008 and 2009, putting women into leadership positions is "becoming an imperative," Brooke says. America has a great deal of ground to make up: As I mentioned, WEF's *Global Gender Gap Report* ranks the United States fifty-sixth in political empowerment of women as calculated by several indicators. If you look only at the number of women in Congress, we do even worse: The Interparliamentary Union, an association of parliamentary bodies around the world, ranks the United States seventieth in the world for the number of women in national government bodies. Among the many countries that have elected a greater percentage of women are China, Mexico, Pakistan, Venezuela, even the United Arab Emirates. But Brooke believes the United States will soon see more women at the top—in politics, in business, and in all areas of society. She says, "We're struggling to come to a 'new normal' now, and we're never going back to the way it was."

Why Women Leaders Matter, or "Old, Fat, White Guys Don't Get Stalked"

The day before I talked to her, Congresswoman Debbie Wasserman Schultz had broken her leg sliding into second base at the first ever congressional women's softball game in Washington, D.C., a game that benefited the Young Survival Coalition, a breast cancer advocacy group. But even just a day after her injury, the broken leg hadn't slowed down this mother of three from Weston, Florida. She'd shown up for her scheduled 8:30 A.M. meeting and completed a series of five congressional votes before our chat. Fortunately, it was July, so she didn't have to review her ten-year-old twins' homework or admire her five-year-old daughter's artwork via video call home to Weston. Instead, her family was with her in Washington, her older daughter in the room while we talked.

At forty-two, an age when many women first enter politics, Wasserman Schultz has already had a distinguished political career, including eight years in the Florida state assembly, four in the state senate, and election to the U.S. House of Representatives. And she's overcome countless stereotypes already. At age twenty-six, she shocked critics by entering and winning the statehouse race (after knocking on twenty-five thousand doors in the Florida heat). She became a mother while serving in elected office: She was pregnant with her youngest when she ran for U.S. Congress. Today, she makes the commute to D.C. every week, while her husband, a banker, holds down the fort at home.

Wasserman Schultz is one of 73 female members of the 435-member U.S. House of Representatives: Women are just 17 percent of the total congressional representation, and every day, Wasserman Schultz sees the impact of the shortage of women in Congress. "We need to boost our numbers," she says. "If we do, our issues will rocket to the top of the legislative agenda. Just look at what Nancy Pelosi's done as speaker. The very first bill that Barack Obama signed was the Lilly Ledbetter Fair Pay Act." If just *one* powerful woman in a key position can make big changes, imagine the change in priorities if women held half the offices in Congress. Or even a third. Even a quarter.

"Women at any power table bring new ways of doing things," says Marie Wilson. "But women can only bring those new ways if there are enough of them, so that they're listened to and not shot down or 'genderized'"—that is, their point of view is not dismissed as representing only women.

Wilson points to research suggesting that any minority needs to reach critical mass—somewhere around 30 percent—to effect change. When that happens, suddenly it's easy to see women's influence at work. In 1998, for instance, the Indian region of West Bengal reserved one-third of village councillor positions, including the head councillor role, for women. Those councils then began to invest more in water, fuel, and roads—services that improve the lives of rural women and their families. In villages where the leaders of the councils were female, other women were more likely to take part in policy making.

A critical mass of women in lawmaking may bring other changes, too. One study by researchers from the Abdul Latif Jameel Poverty Action Lab at the Massachusetts Institute of Technology found that villagers are less likely to have to pay bribes in villages reserved for or headed by women. Other research, from the London School of Economics and Political Science, analyzed Indian elections between 1967 and 2001 and found that boosting female political representation in urban areas by 10 percent "increases the probability that an individual will attain primary education in urban areas by six percentage points." That's enough to close an impressive 21 percent of the gap in primary education that exists between the richest and poorest Indian states.

In the United States, New Hampshire has suddenly provided a striking example of the change that women lawmakers can bring. In 2009, the state senate became the first legislative body in the United States to have more women than men (thirteen women, eleven men), and together the senate and assembly membership became almost 38 percent female. Within a few short months, both branches voted for same-sex marriage and to repeal capital punishment, allow medical marijuana use, and boost the gas tax by 15 cents. Until recently, New Hampshire was the only state in the United States that did not provide free public kindergarten. But in 2009, New Hampshire began creating grants and other incentives for districts to provide kindergarten classes. The point isn't that electing women will create a liberal revolution (although the Democrats do field many more women candidates). Instead, the headline here is that conversations change when a critical mass of women enters the room.

It's not just the policies that change. It's the whole tone of the conversation. "There's always a lot more consensus building among women," says Wasserman Schultz. "Among my women colleagues and with Speaker Pelosi's leadership and other women committee chairs, there's a much less dictatorial, top-down style," she says. "Men are used to making a decision and handing that decision down to the group and having it executed. Especially in the legislature, consensus building is important, and it seems to come more naturally to women."

That seems to be true in international dialogue, too. "When I sit down with a group of women to work, there's very little jockeying for position," says Jody Williams, winner of the 1997 Nobel Peace Prize for her campaign to ban land mines, and a founder of the Nobel Women's Initiative, which works to advance peace around the world. "Women really think about how the whole thing moves forward, and share ideas about how we can advance the issue we're working on." In Jordan, the small but visible group of women lawmakers elected since the 2003 quota is creating a separate women's caucus to discuss the impact of rules and policies on women. "We come from different parts of the country but when we sit to discuss the law, we stand together," says Al Amro.

Of course, no one can *ever* say definitively, "A group of women behaves this way, and men that way; women build consensus and men don't." There's a spectrum of human behaviors, values, and characteristics, and while many women or many men may have more finely honed skills on one end or the other, generalizations never hold true for everyone. Case in point: During the 2008 primary, more than one pundit observed that Barack Obama showed a more collaborative, consensus-building, "feminine" style of leadership, while Hillary Clinton took a more traditionally "masculine" approach.

The important point isn't that women always believe and vote XX, while men vote XY. What's most important is that more women in elected office means a change in the conversation. They bring more and varied experiences that enrich discussions about policy, people, and the future of nations. More diversity means more potential solutions. *That's* the point.

"Everyone brings to Congress their life experience," says Representative Carolyn Maloney of New York, who has served in the House since 1992 and been a staunch champion of bills to improve life for women and families. Just a few bills she's supported or sponsored include the Family and Medical Leave Act, the Federal Employees Paid Parental Leave Act, and the Breastfeeding Promotion Act, protecting nursing mothers from workplace discrimination and requiring large companies to provide time and private space for pumping. She also cofounded and cochairs the Congressional Human Trafficking Caucus, which seeks to end forced prostitution of women around the world, and she coauthored two reports on the glass ceiling.

"Life experience matters. Absolutely," Maloney told me.

When she's working in Washington, Maloney shares a house with Wasserman Schultz and Congresswoman Melissa Bean. The three have spent many a late night perched on the end of one another's beds, eating popcorn and chewing over their days in one of America's most prominent male-dominated workplaces.

More women, Maloney notes, want to run—but can't, because they're maxed out with work and home life. But if more women ran for elected office and won, a virtuous cycle could take place. Once in office, these women could champion work-life balance policies to make life a little easier for all women. And then more women would be able to run for office. And those women could make even more work-life balance changes in society. And so on. And so on.

A New Point of View

Whether it's New Hampshire or India, when women move into elected or appointed office, things change. Not because women always advance education over war, or clean water over weapons, but simply because women bring additional points of view and previously unconsidered or ignored ideas to the table.

"Women bring a different perspective," says Congresswoman Cathy McMorris Rodgers. "Women make the vast majority of health-care decisions, and 80 percent of checks are written by women. So on issues where women are front and center—making financial decisions for the family, setting priorities, determining how their family is going to get the health care they need—it makes sense for women to be among the decision makers. They're going to bring a passion to those issues when elected to Congress."

McMorris Rodgers understands, maybe better than anyone, how greatly personal experience can change your point of view. She'd been in politics for more than ten years, first as a Republican state legislator for Washington State, then as a U.S. representative, before she became a wife and a mother. Having children changes everything—especially if that child has special needs like McMorris Rodgers's son, Cole.

McMorris Rodgers met her husband, Brian, a retired navy commander, at one of her own fund-raisers. "One of my assistants had brought him to meet someone else, but at the end of the party, he said, 'Actually, I'd really like to meet Cathy.'" They married in 2006, and she got pregnant during her first term in Congress. Shortly after Cole's birth, he was diagnosed with Down syndrome.

"The fact that he has special needs has given me a whole new purpose in Congress," she says. Together with several other representatives who have children with special needs, she formed the Congressional Down Syndrome Caucus to lobby for better help and care for children like Cole.

"It's given me a platform to talk about an issue I would otherwise have had no experience with," she says. "When I speak on issues related to Cole, it's amazing how people listen." From her first days as a new mother in Congress, McMorris Rodgers has been struck with wonder at how Cole has changed her life as a representative. "It's been amazing to me how people have responded. He's introduced me to members I never would have met otherwise, across the aisle and in the Senate. People know about Cole and they want to see him when I bring him to the floor. I never expected this and never dreamed of this, but it's amazing to me how he's already making an impact."

As a mother, McMorris Rodgers has found it's become even more clear to her how women lawmakers, who view work and family issues as serious issues, bring those topics smack into the center of policy making. "I'm balancing the demands of being a wife and taking care of my family with the demands of my job. That's an important perspective we bring to the legislative process."

When it comes to showing how women bring important legislation to the table that men failed to imagine, my favorite example comes from Deb Sofield, president of the Women's Campaign School at Yale University, an annual weeklong campaign training program for women from the United States and overseas: Before women were voted into the state legislature in South Carolina, the state had no laws on its books dealing specifically with the crime of stalking. Now that the state assembly has a handful of women, they do have stalking laws. Why didn't the men pass something earlier? "The guys said they just never thought about it. They weren't against it. It just never crossed their minds," says Sofield. "The women joked, 'Yeah . . . because nobody stalks old, fat, white guys.'"

Diverse points of view bringing different types of life experiences to the table are key components to reaching the best solutions. Academic research by Scott Page, a professor of complex systems at the University of Michigan at Ann Arbor and author of the book *The Difference: How the Power of Diversity Creates Better Groups, Firms, Schools, and Societies*, shows through mathematical models that a group of average people with widely diverse ways of thinking was far more effective at solving complex problems than a homogenous group of the best individual problem solvers. Page says, "It isn't a feel-good mantra, it's a mathematical fact." The "smart" problem solvers tended to think too similarly and were more likely to get stuck than the diverse group.

In the corporate world, a kind of success that I like to call "the diversity dividend" is already coming to pass: Study after study finds that companies with more women on their boards, and more diverse boards, perform better than those with just a homogenous group of mostly middle-aged white guys.

The U.S. government has lacked diversity in its representatives for centuries. (The Pulitzer Prize–winning author and humor columnist Dave Barry once knocked the Senate, accurately, as "100 white male millionaires working for you.") Fortunately, American women are starting to bring their rising economic influence to bear on America's lack of diverse political representation.

Power Shifts Afoot: Tapping Women's Economic Power

During her first campaign for the Florida state assembly, Debbie Wasserman Schultz raised just $21,000. During her 2008 run for Congress, she raised more than $2 million ($1.7 million for her campaign, plus $500,000 for her leadership political action committee). She parlayed that money into political influence of the most powerful kind.

"My goal was to get as far out in front as I could and avoid a Democratic primary," she says. It only made sense: She was pregnant with her youngest daughter. Why not make life easier? She poured on her fund-raising efforts and raised her money very quickly. Rather than spending that capital, she used it to strategically enhance her influence. "I convinced Speaker Pelosi to endorse me in the primary, which is unusual. The argument I made was that it made no sense to spend $2 million in a primary when I could raise that money and use it to help my future colleagues." Indeed, no one filed against her for the primary, she won her seat, and she strengthened her ties with Pelosi.

Ask any successful female politician about the most important fundamental to master in order to get elected, and money's the first thing she mentions. Money's not the *only* force that's kept women out of politics, or even the most important one. It's tough for anybody, male or female, to defeat an incumbent. There's a shortage of female role models. There aren't enough women candidates in the pipeline. The "second shift" problem leaves women with little extra time to enter politics. But solving the money problem makes those other barriers easier to leap— and women donors are just starting to put their money where their votes are.

"Women are definitely playing a bigger role in fund-raising than in the past," says Debbie Walsh, director of the Center for American Women and Politics. In 2008, women gave *more than twice* what women gave in 2000, a whopping $749.2 million donated to candidates, parties, or political action committees. (This amount counts only donors who gave more than $200, because only campaign contributions of $200 or more are itemized. It is important to note that generally women give in smaller amounts.) Somehow, in the midst of a global recession, women reached deep into their pockets and gave more than double the $306 million they donated during the boom times of 2000. And women's political donations increased more than men's did, growing from 24 percent of the total in 2000 to 30 percent in 2008.

Women are still giving much, *much* less than men, but the rate of change—*more than a 100 percent increase in eight years*—is astonishing. Especially when you consider that women, overall, earn less than men and that more women live in poverty and aren't exactly in the position to give to anybody. Despite all this, women are starting to flex their political muscles. *Half* of the money raised for Hillary Clinton's primary run came from women. *Forty percent* of donations over $200 to Obama's campaign came from women. And 30 percent of Obamas *biggest fund-raisers* were women.

Only 10 percent of Senator John McCain's presidential campaign contributions came from women, and only 28 percent of his donations over $200 came from women. Both Obama and Clinton did a better job capturing dollars from women than McCain did, and capturing votes, too—a big deal since more than half of voters in 2008 were women. In the end, 56 percent of women voters voted for Obama, and only 43 percent for McCain.

Meanwhile, women are not only giving more to candidates, they're giving much more to groups, causes, *and* candidates that support the issues women tend to care about. In 2008, nearly $20 million in donations went to support what are considered women's issues, including pro-choice and pro-life issues, women's rights, the interest of women business owners, and other issues supported by women's political groups and associations. That's *four times* as much as went to women's issues in the 2004 election cycle. Is it coincidence that Obama's first signed legislation was a bill enhancing women's economic power? That 30 percent of his initial cabinet were women? That he immediately commissioned the White House Council on Women and Girls? Women are voting with their dollars, and their money is talking, louder than ever before.

EMILY's Legacy: Creating the Year of the Woman

It's no mystery where this phenomenal growth started. We know the precise place and day—a now-famous meeting in the basement in the home of former Carter White House staffer (and an heir to the IBM fortune) Ellen Malcolm. "In those days, women weren't giving to political candidates at all," she told me. Back then, not a single woman Democrat had ever been elected to the Senate in her own right, or been elected governor of a large state. Because women lacked funding early in the process to conduct polls and build momentum, women candidates weren't being taken seriously by the men who ran the political parties. So in 1985, Malcolm invited twenty-five friends to write letters to other friends about a new network to raise money for pro-choice Democratic women candidates. "It was $100 to join, and then we asked members to write checks to two or three women." The network chose the name EMILY's List. Emily is an acronym—"Early Money Is Like Yeast (It Makes the Dough Rise)." The rest is history.

In 1992, EMILY's List contributed some $6.2 million to women candidates. Twenty women were elected to the House, four women to the Senate. Scholars still call 1992 "the year of the woman." U.S. elections of female Senate candidates have not moved forward as dramatically since then, but they haven't lost ground either. Meanwhile, EMILY's List has helped elect 80 women to the House, 15 to the Senate, 9 to governor's offices, and 473 to state and local positions. Today, EMILY's List is among the largest political action committees in the country. In the 2007–2008 election cycle, it raised more than $43 million from 100,000 members.

And since EMILY's List began, other political action committees (PACs) and organizations for women have cropped up. "EMILY's List educated women about the importance of giving to women," says Debbie Walsh. PACs for women are not just on the Democratic side anymore either. Today, the Susan B. Anthony List raises money for pro-life women candidates, and the Republican WISH List raises funds for pro-choice women Republican candidates. Says Walsh, "Ellen Malcolm and her work with EMILY's List has taught women that if you care about something and want to see change, you need to write a check, and a significant check."

What's significant? In the 1990s legendary Texas governor Ann Richards urged women to write a check for the amount of money they'd spent on their outfit that day. That might be $25, but it might well be $2300, too. "There are an awful lot of women who can write the maximum check," says Walsh.

The Networked Revolution: Technology Changes the Game

EMILY's List remains an important force, raising huge amounts of money for women candidates and providing them and their potential campaign staff members with rigorous training in campaign planning, budgeting, media and field skills, and in how to do yet more, non–EMILY's List fundraising. But grassroots online groups have also begun to sweep a new wave of women into political action.

"We're seeing a rebirth of the feminist movement and a revolution played out on laptops everywhere," says Carolyn Maloney.

Groups like MomsRising and MoveOn.org are using cutting-edge technologies and marketing techniques, tailored to women's media habits and giving patterns, to make it easier for women to research issues they care about and take action—including financial action.

"When MomsRising takes a position on something, the members of Congress hear from mothers across the nation," Maloney says. When she sponsored the Federal Employees Paid Parental Leave Act, which the House approved in June 2008, "my colleagues were hearing from their constituents because MomsRising said it was an important bill."

I described some of MomsRising's tactics in Chapter Five, when I talked about women and marketing: MomsRising created that hilarious viral fake news video about the Mother of the Year award. As we'll see below, they're brilliant at reaching mothers through e-mail and the Web, using the venues that moms frequent, with content they enjoy, and providing lots of links to more information and quick, practical suggestions for how women can make a difference. That might include sending a fortune cookie with a custom message to an elected official, or decorating (or just donating money for the decoration of) a baby outfit (a "onesie") to make a chain of baby clothes to be strung outside the Capitol building to demonstrate "the power of ONEsies."

As it turns out, the communications tools and marketing approaches of MomsRising and other grassroots groups, including MoveOn.org, dovetail perfectly with the way that women decide how to spend their money.

In Chapter Two, I told you about research into women's financial profiles. When it comes to finances, the single largest group of women, 35 percent of the women we surveyed, is the Perceptive Planner group, the women who prefer to do extensive research and planning before making a financial move. This profile matches up *perfectly* with the kind of tools that grassroots, online advocacy groups are using today.

"You see the Web giving an opportunity to allow women to do the research they need to do, to be able to engage their friends and family," Ilana Goldman, former president of the Women's Campaign Forum, told ABC News in 2008. Women want to research issues and candidates thoroughly before donating. These groups, and grassroots giving sites like ActBlue .com, make it easy to do both.

Online fund-raising also matches well with women's giving prefer-ences. "I think women give in different patterns than men," says Ellen Malcolm, the founder of EMILY's List. "They don't tend to be the $2300 max-out donor. We see women giving multiple times with smaller checks. They might get to $2300, but they get there by giving $100 or $250 mul-tiple times. This pattern of fund-raising worked for Obama and Hillary, too." The grassroots groups specialize in urgent, timely pleas for specific, small amounts—for $25, say, to help fund a newspaper ad in the *Wall Street Journal.*

MomsRising in particular—because it's run by moms—is highly at-tuned to the lives of many modern women, and the masterminds at Moms-Rising are expert at finding ways to engage women on women's own terms. "Three-quarters of moms are in the labor force, so the majority of people can't come out and do advocacy during the day. Women are jug-gling an unprecedented number of roles at the same time," says Kristin Rowe-Finkbeiner, cofounder of MomsRising. "We look at ways to have people's voices heard even when they can't physically be there." Thus, the fortune cookies and the "power of ONEsies" displays.

Moms' online political activism has only just begun. In 2008, Moms-Rising's 160,000 members took more than a million actions—from send-ing e-mails to their representatives, to decorating and donating baby clothes for display, to bombarding John McCain with résumés when he suggested women earned less because they weren't well educated or qual-ified, to sending those customized fortune cookies to elected officials. MomsRising members made 200,000 contacts with their elected officials on the Lilly Ledbetter Fair Pay Act of 2009 alone.

That was in 2008, when MomsRising had 160,000 members. By May 2009, the organization had grown to include *one million* members. If you think we've already seen the true power that grassroots online organizing can unleash—both financially and politically—just wait until the next election cycle.

Waiting for an Invitation:
Recruiting Candidates

Penny Bernard Schaber got her first vote without even running for office. She and her husband were walking home from their polling place, a school near their home in Appleton, Wisconsin. They were both unhappy with their choices for state representative. "You know, I couldn't vote for him," her husband said of the incumbent. "So I wrote your name in."

Schaber, a physical therapist by training, had never run for office, but her husband got her to thinking. Years earlier, she'd worked in the Peace Corps in Brazil and seen the importance of working for local change. As a physical therapist, she'd worked in all kinds of health-care settings, from hospitals to nursing homes to schools, and she understood organizations and management. As a Sierra Club member, she got involved in land use and transportation planning sessions, and attended city council and county board meetings regularly. "I found myself getting frustrated and complaining about what I saw happening in politics," she says. "A woman friend of mine said, 'If people like you don't run for office, then nothing will change.'"

So in 2006, Schaber ran for state assembly. She lost, but she made a great show, recruiting two hundred volunteers and earning 46.7 percent of the vote—an impressive feat against a ten-year incumbent.

And that wasn't the end of her story. Soon after her loss, Schaber received a phone call from a new political action organization called Emerge America. They wanted her to run again. They wanted to train her to win. And in 2008, after the group's seven-month training course, Schaber did win.

"One reason there aren't more women in elected office is because women are not running in the same numbers as men," explains Andrea Steele, founder of Emerge America. Steele wanted to change that, so she looked at why women weren't running. Research suggested two major reasons: "The number one reason is they don't feel as qualified as men in general. A woman and a man can have exactly the same résumé and a woman won't feel as qualified. If the job description has one thing she can't do, she won't apply. Whereas if a man sees one thing he can do, he applies."

The second reason there aren't more women in elected office? "Women are not recruited in the same numbers as men," Steele says. "Women don't self-nominate like men, so they need to be recruited. And party leaders, leaders in the community, don't go up to women as often and say, 'I think you should run.'"

Or, as Deb Sofield puts it, "Women don't wake up in the morning thinking they should be governor. Men do wake up in the morning thinking they should be president."

Emerge America has tried to address both problems. First, the program seeks out women with the potential to win. Second, it provides intense training through a seven-month program of monthly weekend boot camps. That's much more in-depth than traditional campaign schools, which may last just a day or week. Since its founding in 2005, Emerge's program has trained 376 women to run for office.

The training works. Of the Emerge America trainees who have run so far, half have been elected. "The first time I ran, I didn't have a lot of political connections or networks to use. Emerge helped me develop those networks," Schaber says. She learned to approach community leaders she didn't know and present a convincing argument for herself. She learned about fund-raising, communications, and staffing. "They helped me move up the curve faster."

Along the way, she became increasingly aware of the importance of women running for office.

"Women coming up, including myself, we're used to seeing women in positions of power, because they broke the barriers a long time ago. We don't think we need to be there," she says. But the percentage of women in statewide elected offices like governor stalled out at a high of about 27.6 percent, and actually started sliding backward in 2001. Today just 23.6 percent of statewide elected offices are held by women.

"We need to come in behind and push hard to make sure that women stay publicly active," Schaber says. "We figure the issues are taken care of and we don't have to worry about them, but it really is our responsibility to run for office and make sure the issues women care about get the attention they deserve."

The Hillary Effect

Maybe it's the impact of Hillary Clinton's presidential run, inspiring women like Ann Lininger to take action. Maybe it's because women's economic power is reaching critical mass. Whatever the cause or causes, there's a surge of interest in candidate training programs for women.

"Our training sessions have doubled their size because more women are interested in politics as a result of this past presidential election," says Marie Wilson, founder of the White House Project. In 2005, the White House Project launched its Go Run training program, which has since trained some six thousand women in leadership and campaigning. In 2007, the White House Project expanded its trainings from urban to rural areas. In 2009, the Women's Campaign School at Yale University admitted seventy women instead of the usual fifty-five to its program. EMILY's List continues to train potential candidates, as it has since 2001; on the other side of the choice debate, the Susan B. Anthony List provides candidate training for pro-life women.

"What's important isn't the two or three women who are already big success stories," says Wilson. "What's important is getting hundreds of women to run. It's the mass, the numbers, that will change things."

To reach that critical mass, Wilson adds, more women need to enter politics at younger ages. Cathy McMorris Rodgers of eastern Washington, for instance, was just twenty-five, working as a legislative assistant for her state assemblyman in Olympia, Washington, when her boss was appointed to a state senate seat. He encouraged her to run for his assembly seat, launching her decade-long career in the state house. Because she started young, she gained seniority and became minority leader in 2002, the youngest leader in either party since before World War II.

Then in 2003, McMorris Rodgers's elected-office mojo happened all over again: The U.S. representative from her district decided to run for Senate and suggested Cathy, then thirty-five, run for his district seat. She resisted at first, but he changed her mind by saying, "You know, Cathy, you're young enough that if you run and get elected, you could be there awhile. You could gain some seniority and really be able to make a difference." She ran. She won. And she's set herself on the path to real political influence: Research at Rutgers suggested that the majority of political leaders in Congress, state legislatures, and municipal councils won their seats at age thirty-five or younger.

"You have to get a lot of young women in, because that's the way you make it to the very top," says Debbie Walsh. Groups like the Women Under 40 Political Action Committee (WUFPAC) are funding women candidates in their twenties and thirties (the group funded both McMorris Rodgers and Wasserman Schultz). Meanwhile, a group called Running Start offers leadership training for high school and college women, encouraging them to close the politics gender gap early. (A survey of student governments on college campuses found that 71 percent of student body presidents were male.)

Getting more women into the political pipeline would help get more women into office. That's even more important for Republicans, who face a bigger gender gap than Democrats. Twenty-two percent of House Democrats are women, compared to just 9.5 percent of Republicans. Thirteen women senators are Democrats; four women senators are Republicans. While both parties need to field more women candidates, Republicans lag behind.

"When I was elected in 2004, I remember walking into my first meeting of the House Republican Conference and seeing a sea of dark suits. There were two hundred and thirty-two members, and twenty-four were women," says McMorris Rodgers. "Since then, we're down to seventeen Republican members of Congress who are women." McMorris Rodgers is working with the Republican National Committee to recruit more women candidates. "Many within the Republican party are conscious that we need more women in elected office on the Republican ticket. We need a more diverse face; we need to be promoting some new faces and new blood within the party."

Prepping the Pipeline Overseas

In many other countries, political parties and voters themselves are also feeling the need for new faces and new blood. That's why 110 countries around the world have adopted laws or voluntary party policies to make sure more women take part in political decision making. In Egypt, for example, a 2009 mandate added sixty-four new parliamentary seats specifically for women; men cannot run for those seats. In 2008, Angola mandated that 30 percent of candidates in national elections be women. In Chile, the major parties promise that 20 percent of their candidates will be women; when Michelle Bachelet was elected president in 2006, she appointed women to ten of her twenty cabinet positions and has continued to maintain high numbers of women throughout subsequent cabinet reshuffles. Germany's parties embrace voluntary quotas of 30 to 50 percent women. With all these boosts for women abroad, no wonder the World Economic Forum's *Gender Gap Report* ranks the United States as fifty-sixth of 130 countries for women's political empowerment. While quotas have their pros and cons, and different types of quotas have different advantages and drawbacks, they all have one thing in common: They're remarkably effective at uncovering untapped political resources. For example, running for office had never even occurred to thirty-eight-year-old Tharwat Al Amro. In fact, she was studying overseas, working on her Ph.D. in the United States, when she got the life-changing call from back home in July 2007.

Her friends and her younger brother home in Al Karak, an area of about sixty-eight thousand people, wanted her to run for parliament. Her clan—the political group that oversees local affairs—thought she had a good chance to win. She was well educated, and her father, though poor, had close ties within the clan. And, of course, she was a woman.

In 2003, Jordan's election law created six new seats specifically for women, raising the number of seats in Jordan's lower house from 104 to 110. Whichever six women in the country received the highest percentage of votes in their district would win a seat. So if Al Amro could win a high percentage of votes, her district would essentially have two representatives—Al Amro, who would land one of the women's seats, plus whatever candidate won the most votes for the district (who would most likely be male, since only one woman has defeated a man for a district seat thus far).

Al Amro talked it over with her family, then flew home to meet with members of her clan, who explained how many votes she might win from each village. "I began to understand how it was that I could win," she says. She decided to run.

As Al Amro found, quotas do make it easier for women to get elected—but many other barriers still get in the way. Al Amro's advisors told her she'd need 30,000 Jordanian dollars to run a campaign that included TV and newspaper ads, posters, visits and events in the thirteen villages in her district, and renting campaign headquarters. Coming from a poor family, Al Amro had only about 3,000 Jordanian dollars, from family and friends, and no way of raising more.

"People now accept that a woman can run, but they don't accept that she can ask for money," she says. "They give gifts to men, they accept men and help them with everything, but not women."

So Al Amro campaigned on a shoestring. Instead of renting a space for headquarters, she ran the campaign from her parents' house. Instead of throwing expensive events, she invited voters to her own living room and explained why she'd be a good member of parliament. She did make a few campaign visits outside her home, with her brother as escort, but with little money or visibility, her chances seemed shaky. Her male opponents were spending 30,000 to 100,000 Jordanian dollars. On election day, she followed the poll results anxiously. By 4 P.M., she had only about half the votes she'd need.

Suddenly, the clan elders—all men—rallied to her support. "At four P.M., they got into their cars and went around to all of our villages and asked people to come vote. 'She will win, she will win!' they said." Between 5 and 7 P.M., the tide turned, and Al Amro won.

Today, she splits her time between Al Karak and Amman. "There are just seven women in parliament, so we need to band together with the men," she says. The women are still just learning to work together with one another on issues, but already she sees progress. She's working on laws to help divorced women obtain support and rights.

"We are working very hard," she says. "We have to succeed."

Show Us the Money

Al Amro's shoestring campaign worked, but her budgetary woes highlight a major problem for women candidates, particularly in countries with no laws or mechanism to provide them with public funds and no cultural precedent for Western-style fund-raising—especially not for women. Still, even in countries where women have access to few financial resources, women candidates, and the men who support them, are finding ways to come up with the funds to get women elected.

In Morocco, for example, "money is one of the great barriers to women aspirants," according to a study by the National Democratic Institute for International Affairs. In an effort to encourage more women to run—a goal endorsed by King Mohammed VI in October 2008—the government announced it would begin offering financial incentives to the parties that successfully fielded the most women candidates for local elections in June 2009. (This is the exact opposite of another financial incentive system in France: Half of the candidates on party election lists must be women. If they are not, parties face financial sanctions.) And in Indonesia, women candidates sometimes participate in a cultural traditional known as the *arisan*—a networking group where members contribute weekly to a community pot of money that each member will win at least once. Winners don't have to use the money for a political run. "It's not specifically to run for office," explains the National Democratic Institute's report. But the funds from this process can be used to support a campaign, and political parties have been using it to network and to build support.

Back in Jordan, Tharwat Al Amro may benefit in her next election, in 2011, from a group called the Women Helping Women Network (WHWN), modeled on EMILY's List in the United States. "We wanted to do three things. To get women elected either by supporting other women's campaigns or by running for office themselves, to send a positive message about women's political participation, and third, to let people know that women can help women," says Roula Attar, resident director of the Jordan office of the National Democratic Institute (NDI), a Washington, D.C.–based nonprofit, nongovernmental organization that encourages civic participation, open political systems, and representative, accountable government in countries around the world. Two and a half years ago, Attar launched the Women Helping Women Network with an executive committee that includes Jordanian women leaders from business, politics, academia, and law. The group offers women candidates much needed training in media relations, campaign messaging, and fund-raising.

Fund-raising and campaign training efforts like these, many launched by regional women-to-women support groups and sometimes funded by NGOs like NDI (which receives funding from the U.S. Agency for International Development and the U.S. State Department as well as international development agencies and private foundations), are under way in more than sixty countries worldwide. As women's economic power builds around the world, organizations that learn to tap that power and channel it to women candidates will have a powerful impact on boosting women from independence to influence.

The Woman's Touch:
What Women Do with Power

Cathy Allen's résumé reads like an atlas. Chile, Morocco, Spain, Holland, Yemen, Qatar, Dubai, Egypt. As president and CEO of the Connections Group, a political consultancy in Seattle, she's helped women get elected in all of those countries and more. For twenty years, she's worked as a political consultant around the world, training women in leadership and campaigning. And every time a country adds a measure to boost women's political participation, her phone starts ringing.

For instance, in 2002 the political parties in Morocco signed an agreement reserving thirty seats for women in their national elections. Suddenly, the parties needed women. For five years, Allen coached women candidates on presenting their message, on reaching the right people at the right time. "Just a few years ago, there were only three women in parliament in Morocco, and now there are thirty-five," she says with satisfaction.

Her sense of triumph doesn't come simply from winning races. Time and time again, she's seen the election of women to ruling bodies transform communities, improving health, education, and infrastructure and making lives better for women and families. Before women were elected in larger numbers, for example, "less than 6 percent of rural girls in Morocco had access to education," she told me. "Now 38 percent are in school. When women get elected, more kids get educated and that has a direct effect on the economy."

That's an enormous change in a short time, and it's brought other changes with it. Sexual harassment is now a crime in Morocco. In 2006, the Moroccan minister of social development, family, and solidarity created a national organization for fighting violence against women, providing social services and follow-up on cases of abuse. And in 2004, Morocco raised the marriage age from fifteen to eighteen and gave women equal rights to property after divorce. In 2009, Marrakech elected its first woman mayor. In the same election, twenty-one-year-old Fatima Boujenah became the youngest local council leader in Morocco.

Women are making similar inroads into political and government leadership positions all around the world, most dramatically in countries where elections themselves are relatively new. Women gained the right to vote in Kuwait in 2005; just four years later, four Kuwaiti women won parliamentary seats for the first time. One of the women elected, Massouma al-Mubarak, was also the country's first female cabinet minister. In Afghanistan, women couldn't even attend school in 2001, and the country's first presidential election didn't take place until 2004. In the summer of 2009, a whopping sixty-three women were running for nine provincial council seats set aside for women—despite harassment, threats, and continued repression. "I'm determined to see future generations of girls like my daughter gain confidence by seeing me and other women taking these steps," candidate Farida Bayat, thirty-seven, of Kabul, told National Public Radio. "Women are half the population of this country and should be taking part in politics and everything else."

Afghan women like Bayat are plunging into the fight for leadership positions at the risk of their own safety, even their own lives. Since she started campaigning, Bayat's received harassing phone calls and at least one death threat. Other female candidates have been harassed to the point where Afghanistan's ministry of the interior agreed to assign police protection to any female provincial candidate who asked for it.

In many other parts of the world, too, women's political participation is still risky, even life-threatening. In Iran, the offices of women's rights advocate and Nobel Peace Prize–winner Shirin Ebadi were raided and closed down in 2008, and twenty-six-year-old activist Neda Agha-Soltan was shot and killed while protesting the controversial 2009 presidential election results. But even in the most unlikely and dangerous settings, women are demanding a seat at the table and inspiring other women around the globe.

"The proportion of things happening all over the world is far greater on the positive side," says Cathy Allen. "Even moments that look like a backslide can be part of an inspirational moment. Even when a woman is killed in Iran, I guarantee you, a little girl in South Africa sees that on YouTube and says, 'I'm going to do this job.' When women are pushed down someplace, there are far more places where other women will be inspired."

Even in countries that don't yet have quotas or women in office, efforts are increasing to create a pipeline of future political leaders. Women's Learning Partnership for Rights, Development, and Peace is training women in twenty-two countries to work together to achieve local goals through better communication and group leadership.

"The leadership model we use stresses the practice of democratic decision making, communication, participatory and collective decision making," says Mahnaz Afkahmi, founder and president of Women's Learning Partnership. She previously served as Iran's minister of state for women's affairs and secretary general of the Women's Organization of Iran. "Everyone wants democracy, but they think it's putting a ballot in a box or getting people they like elected. They need to learn to do this through communication and dialogue and respect for each other."

Cathy Allen is training young women to become community leaders in Algeria, Tunisia, and other countries where women's political participation is still limited. "In some places where they don't have elections yet, but we believe they will get there, we want a class of young, bright women who have distinguished themselves in their own backyard. We're hoping to help them pull together community projects, from AIDS prevention to water quality inspection to young girls' reading programs. These are community projects that won't get them arrested but will make them visible, so when democracy happens, they're ready."

Programs like Women's Learning Partnership, Jordan's Women Helping Women Network, and others are putting qualified women leaders into a pipeline that can be tapped as needed. In Rabat, Morocco, one new program called Youth of Today, Leaders of Tomorrow is bringing together ambitious young women, ages twenty-two to thirty-four, from Algeria, Egypt, Libya, Morocco, and Tunisia. These young, educated, multilingual women are creating an international network of young women making changes in their community.

"The program provided us with training on personal and leadership qualities, how to be a successful advocate, and how to obtain grants," says Naagla El Dawy, thirty-four, of Assiut, Egypt. She runs a nonprofit in Assiut dedicated to human rights and community development, and attended the training to learn how other organizations in other countries were solving the same problems she faces. She's been inspired by the changes she's seen in Egypt during her own lifetime: "In the past, most girls in my village did not go to school. Now nearly all girls go to school." And she holds big ambitions. In five years, she told me, "I would like to be a member of the Shura Council," a house of Egypt's parliament. Why? Her words echo those we've heard from women in Afghanistan, in Jordan, in Portland, and Appleton, Wisconsin. "Women represent 49 percent of the population," she told me. "If we have more women in elected office, women's issues will receive much more concern, and laws concerning women will be enacted."

Equality Leapfrog

What's most striking about countries like Jordan and Morocco and Kuwait isn't how far behind they still are. It's how fast they're moving. The speed of this change reminds me of the lightning-fast spread of cell phones in developing countries that never had good landlines to begin with. When you start with a blank slate—without old infrastructures or habits to dismantle or alter—change can happen particularly fast.

Of course, in the United States, our slate isn't blank, nor would we want it to be. Many experts argue that quotas aren't needed in the United States—and that even if they were, they'd never be adopted because of America's squeamishness about affirmative action. Still, quotas requiring that women win a specific number of seats are a stunning example of how quickly change can happen. And they're not the only option.

"Quotas are one way to leapfrog ahead, but there are other mechanisms and systems that are friendlier to people who aren't historically in power," says Laura Liswood, secretary general of the Council of Women World Leaders. For instance, the prime minister of Spain promised that half his cabinet would be women. Many political parties abroad adopt internal policies promising that 20 to 30 percent of their candidates will be women.

But regardless of the mechanism for empowering women leaders, the need for new representation had never been more apparent than in 2008 and 2009, when the global economic crisis, environmental concerns, and political corruption blatantly exposed the shortcomings of status quo leadership.

"Women make particularly good candidates at about this time. People are sick and tired of the status quo, all over the world," says Cathy Allen. She's conducted focus groups in forty countries, including the United States, about voters' attitudes toward women. "Universally, there's an acceptance of women's characteristics. If you have a woman and a man and people know nothing about either, they ascribe certain characteristics to them. For women, it's that she listens better, that she asks the kinds of questions I'd like to ask, that she favors more transparency, that she'll reach out to other groups not at the table. These perceptions seem to be universal and they give women a hand up." There are some negative perceptions of women, too: Allen says voters think men are better with finance, more focused on the big picture.

True or not, stereotypes are giving women an edge right at the beginning of the twenty-first century. Increasing numbers of voters believe that women have the best leadership qualities during a time of economic crisis and disillusionment. And these perceptions seem to be helping women get into office—which, in turn, inspires other women to run.

"In so many communities, women are beginning to feel the strength of their own power," Allen says. "[This awakening] is moving internationally faster than nationally. The world is getting smaller every day. People in the poorest of places have access to TV or computers, and they see what choices women have elsewhere. When you see the top two parties in Mexico electing so many women, when you see women prime ministers and presidents in Germany and Liberia and Chile, it has an increasing effect on women's empowerment everywhere."

At home and abroad, pressure is growing. Soon the pressure to elect more women will prove irresistible. Much of that pressure comes from women themselves, seeing other women elected and asking, "Why not me?"

"Women in even the poorest places see that women around the world have choices, and say, 'Why don't I have choices?' When that happens, they dare to dream bigger," says Allen. "Those dreams," she says, "can set off a chain reaction leading to better conditions for everyone—and, ultimately, a healthier economy. My conjecture is that when women are elected, it has a positive effect on international corporate interests. I see companies starting to head to countries where women are beginning to feel the strength of their own power." Her theory: Women's demonstrated effect on improving education for children translates into better jobs for young women and ultimately improves their buying power—capturing the attention and investments of Western companies.

Whether the economic impact of women's growing political influence is as direct as Allen suspects, or whether it's more gradual and subtle, it's very clear that the more women lead, the faster their move to economic influence will take place—and the more economically influential women become, the smoother and more inevitable their political empowerment will be. It's a virtuous cycle, one that will ultimately benefit women *and* men, their families and their national economies. But it's far more than money that's driving this power shift: It's simple fairness. Women make up more than half the global population and a growing number of its workers: It's time that they share half the power.

NINE

Legacy

WHAT INFLUENCE LOOKS LIKE

At five-four, with a frank gaze, a hoarse bark of a laugh, and a ready store of wisecracks, Dr. Catherine (Cathy) DeAngelis, age sixty-eight, embodies the word "scrappy." The first woman editor in chief of *JAMA, the Journal of the American Medical Association,* she's been known to blast "The William Tell Overture" through the office sound system to shake up the place on a slow day. So it wasn't hard for me to imagine her as a young pediatrician, in 1973, barging into the office of the chair of pediatrics at Columbia University Medical Center.

"Tell him I'm holding a check for $50,000 and I don't know what to do with it," she announced to the secretary.

That's a lot of money today; it was even more back then.

Moments later, the chair came running out of his office.

"A check for $50,000?" He was animated and confused.

"Yeah, I just got a grant," DeAngelis said. "What do I do with it?"

"But how? Did you put it through the grant office?"

"There's a grant office?" she said.

DeAngelis was a brand-new faculty member at Columbia's College of Physicians and Surgeons. After high school, she'd become a nurse, then put herself through college and medical school. While completing her residency in pediatrics at Johns Hopkins University School of Medicine, she was troubled by the divide between doctors and nurses. The vast difference in their levels of authority wasn't helping patients, she thought. If pediatric nurses had just a little more training, they could diagnose and treat a lot of common childhood problems. More experienced nurses would cost less than doctors and provide better, faster care for kids.

She continued to ponder the question at Harvard, where she went to pursue her master's in public health. While there, she wrote a course description and a textbook to train pediatric nurse practitioners to work with doctors. Then she applied to a foundation for money to start a nurse practitioner program in Harlem.

Just as she started her new job at Columbia, the foundation called. "We don't fund things quite like this," the grant officer told DeAngelis. "But I want you to wait one hour. Then call this number at the New York Community Trust. Tell them you need $50,000."

Less than twenty-four hours later, DeAngelis brought the check to the pediatrics chair at Columbia and explained where it came from.

There was a long moment of silence.

Finally, he said, "But . . . funding doesn't work that way."

"I'm sorry," she replied. "Here's the check. Now what should I do with it?"

Spending the Check

I laughed out loud when DeAngelis told me about that moment. Of course, DeAngelis knew what she wanted to do with the check; she simply didn't know where to deposit it. She had a technical question, really. But for me, the check story is a tale of women's rising economic influence in a nutshell. Since the 1960s, women have been quietly socking away education, experience, and earning power, solving problems and inventing new ways of doing things. And now the question before us is this: What do we do with the check? How do we want to use our economic influence to shape the world?

Catherine DeAngelis has asked and answered that question many times in her long career; as we'll see, her answers have changed medicine for the better not once, but many times. Even now, past the age when many Americans retire, she's not slowing down; she's still thinking of the bigger picture, of how she can make a larger impact on medicine, help more patients, change the world.

Other women you'll read about in this chapter found their own ways of spending the check, each using her economic and personal influence to change the status quo in startling, sweeping ways. These are women who climbed the pyramid of economic power, developing their own earning potential and moving from confidence to full-blown influence. It's not that they are rich—most of them aren't—but they understand economic influence and how to use it. Their stories show economic empowerment in action.

Although this chapter tells the story of just five women, they'd be the first to tell you that they're a few among many thousands of other women who are using their economic influence to reshape the world. In turn, those thousands stand as beacons, inspiring millions more who are just now beginning to ask, "How am I going to spend this check?"

If only a tiny percentage of those women answer that question as wisely and as well as these five women did, the world will never be the same.

Influence from Within: Changing Medicine from the Inside Out

The pediatric nurse practitioner program that DeAngelis launched at Columbia is still going strong. In a striking coincidence, when she took the helm of *JAMA* nearly thirty years later (becoming one of the world's most influential voices in medicine), the magazine was about to run a story praising the nurse practitioner role and referring to the program she'd launched.

In the three decades between those moments, DeAngelis had improved medicine again and again, standing up to sexism, discrimination, and personal attacks. "I don't scare easily," she says.

Raised in a poor mill town in Pennsylvania, Cathy DeAngelis came from a family that valued education, although neither of her parents went to school past eighth grade. So when she announced at age four that she wanted to be a doctor (and began practicing surgery on her dolls), her father started saving his lunch money. In high school, well-meaning advisors nudged her toward nursing school. "Somebody told me the way girls become doctors is to be nurses first," she says. "They probably knew my parents couldn't afford four years of college."

But becoming a nurse turned out to be a valuable sidetrack for DeAngelis. She used her earnings as a nurse (supplemented by Dad's lunch money) to pay for her first year in college. From there, she won enough in scholarships to graduate with no debt and continue on to medical school at the University of Pittsburgh. That's where she decided she wasn't going to let anybody, ever, scare her away from her chosen path.

During her first year, she took a research course with a teacher who was uncomfortable with the idea of women entering medicine. He gave DeAngelis a zero on her first paper. She was shocked. She'd spent her summers in college working at the National Institutes of Health on research projects, and she knew her research skills were more than up to scratch. "It was Friday, and he told me to have a new paper on his desk on Monday afternoon." With biochemistry and anatomy exams on Monday morning, DeAngelis felt trapped and desperate. "All I really wanted to be my entire life is a doctor, and one way or another, I was about to fail out of med school," she recalls.

That night, she fell asleep studying and woke in the wee hours. She went down to the dorm bathrooms to wash her face. Miserable, she ran her hands under the warm water and noticed by the sink a jagged piece of glass from a broken mirror. "For one split second, I looked at that sliver and I thought, 'It would be so easy. I wouldn't have to worry about this anymore.'"

Then she got very, very angry. "I looked at myself in the mirror and I said, '*Nobody ever* is going to push me to that point.'" She went back to her room and slept. She aced her exams on Monday, then she marched into her professor's office and put her paper on his desk. "I tell you what we're going to do," she said. "You're either going to give me the fair mark I deserve, which is at a minimum a B, or we're going to the dean's office together" to have her paper, and those of her classmates, graded again, by an independent panel. "Are you ready to do that?"

He gave her an A. She never let anyone threaten her again. "What are they going to do to me?" she says now of her critics. "They can take my job, but they can't take the two things that mean the most to me: my family and the knowledge I have."

That courage, as well as her mastery of the inner workings of the medical field and academia, have helped her make major changes in medicine. As deputy chair of general pediatrics and adolescent medicine at Johns Hopkins, she attended a meeting in the early nineties where the mostly male department heads were outraged by a report alleging that women faculty members weren't being paid or promoted fairly. DeAngelis proposed to do her own study. With the backing of the dean and the department chairs at Johns Hopkins University School of Medicine, she sat down with each department head and reviewed the methodology she planned to use. Having approved her research plan, the men could hardly criticize her when her study showed that, indeed, women faculty members were being paid far less and promoted far less often than their male peers. Later, she became vice dean of the school, and within a few years, women faculty were earning more and their promotion rate increased. In 1991, she launched an annual report on the status of women, listing salaries and promotions. By 1994, most of the discrepancy was gone. Sixty percent of all women who've *ever* been promoted to professor at Johns Hopkins got their promotions during DeAngelis's nine years in the dean's office.

Along the way, as I mentioned in Chapter Four, she focused on building up women's networks. On every committee and leadership group, she stresses, "You need two or three women, because there are so many more men. So each woman has to pick one man and win him over. If you get on a committee as the only woman, no one will listen to you; if two of you get on a committee, the men will pit you against each other. But if there are three of you—and you each make an effort to befriend or associate with a male colleague—you will be heard." In this way, women were able to participate more fully as faculty members and get the backing they needed for promotions. DeAngelis gave women faculty members at Johns Hopkins tools that enabled them to succeed.

Meanwhile, she reformed the medical school curriculum at Johns Hopkins, making students spend more time with patients and learn the basics of compassionate care, not just high-tech science. Her focus on patient-centered education set a model for the rest of the country.

Today, as editor in chief of *JAMA*, she's making waves again, adopting policies to bring more transparency, honesty, and full disclosure to the results of medical research by pharmaceutical companies.

"If I publish something and I didn't do everything I could to make sure that it's as accurate and honest as it can be, and a patient gets hurt, then that's no different than if I sat there and treated the patient according to what I published. I'm just as responsible," she says. Among her reforms: She decreed that no study would be published in *JAMA* unless drug companies published *all* their research findings about a drug and stopped suppressing negative results. In 2004, she urged the International Committee of Medical Journal Editors to adopt the same standards.

Pharmaceutical companies have had to comply: They can't afford not to. They need the credibility and seal of approval that comes when *JAMA* and other major medical journals publish studies on their drugs. Their profits depend on it. So they play by the new rules. Although DeAngelis's tough standards and no-nonsense talk have won her enemies and sparked controversy at times, there's no denying that her savvy use of economic influence has changed medicine for the better.

In many ways, DeAngelis is extraordinary. Yet her story is just one example of how women are using their economic influence to transform the world. She's a woman who moved herself up economically from survival, but didn't rest on the comfortable plateau of financial security and confidence. Instead, she used her education, security, and understanding of the flow of money to influence the world. Not just for her patients and others (although she launched programs that have helped countless children), not just for the women she worked with (although at Johns Hopkins, she dramatically improved women's pay and promotion rates), but for patients everywhere. Along the way, she's shown just what women can do when our workplaces, our universities, our society let us get a foot in the door.

Influence from Without:
Redefining the "Bottom Line" in Pharmaceuticals

There's something restless about Victoria Hale, with her wide-set sincere eyes and mass of dark curls. Even when she's talking about her impressive accomplishments bringing affordable, life-saving drugs to poor families around the world, she sounds ever so slightly antsy, full of pent-up energy for her next project. Yes, at age forty-eight, she's already secured more than $100 million in grants from the Bill & Melinda Gates Foundation. Sure, she's also won the so-called genius grant from the MacArthur Foundation, a $500,000 award with no strings attached. But the energy that's brought her this far drives her relentlessly on to the next project.

Like DeAngelis, Hale started out low on the hierarchy of economic influence. Her parents were struggling government workers. Growing up in Maryland, Hale was often sick. She became fascinated by the way the body and drugs interact. "Most kids don't know about antibiotic resistance at age eight. I did," she tells me. At the state university, which she says, was "my only option because of our financial situation," she decided to study pharmacy. Her parents approved: A well-paid, secure job as a pharmacist seemed like a smart choice.

But going on to graduate school? Her mother, at least, wasn't so sure about that. When Hale broached the idea, her mother didn't say anything at first. Later, she pulled Hale aside.

"If you get that Ph.D.," Hale recalls her saying, "no one will want to marry you. You're already so strong-willed; with a Ph.D. on top of that, you're going to be single."

That was the early eighties, and the myth that strong, educated women didn't get married hadn't yet been fully dispelled.

Hale, who knew she wanted a family, was worried by her mother's concern.

So it took some courage for her to head for graduate school anyway. In the end, not only did her mother's dire predictions fail to come true—she met her husband, a doctor, just before starting her Ph.D. program—but ultimately, it was Hale's combination of Ph.D. *and* family that drove her to turn the entire business model of drug development on its head. She and her husband have two boys, Elliott, ten, and Gabriel, seventeen. Her love for her boys has shaped the course of her career.

As a friend of Hale's pointed out to her, "Of course you're passionate about saving children's lives. Once you're a mother, you're a mother to all children. It doesn't matter whose child it is."

After graduate school, Hale became a fast-rising star in drug development, working at Genentech and the U.S. Food and Drug Administration (FDA). "I'm a great drug developer," she says. "I could tell at the FDA early on which drugs would hit walls and which would succeed. I'm great at picking winners." But the more winners she picked, the more she became haunted by those people who were losing out.

"Only a limited number of people in the world can develop drugs, and most of them are in the United States or Europe. A few are in Japan. So you're working in this exclusive club," she says. And the club was neglecting millions of people. Even today, only 10 percent of global health research and development dollars go toward the conditions that make up 90 percent of the world's health problems. All over the world, in developing countries, millions of children a year die from diarrhea, from parasites, from malaria—illnesses and diseases that the right drugs could cure.

"At the executive level, it's almost all men," she says of the pharmaceutical industry. "These executives decide which diseases to tackle, which products to develop." Sometimes the numbers don't add up to a profit. Sometimes the research risks are too high. She points to eclampsia, a life-threatening pregnancy complication: Treatments could be developed, but the risks of testing drugs on pregnant women are too high for the taste of most lawyers and the companies they counsel.

Hale was troubled. Was it really true, she wondered, that pharmaceutical research and development were simply too expensive to create desperately needed medicines? Could a different business model challenge that paradigm? What if a company collected smaller revenues from a much larger number of people? Did a drug company have to earn profits *at all?*

The questions ate away at Hale, even as her career continued to thrive. She knew there had to be another way.

"To not do drug trials with pregnant women because you'll get sued? That's not in my reality," she says.

Then tragedy refocused her life. After a heartbreaking miscarriage in 1997, she left her job. She needed to think. She needed to spend time with her husband and five-year-old son, Gabriel, and to find more meaning in her life, her work.

And she did. Within a few months, she'd written the business plan for OneWorld Health, an institute to develop safe, effective, and affordable new medicines to fight infectious diseases in the developing world.

"The proposal came pouring out of me," she told me.

The idea was simple: Build a team of pharmaceutical scientists, ask drug companies to donate time and intellectual property, and reach out to developing countries where nonprofit hospitals and government organizations could help conduct trials and distribute medicines. Keep U.S. overhead low and hire as many overseas workers as possible.

"People said it would never work," Hale recalls. Then, in 2000, she realized she didn't need the support of any of the naysayers. She was riding to a conference in New York, chatting with her cabdriver, from Nigeria, when she mentioned she was a drug developer. "Oh, you have all the money!" he said.

And she realized she *did* have all the money—or at least the ability to earn it. She could use her own economic power to launch the idea. She took on lucrative consulting projects to fund the launch of her company. In 2001, the Institute for OneWorld Health became the first nonprofit pharmaceutical company in the United States. A year later, the Bill & Melinda Gates Foundation agreed to fund development of drugs to fight diseases that kill extremely poor people in India, Nepal, Bangladesh, and other developing countries.

Over the next few years, drug development proceeded and Hale received awards and accolades, including the MacArthur "genius grant." Meanwhile, she and her husband—a physician who now works for her company—had their second son, Elliott. "A lot of things lined up for me. I'm healthy, I have a good husband, a lot of people support me. If I were born twenty years earlier, if I were born into another family, this might not have happened," she says. In her house, gender roles are "sort of blurred. I'm the tough one, my husband's the sweet one," she says. She doesn't cook or clean during the week. But she's setting an example for her sons and teaching them to think about those in need. "We've taken them to Bangladesh, Nicaragua, Thailand," she says. She wants them to understand how lucky they are to have the advantages they do.

Still, as the Institute for OneWorld Health thrived, Hale felt restless. "With OneWorld Health, a lot of proof-of-concept was demonstrated. We showed that a nonprofit can develop a new medicine. But in the end, One-World was still dependent on philanthropy," she says. The next step was to prove that a pharmaceutical company can develop affordable drugs that help poor women and children and also operate at a profit. Instead of making tens of billions by developing blockbuster drugs, the company could aim for tens of millions and make sure that the well-being of women and children came first, before big profits. So, while remaining on the board of OneWorld Health, Hale launched Medicines 360, with the mission of becoming a sustainable company, developing needed, affordable drugs without asking for charity.

Fittingly enough, Medicines 360's first projects will focus on maternal health.

"I believe the way to make the world healthy is to heal children and families and communities by making women healthy and strong and empowered, so they can go on and make decisions and change the world," she says. Medicines 360's first product will be a new kind of affordable, highly effective contraception. Hale knows contraception is a hot-button topic, both in the United States and overseas. But worldwide, she points out, some 25 percent of pregnancies are unplanned. And unwanted pregnancies often lead to abortion or greater poverty. Preventing both those painful outcomes seems like worthy work.

Hale's desire to create a self-supporting pharmaceutical business, one not dependent on handouts, is part of the larger movement of social entrepreneurship, where start-up founders use the rules of market economics to improve the world. With their own children and the children of others on their minds, with their historic involvement in not-for-profit leadership and their growing professional success, it's not surprising that many social entrepreneurs are women, using their newfound economic influence and workplace experience to harness the power of the market for social good. Women like Hale are pioneering business models that earn profits, without letting profit alone dictate decisions. It's a delicate balance: Making money is hard enough without tracking the so-called triple bottom line—the financial, social, and environmental impact of a company. But the risky and rewarding work of social entrepreneurs like Hale is inspiring women like Priya Haji of Berkeley, Sweta Mangal of Mumbai, and the millions of women entrepreneurs helped by Grameen Bank and other microfinance institutions to become more savvy about the ways and workings of money, and to find innovative ways to generate it and channel it toward good.

Influence in Business: Harnessing the Market for Good

With her long dark hair and a fondness for beads and flowing fabrics, Priya Haji, thirty-seven, looks more Bohemian than boardroom. But those aren't just any beads she's wearing. They came from one of the dozens of artisan cooperatives she works with through her company, World of Good. That means the beads are not just beautiful but are "fair trade" products—the women who made them may have lived in Cambodia, Thailand, India, or thirty other countries, but they were paid fairly and not exploited.

You can wear Haji's beads, too, if you live near a Whole Foods Market or one of fifteen hundred other retail outlets where World of Good products are sold. Since its launch in 2004, the company has been phenomenally successful at bringing hundreds of products into the U.S. market and putting them on the shelves of mainstream stores. Haji and her team have also struck supplier-retailer partnerships with large corporations, including Disney and Hallmark, which now sell the company's beautiful, authentic handcrafted wares.

All of these business deals are part of a vision breathtaking in its ambition, a plan to turn World of Good into a household name brand, offering gift products from around the world produced by women paid fairly and treated well. If this vision becomes reality, Haji will not only build a thriving, profitable business but radically transform an entire sector of the global economy and help women around the world. Her mother is from India and her father is from East Africa. "But I've always been a person who swings for the fence," Haji says. As a teenager, she worked with her father, a doctor, to launch a low-income health clinic. In college, at Stanford, she helped create an addiction treatment program that now serves as a national model.

So when she turned her attention to fair-trade issues while at business school at U.C. Berkeley, she and her cofounder, Siddharth Sanghui, didn't open a single boutique or Web site. Instead, they imagined a profitable mainstream brand, selling through major retail outlets and assuring customers that they weren't supporting oppressive treatment of women overseas. "It's about creating a bridge between the women here who buy the products and the women who make them," she says.

Haji's ultimate goal is to use the power of profit to help solve a growing problem, one that reaches into your closet and mine.

As I write this at home in Orinda, California, I'm wearing a silky white shirt with a dark blue, hand-embroidered design on the collar, neck, and cuffs. I'm not sure where I got it—probably from the Gap or Banana Republic. The shirt certainly came from a factory, but those little patterns were very likely embroidered by a woman working in her home, in India or Bangladesh or El Salvador or Lesotho or elsewhere. In fact, 40 to 60 percent of globally outsourced production from big Western companies happens not in the factory but in the home, says Martha Alter Chen, a public policy lecturer at Harvard's John F. Kennedy School of Government. "And 80 to 90 percent of those workers are women."

These women are embroidering, beading, stitching soccer balls, assembling electronic parts, all at home. Sometimes they're paid fairly and treated fairly. In a few countries, shining examples of labor organizations, like India's Self-Employed Women's Association and Bangladesh's BRAC Bank, are finding ways to organize, help, and protect home workers. But for the most part, these skilled craftswomen are underpaid and exploited.

"Compared to other workers, the situation of home workers is so difficult," says Chen. Not only do they often earn less than $2 a day, but they pay for their own equipment, their own electricity and utilities. They're the first to be fired, the last to be paid. Of some three hundred million home workers worldwide, most are poor women, and many of those are women and teenage girls living in poverty.

It's a human tragedy. It's a gender tragedy. And, incidentally, it's a serious public relations threat for U.S. companies that want to be perceived as good corporate citizens. "If you're a responsible company," Haji says, "you want to be sure that those home workers are compensated fairly and have good working conditions and no child labor and so on."

You certainly *don't* want the kind of scandal Gap endured in 2007, when a British paper printed pictures of children embroidering clothes for GapKids in India. Embarrassed and facing potential boycotts, the company quickly announced measures to improve working conditions and better monitor who's doing the company's handwork and under what conditions.

No mom wants to buy clothes for her children that were made by child labor. And if they knew about it, I think most women wouldn't want to buy any product that pays workers so little that they're trapped in the unrelenting cycle of poverty.

This common sense is what Haji's banking on. By giving women an easy way to shop their conscience—and still get cute gifts—she hopes to harness the power of profit and use all her business savvy to help women home workers around the world.

"For me, what was engaging was asking, 'Can you really pop the top off this thing?'" she told me. "Can you really build something that takes [fair trade] to a whole new level, gets it to a whole new audience, and creates a commercial enterprise on an unprecedented endeavor for all these small communities at once?"

At World of Good's company headquarters in Emeryville, California, rows and rows of tall shelves hold cardboard boxes bursting with treasure: vibrantly colored tote bags made from grocery bags collected, washed, melted down, and woven by women in Delhi; gracefully curved bamboo plates patiently polished by women in Vietnam; olive green messenger bags from India; gleaming emerald trays from Kenya; orange striped scarves from Egypt; pendants of resin, glass, and cinnamon from Bali. Entrancing as the collection is, Haji realized from the start that no matter how popular her items were, World of Good's sales would influence only a tiny fraction of the $55 billion U.S. market for informal economy goods. And her dream was bigger. Much bigger.

That's why, at the same time she started up the company (bankrolling it with her own savings), Haji launched its sister nonprofit, the World of Good Development Organization, which receives 10 percent of the company's profits. The nonprofit was built right into the very structure of her start-up. To date, the nonprofit side of World of Good has built an online database called the Fair Wage Guide, including twenty-two thousand entries from sixty-one countries, showing how much each individual worker was paid for a given piece of work. Some 750 companies have used the Fair Wage Guide to make sure they're paying fairly: A survey of the site's users showed that 80 percent of those companies raised their payments to artisans, sometimes by as much as 200 percent, after reading the guide. These raises have meant increased wages for more than fifty thousand low-income home workers in sixty developing countries.

The World of Good Development Organization, which also raises funds separately from those provided by World of Good's profits, is now working on using text-message technology to connect home workers in developing countries to one another and to information about fair wages and conditions. (These workers are much more likely to have cell phone access than computer access, so text messaging is the form of electronic communication most likely to reach them.) World of Good Development Organization is also gathering information for a living wage database, so employers can figure out the cost of living in various countries. And the World of Good nonprofit also funds projects like schools and wells in the communities where it employs women.

Imagine approaching investors with this pitch: "I'm going to build a major brand to convert more shoppers to buying fair trade products, and I'm going to donate 10 percent of the profits to my foundation." Yet Haji's approach didn't scare off investors. To the contrary. With her Stanford-Berkeley pedigree and her well-thought-out business model, she won major business plan competitions and attracted major investors.

"Some investors are interested because of the social mission, and some are interested in the idea of a commercial brand that will become valuable," she says. "They know there's going to be a new set of socially responsible brands that will come forward and dominate the market, like Odwalla or Ben & Jerry's, or Whole Foods," she says. "The idea was to expand that into other categories. Peoples saw the commercial opportunity."

Considering how few women-run companies land venture capital, Haji's success speaks volumes about her talent, and about the business community. Some investors see that helping women economically can also be good business.

At least, that's what the principals at DFJ Frontier, a West Coast venture capital fund, figured when they invested in the company. World of Good wouldn't have the same profit margin on each item as a company that paid rock-bottom prices for its goods. But DFJ Frontier knows that a big profit margin alone isn't the key to business success. Look at Amazon .com: The company makes less per book than traditional retailers; its success comes from creating millions of fanatically loyal customers.

"Sometimes lowering your profit margin slightly can produce better long-term financial results, if it provides incentives for a network of partners to trust each other," says Scott Lenet, cofounder and managing director of DFJ Frontier. "World of Good has done exactly that in the category of ethically sourced products, attracting not only artisan groups in developing countries, but also large distribution partners like eBay and Whole Foods." So what if World of Good makes less per item? So does Amazon. "World of Good is working to accomplish something analogous by ensuring that producers who may be traditionally exploited are paid fairly."

Less profit margin, sure. Loyal customers and suppliers, very likely. Smart business? Definitely.

"Doing this as a solid business helps everyone," Haji says. "Yes, we will empower millions of women around the world, but it's a commercial endeavor—for the women who are making the products and for us."

Women like Haji and Victoria Hale have moved far away from the 1960s activists, suspicious of profit and the capitalist system. Instead, they want to harness its power for good—for the profit of the company and for the world's women. "For me, profit is part of the integrity of it," says Haji. "My life should be tied to this with the same economic pressure that theirs is."

If Haji's business thrives, so will the women at the very bottom of the supply chain. She's reaching from the peak of the economic pyramid down to the survival level and helping women pull themselves up to confidence. *That's* influence at work.

Influence in Investing:
Patient Capital

On November 26, 2008, Sweta Mangal, then thirty-two, of Mumbai, was at a party at Mumbai's Cricket Club when she got a text message from her office, asking her to come in right away. Like the city's other nineteen million inhabitants, she had no idea that terrorists had floated into Mumbai on rubber rafts, armed with assault rifles, bombs, and hand grenades.

But within minutes of the first attack, Mangal and the company she runs, Dial 1298 for Ambulance, found themselves at the heart of the drama. When gunmen opened fire on the crowd at Leopold Cafe, a bystander called Mangal's company immediately, and her ambulances began to arrive within eight minutes of the attack, before police or media. They were also first to arrive at the Taj hotel, where terrorists had seized the second floor.

During the next three days, terrorist attacks would leave 170 people dead or wounded, and Dial 1298 for Ambulance would transport 125 victims, with 30 ambulances and 90 crew members working around the clock at a time when most Mumbai residents were afraid to leave their homes. Mangal spent the whole time in the ambulance dispatch room. "Emotionally, it was good because we ended up helping people. But at another level, I was scared, because our staff was right there where it was happening. I kept thinking, 'What if something happens to our people? How do I help them?'"

Since the company's launch in 2005, Dial 1298 has revolutionized emergency transportation in India. "Before we started to operate ambulances that were equipped with advanced life support systems and doctors and lifesaving equipment, and asked people to pay for it, nobody thought it could be done," says Mangal, who has been Dial 1298's CEO from the beginning.

But Mangal had studied in the United States, getting her MBA at Rochester Institute of Technology; two of her company's cofounders, Shaffi Mather and Ravi Krishna, had also studied overseas. What a difference they'd seen between emergency transportation in India and elsewhere: One night, Mather's mother in Mumbai started choking and Mather couldn't get an ambulance to come. Although his mother survived, it was a harrowing experience. At almost the same time, Krishna's mother had a heart attack in New York; an ambulance pulled to the door four minutes later and saved her life. When these three friends met with two others over dinner in Mumbai and compared these two incidents, they recognized the business opportunity. "We wanted to bring services like 911 to India," says Mangal. They also wanted to figure out a business model that would let them provide reliable, round-the-clock service even for poor callers.

The five friends pooled their money and purchased two state-of-the-art ambulances for $50,000 each in 2005. At first, the company tried a "pay what you can afford" model, but they found that few people paid when given the choice. Next, they tried charging based on hospital. Wealthier patients wanted to go to expensive private hospitals; poor patients to cheaper public hospitals. Transportation to public clinics was half-price or free, depending on the patient's ability to pay; everybody else paid the full price. It worked.

By 2008, the company was servicing nearly twenty-seven thousand calls—about 16 percent for free. Today, the company has 60 ambulances and 391 employees, and it's making a profit. Local governments have hired Dial 1298 to create similar services in their cities; Mangal and her colleagues have had calls from Sri Lanka and other developing countries asking for help setting up ambulance companies. "Any developing country would rather have a self-sustaining ambulance service than a fully funded ambulance run by the government," she says. "I know that I need to be in a business where it's impacting life, and also making money."

Dial 1298 is a model with big potential. At least, that's what U.S.-based investor Jacqueline Novogratz thinks. She invested nearly $1.6 million in the company, adding it to the portfolio of social investments held by Acumen Fund, a venture fund that takes philanthropic dollars and invests them in sustainable businesses. Dial 1298, she says, "is building a scalable model that can sustain itself."

Mangal's company is one of thirty-five companies that Acumen Fund has invested in, to foster viable businesses that also deliver critical goods and services, often to poor people. In many ways, Acumen is another hybrid, an inspired mash-up between a philanthropic foundation and a venture capital fund. A nonprofit, it takes philanthropic donations, but channels them into savvy, profit-minded companies showing innovative, market-oriented solutions to social problems. With its successful investments, Acumen Fund makes its own endeavor sustainable, funneling any return back into the fund to seed more social ventures.

"The market is a place to start, and it is also limited," Jacqueline Novogratz told me. On the one hand, she believes investing in local companies that make a profit creates sustainable solutions. Local companies are also culturally appropriate, usually created and run by residents of the company's home country.

But Novogratz is not naïve about the market. Far from it. Since her teenage years in Virginia, she's known that the market alone can't solve social problems. When she was eighteen, her father, a veteran, needed triple bypass surgery. "The quality of the military surgical care at that time meant that there was an 8 percent mortality rate. My mother was pregnant with her seventh child," she told me.

Fortunately, a wealthy friend stepped in and paid for her father to have surgery at a hospital where the mortality rate for this procedure was just 2 percent. "I want a world where everyone has access to high-quality health care," Novogratz says. "But not everyone is going to be able to afford it. So can you create systems, using the market, to get as many people as possible to afford it, and then recognize that a good society will create opportunities for all others to get access?" That's what she's trying to do with Acumen Fund, with its hybrid emphasis on companies that can provide low-cost basic services but turn a profit.

Those profits, and any returns to Acumen, can be a long time coming. But in the end, Novogratz believes her hybrid solution makes the most of the strengths of the market, while limiting its weaknesses. She doesn't call her strategy "venture capital"; she calls it "patient capital." "It uses the best of both worlds. It expects low market return and has a very long time horizon, so you have the chance to make some of these innovations work."

Novogratz, forty-seven, who trained as a banker and as an economic development consultant, has a hybrid background herself. As a banker just out of college, she conducted audits for Chase around the world, and saw enormous missed opportunities. "Low-income people in Latin America didn't get access to credit at all. In fact, many of them didn't have the confidence even to walk into the doors of the bank," she recalls. She proposed that Chase extend banking services to poor people. "My thought was that maybe they would pay back more, and that Chase would actually do very well." Had her boss taken the idea, maybe he'd have won the Nobel Peace Prize, like Muhammed Yunus, who launched Grameen Bank to provide microcredit in Bangladesh. Instead, her boss "just kind of patted me on the head." Later, Novogratz worked for international aid organizations and foundations in Africa, learning about the benefits and limitations of aid. "Charity done in traditional ways, as well as aid done in traditional ways, will not solve poverty. In fact, it usually ends up creating dependency," she says.

Her fund picks up where microcredit leaves off. Instead of lending $50 or $500, she invests $500,000 or a million to companies like Dial 1298 for Ambulance. "We are not investing in entrepreneurs that might employ two or three people. We're investing in entrepreneurs that are serving a million." (And the technical expertise and consulting Acumen provides may be as important as the money the fund invests. "Acumen Fund is an active board member who helps give us strategic direction," says Mangal. At the same time, she adds, Acumen "gives us the freedom to make the day-to-day business decisions ourselves.")

The companies that excite Novogratz most are those with the potential to impact the most people in the most places. Another of her pet projects, Aravind Eye Hospital in Madurai, India, treats a million patients and does 250,000 cataract surgeries in a year. Most patients don't pay anything, or just a few rupees, because, like Dial 1298's, the hospital's services are priced on a sliding scale. Wealthy patients pay to stay in private rooms with air-conditioning. The patients treated for free sleep in large rooms on mats. But they share doctors. "You're getting the same level of health care even if you're not getting the same level of amenities," Novogratz says.

Like all venture funds, Acumen won't hit a home run every time, and significant barriers stand in the way of many of its companies. Dial 1298 for Ambulance, for instance, tried to get an easy-to-remember number like 911, but refused to bribe government officials for the number.

"If you're not ready to pay up, you will not get some contracts and some benefits that you would otherwise. But as a group, we do not believe in giving in to corruption. We fight for the right things to be done in the right way," says Mangal. So she and her cofounders got stuck with the not terribly memorable "1298" phone number and have had to rely on their own hard work to make it memorable.

Acumen and its associated businesses also have to navigate treacherous gender territory. In many of the Acumen-funded companies, the vast majority of employees are women. "Acumen and the businesses it funds have about eighteen thousand employees, and anywhere between 80 and 90 percent are female," Novogratz told me. Partly, it's the choice of employers. "If you talk to the entrepreneur who runs A to Z Textile Mills in Tanzania, who employs seven thousand people, 90 percent women, he will say they are better employees. They come to work early. They stay late," she says. The money paid to women goes back to help their families. "The boys will often go AWOL after they get paid. Something like 60 percent of women's income typically goes to the family, compared to 30 percent of men's income."

As women earn more and begin to lift their families from poverty, they encounter cultural resistance. "There are arguments, and many people have made them to me, that [providing fair-wage jobs for women] is a bad thing because you're disrupting family," Novogratz admits. "But I think all change comes with a price. This change is about rebalancing what it means to be human beings, when all human beings are participating in society."

Influence in Global Peace:
The Tea Party That Changed the World

On a hot November day in Nairobi, Kenya, in 2004, the composed, well-tailored Iranian lawyer and former judge Shirin Ebadi took tea with Jody Williams, the brash American activist who peppers her polemics with salty unprintables. It was an unlikely tea party. Yet they were slated to meet again for tea the next day, with a third guest, Wangari Maathai of Kenya, who had just joined Ebadi and Williams in a very small club—women winners of the Nobel Peace Prize.

"In the one-hundred-and-eight-year history of the Nobel Peace Prize, only twelve women have received it," Williams told me on the phone recently. Seven of those women are alive today. Williams and Ebadi received their awards for very different kinds of work—Williams, in 1997, for bringing dozens of NGOs and governments together to oppose the use of land mines in war; Ebadi, in 2003, for campaigning fearlessly (despite death threats, harassment, and imprisonment) for the rights of women and children in Iran. Their backgrounds and personal causes were worlds apart. But in the sunny garden café in Nairobi, as they drank their tea, they came up with a novel idea to advance their shared desire for a more peaceful world.

What if all the living women Nobel Peace Prize winners banded together to promote the role of women in *creating* a more peaceful world? These Nobel laureates realized they could combine their fund-raising power and connections to support the peacemaking efforts of other women around the world. They could bring women from every continent together to share their ideas and to underscore the commonalities between seemingly disparate projects advancing the good of the planet, economic security of families, fairness of government, and peace itself.

It was a simple idea—but one that none of the male Nobel winners had ever launched.

Williams loved the idea. It made perfect sense, she told me a few years after that tea. "Women suffer the most during war, and have the least to say about peace, and struggle to keep things together during war. They don't get recognized. The men who make the war get recognized." Her words echoed the spirit of the United Nations in 2000, when it passed a security resolution acknowledging that women and children account for the vast majority of people harmed by wars, and calling for a greater role for women in creating peace. Although that resolution passed in 2000, little had changed by 2004.

The day after that meeting in the café, Ebadi and Williams broached the idea with Maathai, the first woman in East and Central Africa to earn a doctorate degree and the first woman to chair a department of veterinary anatomy at a major university in the region. Maathai had led poor Kenyan women to plant more than twenty million trees to reforest their country in what became known as the Green Belt Movement. Innocuous as tree planting may sound, Maathai's efforts had far-reaching effects on government, the economy, the status of women, and the health of the planet. The brilliant and colorful Maathai immediately signed on to the plan that Ebadi and Williams proposed. Soon, the three enlisted the help of three more women who had received the Nobel Prize: Guatemala's Rigoberta Menchú Tum, who worked to improve the rights of indigenous people like herself in Guatemala, and Ireland's Betty Williams and Mairead Corrigan Maguire, who shared the 1976 prize for their crusade against sectarian violence in Northern Ireland. (The seventh living woman laureate, Aung San Suu Kyi, remains under house arrest in Burma/Myanmar.)

Funded initially by the Nobel laureates themselves (who each received a prize of about $1.4 million), the Nobel Women's Initiative officially launched in 2006. The six laureates were quickly able to convert their enormous moral prestige into economic influence and soon won additional funding from groups including the Global Fund for Women, UNIFEM (the United Nations Development Fund for Women), the Tides Foundation, and many others.

The group's mission is to promote, spotlight, and grow the work of women's rights advocates and organizations worldwide that address the root causes of violence. "It's about promoting peace with justice and equality," Williams told me. "Peace is not just the absence of armed conflict. That's only the baseline."

Maathai had expressed much the same sentiment when she received the Nobel Prize in 2004, connecting the dots between what had previously been seen as separate silos—government, economics, the environment, and peace: "Managing resources in a sustainable way and governing ourselves in a more democratic, inclusive way where we respect human rights and respect diversity and promote equity—that is very, very important to peace. When you do so, you preempt some of the reasons we fight each other."

The Nobel Women's Initiative came together amazingly quickly: Its first international conference took place in Ireland in 2007, its second in 2009, in the Guatemalan city of Antigua, hosted by laureate Rigoberta Menchú Tum. The attendees who gathered in this cobbled-street town ran the gamut of experience and geography. An Egyptian journalist roomed with the director of a group of Jewish and Palestinian women working for peace; a member of Ghana's parliament rubbed elbows with a political advocate from Kyrgyzstan.

Not every invited attendee could make it: Two Iranian women were stopped at the airport in Tehran and their passports were confiscated. The incident was a reminder to other attendees about just how much change is still needed.

Mingling amid fountains and hanging gardens in the courtyards, or sitting before laptops in conference rooms, this international group discovered that their wide diversity of experience led them to a whole new definition of "peace"—a definition that links economic empowerment for women, financial security for families, the rise of women in parliamentary bodies, the integrity of the environment and natural resources, and the basic human rights of men and women around the world. The meeting culminated with the adoption of a resounding declaration, one that included an eloquent statement of how far we've come and how far we have to go.

"No country or society can claim to be democratic when the women who form half its citizens are denied their right to life, to their human rights and entitlements and to safety and security," the conference participants declared. "Despite this, we women have made extraordinary efforts to democratize the institutions of society that frame our lives and the well-being of all humanity—the family, the community, clan, tribe, ethnic or religious group, political, legal, economic, social, and cultural structures, and the media and communications systems." The assembled leaders made clear their contributions would only grow bolder: "We are in search of democracy that transforms not just our lives, but all society— and we will not be silenced until it is achieved in every part of the world."

Just Imagine

An allegation I sometimes encountered while writing this book was that women "play small," that women focus most on their own families and children, that they don't dream big enough. But the determination of the Nobel Women's Initiative to bring a transformative democratic vision to every corner of the world is a ringing refutation of that allegation.

The more than one hundred interviews with women that I conducted for this book are a rebuttal to that allegation as well. When women are treated fairly, when they don't bear the burden of poverty and they're blessed with education, when they're not saddled with the impossible job of working full-time while doing almost all of the parenting and home-making themselves, and when their safety and even lives are not threatened when they speak politically—when those simple requirements are met, what happens next is so enormous, it looks like a miracle.

Meeting the basic requirements of survival and independence is still a significant challenge for most of the women in the world (57 percent of the world's population lives on less than $2.50 a day; most poor people are women and children). Globally, "women perform 66 percent of the world's work, produce 50 percent of the food, but earn 10 percent of the income and own 1 percent of the property," according to a 2007 report by UNICEF.

But in the stories of Catherine DeAngelis, of Victoria Hale, of Priya Haji, of Jacqueline Novogratz, and of the Nobel Prize–winning women, we can find hope. And in the stories of countless other women, in this book and outside of it, we can see that when laws, community practices, and workplace policies give women even a small opening, lightening their loads even a little bit, women can change the world in ways no one dreamed possible. Yes, some women reach economic confidence and stop there, simply enjoying the benefits of material wealth and security. But a growing number of women are climbing to influence and exercising that influence to create a lasting legacy by transforming their positive personal vision into action in the world.

As I write, the world is at the very beginning of women's shift to true influence. But already, we see that this shift can take many forms. Influence is Kawtar Chyraa coaching high school girls on their college entrance essays while finishing her internship at Toyota of Morocco and applying to business schools overseas. It's Ann Lininger running for city council. It's Cathy Benko designing a whole new career model for women and men at Deloitte. It's Jody Williams bringing about a signed international treaty to ban land mines, then bringing women around the world together to think even bigger about peace.

Women's economic influence is happening at every level of society, in every sphere, starting as a tiny ripple, spreading out ring by ring into waves, surges, tsunamis of new vision sweeping over our world. As I write and as you read, women are just beginning to unleash their economic influence, and the smartest workplaces, legislatures, and families see that they have no choice but to follow: It's the bright thing to do.

Visionary companies, lawmakers, husbands, fathers, and sons are already joining with influential women to make staggering changes. Imagine what will happen just a few years from now, as economic imperatives weed out the underperforming companies that fail to move women to management, as financial realities penalize countries that squelch the talents and resources of half their population.

Imagine what could happen if women didn't have to work the second shift.

Imagine what could happen if women were even a third of the voices in national assemblies.

Imagine if women in the global north looked to their sisters in the southern hemisphere and lent them a hand, choosing to buy products that lift the poorest women and their children from poverty, moving them closer to the day when they, too, can seize their own economic influence.

And to imagine that?

Think big.

What You Can Do

This book is the story of women rising. It's also the story of women waiting. In Uganda, will Joan Ahimbisibwe's daughter take the next step out of poverty? Will Kawtar Chyraa in Morocco win that scholarship to an international business school? Will Priya Haji grow her business into a national brand, and if so, can she continue to balance profits with progress for women?

The power shift is happening. But the speed of that shift is up to everyone. As women unleash the full power of economic emancipation, the world is waiting to see what happens. How will women use their power?

And how will you use yours?

You can speed up the power shift yourself, right here, right now.

You can visit our Web site at www.influence-book.com, for links to blogs and other Web sites, or follow our tweets at MaddyDychtwald. At our site, we've set up easy ways for you to contribute funds and ideas to groups who are advancing women's economic emancipation in the United States and around the world. We're also doing our part to support these organizations by contributing a percentage of the proceeds of this book to support groups we've mentioned in it.

Here are a few suggestions for what you can do to help shift economic power:

1. Foster *financial knowledge, education, and expertise* for women and girls. If you don't feel financially savvy, take a class to get

yourself on the right path. And encourage your children—girls *and* boys—to learn how to manage their financial futures.

2. Support paid family leave, paid sick leave, and other *family-friendly work policies*. Vote for these policies and ask for them at work. One good place to stay up-to-date on these policies is the Families and Work Institute (www.familiesandwork.org).

3. Insist that *great, affordable child care* is a family issue, *not* a women's issue. Join MomsRising at www.momsrising.org. They'll update you on concrete (and easy and fun) actions you can take to improve child care (and many other issues in this list).

4. *Run for office* or support women who do. Contribute to the Women Under Forty Political Action Committee. If you're pro-choice, join EMILY's List. If you're pro-life, join the Susan B. Anthony list. If you're interested in running for office, look into campaign training programs such as Emerge USA, the White House Project, and the Women's Campaign School at Yale University.

5. Buy products that *pay women fair wages*. Buy your holiday presents and other gifts from World of Good (www.worldofgood.com) or the related WorldofGood.com by eBay, or from Ten Thousand Villages, SERRV, or other socially responsible companies. Before buying from big U.S. retailers, read their social responsibility policies online (it takes five minutes and you'll feel much better). Learn more about fair trade at the Fair Trade Resource Network (http://www.fairtraderesource.org/) or the Fair Trade Federation (www.fairtradefederation.org).

6. Invest in companies and enterprises that *help women help themselves*. Support groups we've mentioned in this book, like World of Good Development Organization and Acumen Fund. Or find your own favorite. Kiva.org allows you to make small loans to

women around the world. BeadforLife supports women artisans. Heifer International supplies livestock, seeds, and agricultural training to struggling communities. There are thousands of other groups helping women: Let your dollars help, too.

7. *Mentor girls.* Support or take part in programs that bring girls into the workplace or to universities, and that encourage them to enter math- and science-based fields. Girls Inc., Girl Scouts, and Big Brothers/Big Sisters of America are good places to begin. Or start a mentoring program for young women through your professional organization.

8. *Enlist men.* Encourage your husband, brothers, sons, male employees, and coworkers to take paternity leave, work flexible hours, and help lobby for change. And remember, a "his and hers" world is a win for everyone. Remind the men in your life.

9. *Encourage your company, your community, and your country to support women in power.* Remember that the most successful companies and countries have something in common: They tap the best human talent available from *both* genders.

10. *Spread the word.* Blog, tweet, and spread the word about ideas, initiatives, and efforts to help women help themselves. We've mentioned many in the book. But we want to know about more. Please share your story and other initiatives you've admired at our Web site (www.influence-book.com). And share what you've learned here with the women and men in your own network. Together, we can connect the dots. We can speed up the power shift and change everything, everywhere, for the better.

Acknowledgments

Books, like most creative endeavors, are team efforts. I was lucky enough to have a fantastic team to help turn my idea into this special book. My heartfelt thanks to all those wonderful people who have contributed to this process.

- My husband, Ken, for being my power partner and soul mate for life, showering me with love, laughter, support, and a critical eye when needed.
- My son, Zak, who amazes me every day with his spirit, soul, wisdom, and wit.
- My daughter, Casey, who boldly wears her beauty and imagination on the inside and out.
- Sally and Ray Fusco and Pearl and Seymour Dychtwald, all of whom help me understand the unflinching power of love and family.
- Richard, Linda, Joel, David, and Michelle Kent, as well as Alan Dychtwald, who provide lifetime friendship, support, and love and complete my circle of family.
- Christine Larson, whose shining intelligence, organizational skills, and strong writing chops have made for the perfect partnership.
- My ace research team—David Baxter, Jamie Nichol, Zak Dychtwald, and Rebecca Geiger—who were unrelenting in their search for truth and meaning.
- Elyse Pellman and Sarah Werling, for their excellent work organizing and executing the discussion groups—and everything else—that were essential to this book.

- Robyn Hamilton, for her patience and attention to the smallest details—from creating illustrative charts to tirelessly organizing endnotes.
- Doris Michaels, for her partnership, direction, and advice in finding the best home for this book.
- Barbara Jones, whose enthusiasm, insightful editing, and constant support were my guiding lights. Together with Ellen Archer, she has championed this book from the start.
- Heather Chaplin, who helped me bring this book to life.
- Ger Sindell, who made me dig deep to focus my early ideas and create a potent book vision.
- Shawn Lenise, for her positive nature and for helping to make my life work.
- The more than one hundred incredible women and men who generously shared their time, experience, energy, and candid insights for this book. Words don't begin to cover my gratitude.
- Age Wave and everyone who has been associated with it over the years, for being a source of joy, learning, and many original ideas.

—MADDY DYCHTWALD

My deepest gratitude and love to Richard Rojo and our sons, Alexander and Zachary. A shout-out to Jolie Solomon, David Hale Smith, and Rebecca Geiger for helping it all come together. And my sincere and humble thanks to every person we interviewed, for generously sharing his or her time, expertise, and stories.

—CHRISTINE LARSON

Notes

CHAPTER ONE

4   *A nation's competitiveness*: Ricardo Hausmann, Laura D. Tyson, and Saadia Zahidi, *The Global Gender Gap Report 2007* (World Economic Forum, 2007).

5   *In 2009, in the United States*: Catherine Rampell, "As Layoffs Surge, Women May Pass Men in the Job Force," *New York Times,* February 5, 2009.

5   *The number of women earning $100,000*: Employment Policy Foundation, Analysis of Government Accounting Office Data, 2004.

5   *Between 2000 and 2008*: *Time Wage and Salary Workers by Selected Characteristics, Quarterly Averages, Historic Data, 2000–2008* (Current Population Survey, Bureau of Labor Statistics).

6   *Already, about 40 percent of U.S. private firms*: *Key Facts About Women-Owned Businesses 2007–2008* (Center for Women's Business Research, 2008).

6   *compared to only 26 percent*: *Survey of Business Owners,* U.S. Census Bureau, 1997.

6   *In Cuba, women hold more technical*: Hausmann, Tyson, and Zahidi, *The Global Gender Gap Report.*

6   *In the United States, women already*: Marti Barletta, *Marketing to Women* (Chicago: Dearborn, 2006).

6   *More than $5 trillion*: Jane Cunningham and Philippa Roberts, "Female Consumerism," *Brand Strategy*, December 18, 2006.

6   *$4.9 trillion in 2008*: International Monetary Fund. World Economic Outlook Database, 2009.

10   *Today, women hold 57.5 percent*: M. Planty et al., "Student Effort

and Educational Progress" in *The Condition of Education* (National Center for Education Statistics, 2009).

10   *In the Arab world, literacy rates*: The Global Gender Gap Report *2008* (World Economic Forum, 2008).

13   *When a corporation adds more women*: The Bottom Line: Connecting Corporate Performance and Gender Diversity (Catalyst, 2004).

CHAPTER TWO

18   *Of 1.1 billion people*: Anita Petry, *The Missing Piece of the Poverty Puzzle* (United Nations Millennium Campaign, October 16, 2007).

18   *In India, more than a third*: International Labour Organization, *Global Employment Trends for Women 2009*.

19   *In all developing regions as a whole*: United Nations, *The Millennium Development Goals Report 2009*.

19   *"For the past two decades"*: "Women in the Workforce: The Importance of Sex," *The Economist*, April 12, 2006.

19   *The development of those two booming*: Correspondence with Kathleen DeBoer, Organisation for Co-operation and Development.

23   *By 2006, about 5 percent*: Current Population Reports 2006 (U.S. Census Bureau Statistical Abstract of the United States).

23   *In the UK, women will*: Avivah Wittenberg-Cox and Alison Maitland, *Why Women Mean Business* (New York: John Wiley & Sons [Jossey-Bass], 2008).

23   *Around 40 percent of high-net-worth*: Lloyds TSB Bank, *Women and Wealth* newsletter, spring 2007.

23   *It wanted to sell soaps*: Marti Barletta, "The Real Story Behind the Success of Dove's Campaign for Real Beauty," *MarketingProfs Today* 6, no. 8 (February 20, 2007).

24   *Rwanda's constitution doesn't mandate*: Association for Women's Rights in Development, *Rwanda: The Impact of Women on Policy Legislation* (December 2008).

28   *Women are more likely to enroll*: Gur Huberman, Sheena S. Iyengar, and Wei Jiang, "Defined Contribution Pension Plans: Determinants

of Participation and Contributions Rates," Springer Science + Business Media, 2007.

28   *And they're more likely to buy*: Hewitt Associates, "Hewitt Research Shows Women Much Less Prepared to Retire Than Men."

30   *A survey by Hewitt Associates*: Ibid.

CHAPTER THREE

41   *Compare that revenue to the sales*: Natasha Singer, "Skin Deep: Why Should Kids Have All the Acne?" *New York Times*, October 18, 2007.

43   *In the United States, 85 percent of corporate*: "Statistical Overview of Women in the Workplace," Catalyst, 2008.

43   *Globally, senior male executives*: Ellen Galinsky et al., *Leaders in a Global Economy: A Study of Executive Women and Men*, Families and Work Institute, Catalyst, and Boston College Center for Work and Family (January 2003).

44   *Every day, more than four hundred*: Margaret Heffernan, "Are Women Better Entrepeneurs?" *Forbes*, June 27, 2006.

47   *Nearly half (47 percent)*: Kathryn Kobe, *The Small Business Share of GDP, 1998–2004* (SBA Office of Advocacy, Small Business Research Summary no. 299, April 2007).

48   *Although British women*: Elaine Allen, Amanda Elam, Nan Langowitz, and Monica Dean, *Global Entrepreneurship Monitor: 2007 Report on Women and Entrepreneurship* (The Center for Women's Leadership at Babson College).

53   *The Diana Project*: Candida Brush et al., *Gatekeepers of Venture Growth: A Diana Project Report on the Role and Participation of Women in the Venture Capital Industry* (Kauffman Foundation, 2004).

54   *The industries with the highest percentage*: Alicia M. Robb and Susan Coleman, Kauffman Firm Survey, *Characteristics of New Firms: A Comparison by Gender* (January 2009).

CHAPTER FOUR

62   *"There's really nothing quite like it"*: Paul J. Lim, "Jessica Bilbiowicz, Blazing a Trail of Her Own," *US News & World Report,* November 28, 2004.

65   *"They're college educated Americans"*: Tina Brown, "The Gig Economy," *Daily Beast,* January 12, 2009.

68   *In a 2008 survey of*: Emily Heller, "General Counsel Pressuring Firms Amid Recession," *National Law Journal,* March 2009.

69   *No wonder unemployment among*: Stewart Verney, "Survival of the Flexible: Law Firms Are Shifting Focus to Weather the Downturn," *Jacksonville Business Journal,* May 15, 2009.

69   *The initial trials were so successful*: Michelle Conlin, "Smashing the Clock," *BusinessWeek,* December 11, 2006.

69   *Similarly, at Capital One*: Claire Shipman and Kay Katty, *Womenomics: Write Your Own Rules for Success* (New York: Harper Business, 2009).

70   *By 2016, there will be three million*: Peter McStravick, "The War for Talent," *Talent Management,* January 2007.

71   *In one recent survey of CEOs*: the Conference Board, *CEO Challenge 2007.*

74   *For instance, Scott Page*: Beth Brooke, *Groundbreakers: Using the Strength of Women to Rebuild the Global Economy* (Ernst & Young, 2009).

75   *"What's the point in pouring"*: Christine Toomey, "Quotas for Women on the Board: Do They Work?" *Sunday Times,* June 8, 2008.

78   *PricewaterhouseCoopers*: "PricewaterhouseCoopers Named Among Ten on *Working Mother*'s 100 Best Companies List for Fifth Consecutive Year," *Working Mother,* October 2008.

CHAPTER FIVE

83   *By 1997, the company's revenues*: Brad Wolverton, "Our Sports Gear, Ourselves," *BusinessWeek,* September 1, 1997.

83   *Women are responsible for 83 percent*: Marti Barletta, *Marketing to Women: How to Understand the World's Biggest Market* (Dearborne, 2006).

83   *62% of new cars . . . vacations*: "Who Wears the Wallet in the Family," *BusinessWeek*, August 16, 2004.

84   *90% of food . . . consumer electronics*: "Hello, Girls," *The Economist*, March 12, 2009.

84   *93% of over-the-counter . . . home furnishings*: Barletta, *Marketing to Women*.

84   *In addition, women hold . . . Japan*: Ibid.

86   *Between you and those food*: "Study Reveals Grocery Shoppers' Purchasing Priorities," *Food Navigator USA*, February 6, 2009.

86   *Milk sales appeared to be*: National Milk Producers Association, *Dairy Market Report*, January 2009, and *Dairy Market Report*, January 2008.

87   *The same thing was happening*: "Healthy Baby Boom," *Progressive Grocer*, April 13, 2009.

87   *And the market for all organic*: "Wal-Mart Goes Organic," MSNBC, March 26, 2006.

87   *The amount of land dedicated*: Pallavi Gogol, "Wal-Mart's Organic Offensive," *BusinessWeek*, March 29, 2006.

88   *More than half of "heavy"*: Michael Howie, *Industry Study on Why Millions of Americans Are Buying Organic Foods* (Organic Consumers Association, March 29, 2004).

88   *Instead, Safeway actually*: "Safeway's O Organics, Eating Right Expand in the U.S. and Overseas," Supermarket Industry News, *Progressive Grocer*, May 7, 2009, and Timothy W. Martin, "Safeway Cultivates Its Private Labels as Brands to Be Sold by Other Chains," *Wall Street Journal*, May 8, 2009.

89   *China and India alone*: "The New Global Middle Class: Potentially Profitable—but Also Unpredictable," Knowledge@Wharton, July 9, 2008, and Sandra Lawson and Douglas B. Gilman, *The Power of the Purse: Gender Equality and Middle-Class Spending* (Goldman Sachs Global Markets Institute, August 5, 2009).

89   *By 2015, it will buy 29*: Jehangir S. Pocha, "China's Hunger for Luxury Goods Grows," *Boston Globe*, March 21, 2006.

90   *Average monthly wages*: Susan Fenton, "Women at Forefront of Consumer Spending in China," *New York Times*, September 17, 2007.

93   *One recent survey showed that 74 percent: 2009 Retirement Confidence Survey* (Employment Benefit Research Institute and Matthew Greenwald and Associates, 2009).

93   *Another showed that, after*: Glenn Setzer, "Single Women Home Buyers Finding a Home of Their Own," *Mortgage News Daily*, July 17, 2006; Jim Woodard, "Women Homebuyers Growing in Number," *Ventura County Star*, January 27, 2008.; Walter Molony, *NAR Home Buyer and Seller Survey Shows Rise in First-Time Buyers, Long-Term Plans* (National Association of Realtors, November 8, 2008).

95   *Micro-lending pioneer Grameen Bank*: Interview with Muhammed Yunus, *Tavis Smiley*, January 24, 2008.

95   *In Austria, Raiffeisenbank*: Antoinette Odoi, "Money Men Develop a Female Focus as Women's Economic Clout Grows," *Guardian*, October 30, 2007.

95   *One study suggested . . . family-run farms*: Carla Power, "Middle East: Women's Money Talks," *Time*, July 30, 2008.

97   *All told, women have*: Liza Barth, "Women Car Buyers Mean Business," *Consumer Reports*, March 22, 2007.

98   *The industry's so out of touch*: http://www.msnbc.msn.com/id/32084157/ns/business-autos/.

99   *Chief engineer Grace Lieblein*: James Healey, "GMC Acadia Cruises to Top of Market for Crossovers," *USA Today*, December 22, 2006, and Jamie LaReau, "GM Engineer Grace Lieblein: She's Smart and Cool," *Automotive News*, October 15, 2007.

99   *In its first year on the market*: Laura Clark Geist, "GMC Courts Women with Acadia," *Automotive News*, May 25, 2008.

102   *The success of these women*: Susan Wright, Elisa Camahort Page, "2009 Women and Social Media Study," BlogHer, iVillage, and Compass Partners, 2009.

102   *In 2009, 63 percent*: Bill Heil and Mikolaj Piskorski, "New Twitter Research: Men Follow Men and Nobody Tweets," Harvard Business School, June 1, 2009.

102   Twice *as many women*: "Women Flocking to Facebook," Inside Facebook, August 4, 2009.

102   *As for social media overall*: "Women & Brands Online: The Digital Disconnect Emerges," Q Interactive, September 8, 2009.

104   *Women, understandably, trashed*: Jenna Worthan, "What Do Women Want in a Laptop?" *New York Times*, May 14, 2009.

CHAPTER SIX

110   *This redefinition of fatherhood*: Jeremy Adam Smith, *The Daddy Shift: How Stay-at-Home Dads, Breadwinning Moms and Shared Parenting Are Transforming the American Family* (Boston: Beacon Press, 2009).

111   *Fathers taught their kids*: Ibid.

112   *Since emancipation, black mothers*: Bart Landry, *Black Working Wives: Pioneers of the American Family Revolution* (University of California Press, 2000).

113   *In 2008, the Families and Work Institute*: Ellen Galinsky, Kerstin Aumann, and James T. Bont, *Times Are Changing: Gender and Generation at Work and at Home* (Families and Work Instititue, 2008).

116   *Data on time use in twenty countries*: Oriel Sullivan and Scott Coltrane, *Men's Changing Contribution to Housework and Child Care* (prepared for the 11th Annual Conference of the Council on Contemporary Families, April 25–26, 2008).

117   *Swedish policy ensures*: Jenny Sundelin, "Play: the Swedish Way," *Guardian*, March 11, 2008.

117   *Since Sweden makes combining*: Ricardo Hausmann, Laura D. Tyson, and Saadia Zahidi, *The Global Gender Gap Report 2008* (World Economic Forum, 2008) and Thomas F. Juster and Frank P. Stafford, "The Allocation of Time: Empirical Findings, Behavioral Models, and Problems of Measurement," *Journal of Economic Literature* 29, no. 2 (June 1991).

120   *In most married couples*: U.S. Department of Labor, 2007.

120   *In two-thirds of families*: *The Shriver Report: A Study by Maria Shriver and the Center for American Progress* (The Center for American Progress, 2009).

121   *Back in 1977, only 34 percent*: Ellen Galinsky, Kerstin Aumann, and James T. Bont, *Times Are Changing: Gender and Generation at Work and at Home* (Families and Work Institute, 2008).

122   *Their happiness levels are*: Betsey Stevenson and Justin Wolfers, "The Paradox of Declining Female Happiness," National Bureau of Economic Research Working Paper no. 14969, May 2009.

125   *In the United Kingdom*: Urmee Khan, "Children of Men Who Do Housework Have Higher IQ," *Telegraph*, September 30, 2008.

125   *Girls with involved*: Eirini Flouri and Ann Buchanan, "The Role of Father Involvement and Mother Involvement in Adolescents' Psychological Well-Being," *British Journal of Social Work* 33, no. 3 (2003).

125   *Some studies suggest*: Scott Coltrane and Michele Adams, *Analysis of Data from the Panel Study of Income Dynamics (PSID), Child Development Supplement* (University of California at Riverside, June 9, 2003).

125   *Today, only 13 percent*: Smith, *The Daddy Shift*.

125   *And while about a third*: Melissa A. Hardy, "Making Work More Flexible: Opportunities and Evidence," *AARP Public Policy Institute Insight on the Issues* 11 (November 20, 2008).

126   *In 2002, California added*: "Paid Family Leave Program Statistics, 2009," State of California Employment Development Department.

CHAPTER SEVEN

132   *ranks twenty-seventh of thirty-seven*: Organisation for Economic Co-Operation and Development, "Public Expenditure on Child Care and Early Education Services, as a Percent of GDP, 2005."

134   *Between about 1970 and 2006*: U.S. Census Bureau, Historical Income Table—Families, adjusted for inflation.

134   *when the Joint Economic Committee*: "Equality in Job Loss: Women Are Increasingly Vulnerable to Job Loss," Joint Economic Committee, July 22, 2008.

135   *"Money going to the family"*: Interview with Muhammed Yunus, *Tavis Smiley,* January 24, 2008.

137   *In the United States, nearly*: Rima Shore and Barbara Shore, *KIDS COUNT Indicator Brief Increasing the Percentage of Children Living in Two-Parent Families* (The Annie E. Casey Foundation, July 2009).

137   *In 2007, a whopping one*: Gardiner Harris, "Out-of-Wedlock Birthrates Are Soaring, U.S. Reports," *New York Times,* May 13, 2009.

137   *The United States is one*: Jody Heymann et al., *The Work, Family, and Equity Index: Where Does the United States Stand Globally?* (Project on Global Working Families, 2004).

138   *In a 2009 "report card"*: *State of the World's Mothers: Investing in the Early Years* (Save the Children, 2009).

138   *The total U.S. public expenditure*: Ibid.

142   *In 2009, Colorado's*: Text of bill: *Concerning Parental Involvement in Kindergarten Through Twelfth Grade Education* (Colorado General Assembly, 2009).

144   *In the United States, the median*: *Estimated Median Age at First Marriage by Sex, 1890 to Present* (U.S. Census Bureau, January 2009) and *Current Population Survey, 2008* (U.S. Census Bureau, February 2009).

144   *The percentage of women ages forty-five to fifty-four*: Andrea Ford and Deirdre Van Dyk, "Then and Now: A Statistical Look Back from the 1970s to Today," *Time,* October 26, 2009.

145   *Today, unmarried moms give birth*: Emily Bazelon, "2 Kids + 0 Husbands = Family," *New York Times Magazine,* February 1, 2009.

146   *In Sweden*: Gardiner Harris, "Out-of-Wedlock Birthrates Are Soaring, U.S. Reports," *New York Times,* May 13, 2009.

147   *"On average, women today spend"*: "Mothers Bearing a Second Burden," *New York Times,* May 14, 1989.

148   *Back in 1900*: Centers for Disease Control and U.S. Census Bureau, "Expectation of Life at Birth, 2009."

151   *A study of pension and annuity*: "Employer spending on Benefits, 2007," *Employee Benefit Research Institute Notes* (Employee Benefit Research Institute, November 2008).

152   *There, some countries*: Rebecca Ray et al., *"Parental Leave Policies in 21 Countries. Assessing Generosity and Gender Equality."* (Center for Economic & Policy Research, June 2009).

153   *80 percent of French women*: "Women in French Society Today," Institut National de la Statistique et des Etudes Economiques. Published by the Embassy of France, August 3, 2007.

153   *Germany has had one of the lowest birthrates . . . on the labor market"*: "Dwindling Germans Review Policy," BBC, March 28, 2006.

154   *to rethink their policies*: "Defusing the Time Bomb: Germany Reports Hike in Childbirth," Speigel Online International, August 21, 2008.

156   *More than 60 percent*: Election Eve Omnibus, Rockefeller Family Foundation, November 2008.

156   *As writer Lisa Belkin*: "The Opt-Out Revolution," *New York Times*, October 26, 2003.

CHAPTER EIGHT

160   *The United States ranks fifty-sixth*: Ricardo Hausmann, Laura D. Tyson, and Saadia Zahidi, *The Global Gender Gap Report, 2008* (World Economic Forum, 2008).

163   *In 2008 and 2009 women were serving*: World Leaders (United States Central Intelligence Agency, 2009).

163   *By 2009, women made up*: "Women in Politics," *World of Parliaments Quarterly Review*, no. 33, April 2009.

164   *In Europe, over the last decade*: Julie Ballington and Francesca Binda, *The Implementation of Quotas: European Experiences* (International Institute for Democracy and Electoral Assistance, March 2005).

166   *Wilson points to research*: Raghabendra Chattopadhyay and Esther Duflo, "Women as Policy Makers: Evidence from an India-Wide Randomized Policy Experiment (October 2001)" (MIT Department of Economics Working Paper No. 01-35).

166   *One study by researchers from*: Ibid.

166   *Other research*: Irma Clots-Figueras, *Are Female Leaders Good for Education? Evidence from India* (London School of Economics, 2005).

167   *In the United States, New Hampshire*: Renee Loth, "The Matriarchy Up North," *Boston Globe,* April 30, 2009.

170   *Academic research by Scott Page*: Claudia Dreifus, "In Professor's Model, Diversity=Productivity," *New York Times,* January 8, 2008.

172   *In 2008, women gave: Vote with Your Purse: Harnessing the Power of Women's Political Giving for the 2010 Election and Beyond* (Women's Campaign Forum Foundation, 2009).

172   *And women's political donations*: Center for Responsive Politics, Open Secrets Database, *Donor Demographics 2000 and 2008. See* www.opensecrets.org.

172   Half *of the money . . . over $200*: Fredreka Schouten, "In Fund Raising Ranks, a Gender Gap Is Showing," *USA Today,* July 30, 2008.

173   *In 2008, nearly $20 million*: Center for Responsive Politics, Open Secrets Database, *Women's Issues: Long-Term Contribution Trends.* See www.opensecrets.org.

174   *Twenty women were elected*: Holly Yeager, "Does EMILY's List Still Matter?" *Atlantic,* July 7, 2008.

175   *"You see the Web giving an"*: "Women Increase Political Donations in 2008 Presidential Race," ABC News.com, September 23, 2008.

178   *Today just 23.6 percent*: *Women in Elective Office 2009* (Center for American Women and Politics, 2009).

180   *Research at Rutgers*: Ruth B. Mandel and Katherine E. Kleeman, *Political Generation Next: America's Young Elected Leaders* (Eagleton Institute of Politics, Rutgers, the State University of New Jersey, 2004).

180   *A survey of student governments*: Carol D. Miller and Mindy Kraus, "Participating but Not Leading: Women's Under-representation in Student Government Leadership Positions," *College Student Journal* 38 (September 2004).

183   *In Morocco, for example*: *Assessing Women's Political Party Programs: Best Practices and Recommendations, 2008* (National Democratic Institute for International Affairs, 2008).

183   *This is the exact opposite*: Ibid.

185   *And in 2004, Morocco*: *Women's Issues* (Moroccan American Center for Policy, 2007).

185   *"I'm determined to see future generations"*: Soraya Sarhaddi Nelson, "Threats Cloud Afghan Women's Political Ambitions," National Public Radio, August 5, 2009.

CHAPTER NINE

197   *Even today, only 10*: *Global Burden* (Institute for OneWorld Health).

202   *Of some three hundred million*: HomeNet: The International Network for Home-based Workers, *Progress of the World's Women 2008–2009* (UNIFEM).

204   *makes less per book*: Amazon.com Annual Report, 2008.

212   *"Managing resources"*: "Interview with 2004 Nobel Peace Prize Laureate, Wangari Maathai," interviewed by Marika Griehsel, NobelPrize .org.

213   *Meeting the basic requirements*: Rhoda E. Howard-Hassmann, "The Second Great Transformation: Human Rights Leapfrogging in the Era of Globalization," *Human Rights Quarterly* 27, no. 1 (2005).

213   *Globally, "women perform"*: *Gender Equality—The Big Picture* (UNICEF, 2007).

Index